S Langdale

INTRODUCTION TO
MYTHOLOGY

LEWIS SPENCE

SENATE

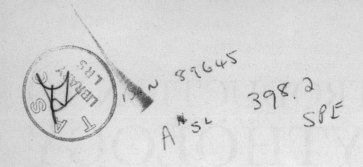

Introduction to Mythology

First published in 1921 by George G. Harrap
& Company Ltd

This edition published in 1994 by Senate, an imprint of
Studio Editions Ltd, Princess House, 50 Eastcastle Street,
London W1N 7AP, England

Copyright © this edition Studio Editions 1994

ISBN 1 85958 000 9

Printed and bound in Guernsey by
The Guernsey Press Co Ltd

PREFACE

THIS volume is an outline of the principles of mythology, chiefly with reference to its more modern developments. Hand in hand with the sister sciences of folklore and comparative religion, it has advanced so rapidly within the last twenty years and altered so greatly from its ancient aspect that it seems an entirely new science. Thirty years ago, if a student of myth had been asked who Janus was, he would probably have replied: "A Roman god of origins." To-day he might see in him a development of the 'kirn-baby.' So does the study of collected facts and analogies enable us to make broad generalizations. Quite recently, for example, Dr Rendel Harris advanced the theory that Aphrodite was originally a mandrake, while Professor Elliot Smith contends that her 'larval form' was that of the cowrie-shell. Apollo, according to some writers, was originally an apple, Bacchus a sprig of ivy, and Zeus himself a flint-stone fetish.

With such metamorphoses of the elder gods a rather long-suffering public has become somewhat ruefully acquainted. But with the value of the new scientific machinery which has discovered these analogies, which has laid bare the true nature of myth, they are not so intimate. The purpose of this book is to provide them with a review of mythic science from its beginnings down to the latest guesses of contemporary authorities. This plan may appear too ambitious, in the present chaotic condition of the science, but a real necessity exists for some such elementary study in order to cast light into the popular darkness on the subject.

The two great drawbacks of mythology are lack of accepted

5

INTRODUCTION TO MYTHOLOGY

definitions and of an historical and philosophical review of the subject on popular lines to co-ordinate the results of research. No science can expand without definition, and the definitions here offered have been accepted by most authorities as good working rules, so that, having won the approval of the ablest and most experienced specialists of the day, they may be regarded as an important help to the study of mythology. A useful series of definitions was brought forward with the countenance of the Folklore Society, but the mesh of most of these was far too wide. Seemingly prepared during personal consultation, they suffered in consequence, and the general result was surprisingly inadequate. How different it has been when written opinions have taken the place of verbal discussion may be observed by anyone who cares to compare them with the present series.

The author would note here that he desires to illustrate his theories as far as possible by myths which have come under his own notice and have been collected by himself, not wishing to have directed against him the usual criticism of the mere collector of *Märchen*, who appears to regard the theoretical writer on mythic science as an arm-chair plagiarist. But he has also used as examples many myths which appear in the several volumes of this series, and is further obliged to the published writings and personal correspondence of the late Mr Andrew Lang, Sir James Frazer, Dr Marett, Mr Sidney Hartland, the late Sir George Laurence Gomme, Professor G. Elliot Smith, and many others. He has to thank Messrs Longmans, Green and Co. for courteous permission to quote from Lang's essay "The Ghastly Priest" in his *Magic and Religion*.

Lastly, he would plead for a kindly consideration of his own system of mythological elucidation—the eclectic, embracing all he thinks best in other systems, whereas it is the bane of most writers upon mythology and allied subjects that the

6

PREFACE

pride of some one theory is strong in them. If it be asked how one is to be certain of selecting the best from each system, the answer is that one must walk in these caverns by the light of one's own common sense.

It is hoped that the comparative tables will be found of use to students. Much care has been taken in compiling them, but it is not claimed that they are in any way exhaustive.

L. S.

CONTENTS

AN INTRODUCTION TO MYTHOLOGY

CHAPTER I

INTRODUCTORY

THE function of mythology is the investigation and explanation of myths or tales relating to the early religious and scientific experiences of mankind. It throws light upon the material, methods, and progress of primitive religion and science, for many myths are an attempt to explain physical as well as religious phenomena.

Myth is one of the great objects of the science of 'tradition' (Lat. 'that which is handed down'), the others, with which myth is only too frequently confounded, being folklore and legend. It is hoped that the following list of definitions will prove of value to students of the subject, as it is certainly the most precise and embracive yet advanced.[1]

DEFINITIONS

Myth, folk-tale, and legend may be generally defined as traditional forms of narrative. That is, all are embraced within the term 'tradition.'

Myth. A myth is an account of the deeds of a god or

---

[1] In order that the beginner in mythic science may be enabled to comprehend its scope with some degree of precision, the writer has framed definitions as closely approaching accuracy as the present state of knowledge and research will permit, and has obtained the advice and assistance of most of the leading authorities. The method adopted was as follows. A table of definitions was placed before each authority, and he was invited to comment upon it. Such comments and criticisms on certain portions of the definitions either displaced the original material or were incorporated with it, first of all being reduced to a brevity suitable to explanatory phraseology. The result was the above list of definitions.

In the *Handbook of Folklore*, Appendix A, a number of definitions bearing upon mythology are provided, drawn up at a conference representing the editors of supernatural being, usually expressed in terms of primitive thought. It is an attempt to explain the relations of man to the universe, and it has for those who recount it a predominantly religious value; or it may have arisen to 'explain' the existence of some social organization, a custom, or the peculiarities of an environment.

Mythology. Mythology as a term implies (*a*) the mythic system of any race; (*b*) the investigation of myth.

Folklore. Folklore means the study of survivals of early custom, belief, narrative, and art.

Folk-tale. A primitive tale (*a*) of mythical origin; (*b*) of purely narrative or æsthetic value.

Legend. A story, generally of real places, often (though not necessarily) of real persons, handed down by 'tradition.'

MYTHOLOGY AND FOLKLORE CONTRASTED

Mythology is the study of a primitive or early form of religion while it was a living faith.

Folklore is the study of primitive religion and customs still practised.[1]

Some authorities regard folklore and mythology as almost interchangeable words; others look upon myth as the groundwork of folklore; but for purposes of study we shall be wise if we regard as fundamental myth any tale in which a god or demigod figures which explains the making of the world, or the origin of some primitive custom among the peoples of antiquity or the backward races to-day, while folklore may denote the study of *fragments* or *survivals* of old belief or custom found among uneducated or semi-educated people in

the *Handbook* and others. Several of them bear the sign of over-caution. For example, we read on p. 300: "Myth, a story told to account for something." Although sufficiently wide, the phrase is sadly lacking in definiteness, and might equally apply to an effort of mendacity !

[1] " Definitions and rules are needed. No student can attack so immense a subject without the aid of such necessary machinery, and it is because the attempt has been so often made ill-equipped in this respect that the science of folklore has suffered so much and has remained so long unrecognized." (Gomme, *Folklore as an Historical Science*, p. 127.) Some high authorities with whom the writer communicated appear to consider the formulation of definitions as a ' waste of time ' ! This attitude in the case of the leaders of any other science would surely be considered as retrograde.

INTRODUCTORY

civilized countries. Thus it is correct to speak of the folklore of England, Germany, or Italy, applying the word to the surviving superstitions and fragments of older faiths to be found in these modern countries among the uncultured classes; but to speak of the folklore of African, Australian, or American savages when we are dealing with the living religious beliefs of these people is highly incorrect. True, fragments of older belief are frequently discovered among primitive people, but the expression should not be used to designate their living religious beliefs.[1]

It will now be clear that in the present volume our concern is with the science of myth alone—that is, with religious beliefs and conjectures as to the nature of things of primitive, ancient, or barbarous peoples, and *not* with modern religious science, philosophy, or theology.

The questions touched upon in this introductory chapter will be more fully outlined later on, and are here presented in order to familiarize the reader with the general subject-matter of the science before entering upon more detailed discussion.

MYTH AND RELIGION

The sciences of mythology and comparative religion overlap at many points, but comparative religion is a branch of religious science or philosophy, whereas mythology deals with mere myths, or, under the more antiquated designation of 'comparative mythology,' compares the myths of different races. In myths too, however, we hear of the birth and nature of gods, the creation of the earth, and the primitive 'reason' for certain ritual acts. As these matters are also discussed by comparative religion or religious science, mythology and comparative religion often contemplate the same phenomenon at the same time. Mythology is therefore a part of religious science. This leads us to our next heading:

[1] In truth, 'folklore' is a most unfortunate denomination, as the science it designates has greatly outgrown the name. Neither 'folklore' nor 'mythology' is capable of defining the study of the religion, fiction, usages, laws, and general mental equipment of savages and primitive people. By far the best term is 'tradition,' and the one barrier to its use seems to be its simplicity.

INTRODUCTION TO MYTHOLOGY

WHAT IS RELIGION?

The attempt to define religion has exercised the philosophic mind through centuries, and never more so than at the present time, although it is now generally recognized that all purely scientific attempts to determine it are doomed to failure, as its origin and nature must be sought conjecturally through psychology. Dr E. B. Tylor proposed as a 'minimum definition' for religion "the belief in spiritual beings"; but this does not embrace ritual, which Robertson Smith thought [1] of first consequence in primitive religion, dogma and myth being secondary.[2] Sir J. G. Frazer considers religion "a propitiation or conciliation of powers superior to man,"[3] a definition not always appropriate. Crawley (in his *Tree of Life*, p. 209) defines the religious object as "the sacred," a very obscure definition. Herbert Spencer derived all religion from the worship of the dead. Max Müller considered that "Religion consists in the perception of the infinite under such manifestations as are able to influence the moral character of man." The fact is that our present knowledge of the human mind does not permit us to make any final definition of the word 'religion.'[4]

The study of myths, then, is assisted by comparative

[1] *Religion of the Semites*, pp. 18 *sqq.*

[2] Gomme, quoting and following Robertson Smith, believes that "mythology was no essential part of ancient religion, for it had no sacred sanction and no binding force on the worshippers." Why then the insistence by most priesthoods on the absorption of myths by their neophytes? Why their 'renovation' of myths? Myths were early efforts at a reconciliation of the tales of gods with the religious sentiment; ritual, as Gomme admits, was merely the outward expression of tradition. On p. 141 of the same work (*Folklore as an Historical Science*) he speaks of "those who believe in the truth of the myth," of its "sacred character," of "traditions which have become sacred." On p. 149 he speaks of myth as "revered," and told in "the hushed sanctity of a great wonder." Yet he believes that it had "no binding force"! On p. 150 he writes of the preservation of primitive myth "for *religious* purposes." Robertson Smith's reasoning was, of course, based on pure theory and upon limited as opposed to universal examples of the connexion of myth with religion, of which it is an integral part. The wonder is that this circumstance was not patently visible to the distinguished folklorist who comments upon and accepts his dictum.

[3] *The Golden Bough* (2nd ed.), vol. i, p. 63.

[4] My own 'minimum' definition of religion is, "The result of man's attitude to the unknown."

14

religion, while myths in their turn often explain gods,[1] men, and the universe, and customs and organizations of society. Many of them, indeed, are early efforts at a reconciliation of the tales of gods and heroes with the religious sentiment, which recognized in these beings objects for worship and respect.[2]

THE 'SAVAGE' ELEMENT IN MYTH

But these tales remained full of irrational and savage notions, a legacy from primitive ancestors. They chimed ill with later religious sentiment, which was shocked and puzzled by them, and priests and poets attempted to explain them away. Thus, among the Greeks, Theagenes of Rhegium (c. 520 B.C.) considered the tale of the battle of the gods 'unbecoming,' and represented it as an allegorical account of the war of the elements. The Egyptians, according to Plutarch, puzzled by the circumstance that so many of their gods were pictured in animal form, invented as an explanation the tale that in a moment of danger the gods concealed themselves in the bodies of animals. As peoples grew more civilized they attempted to cleanse their national or tribal myths from the coarse and barbarous tone which savage predecessors had given them, and many of the myths of the higher civilizations of

---

[1] Dr Marett, in a letter to the author dated November 30, 1914, states that he "thinks it a mistake to state by way of definition that myths are ætiological" (explanatory), on the ground that explanation is not a fundamental of myth and that a theory is thereby involved. Says Gomme : " Every tradition . . . myth or story contains two perfectly independent elements—the fact upon which it is founded and the interpretation of the fact which its founders have attempted." (*Folklore as an Historical Science*, p. 10.)

[2] As regards the relation of myth to history, Gomme has happily said that myth "must not be identified with history. This claim is based upon two facts, the presence of myth in the shape of the folk-tale [which he believes to be a late form of myth] and the preservation of much mythic tradition beyond the stage of thought to which it properly belongs by becoming attached to an historical event or series of events, or to an historical personage, and in this way carrying on its life into historic periods and among historic peoples. The first position has resulted in a wholesale appropriation of the folk-tale to the cause of the mythologists ; the second position has hitherto resulted either in a disastrous appropriation of the entire tradition to mythology or in a still more disastrous rejection both of the tradition and the historical event round which it clusters." (*Folklore as an Historical Science*, p. 128.)

antiquity, as they have come down to us to-day, have obviously passed through one or more stages of refinement and revision at the hands of some priest, poet, or philosopher anxious to free his race from its supposed coarse and savage pristine history.[1]

A PERUVIAN PRIEST-MYTH

A good example of how older myths are accounted for by a modern priesthood [2] is the story of Pacari Tampu, the 'House of the Dawn,' a legend of the Collas, a Peruvian tribe. From the caverns of Pacari Tampu issued four brothers and a sister. The eldest ascended a mountain and cast stones to all the cardinal points of the compass to signify that he had taken possession of the land. The other three were envious of him, and the youngest succeeded in inducing him to enter a cave, whereupon the youngest brother closed the mouth of the cave with a great stone and imprisoned the eldest there for ever. On pretence of seeking his lost brother he then persuaded the second to ascend a high mountain, from which he cast him, and, as he fell, by dint of magic art changed him into a stone. The third brother, scenting treachery, fled. The first brother would appear to symbolize the oldest known Peruvian religion, that of the thunder-god Pachacamac, the second that of an intermediate fetishism or stone-worship, the third the cult of Viracocha, the water-god, while the fourth seems to be the more modern sun-worship, which in the end triumphed officially over all, as is proved by the name of the youngest brother, 'Pirrhua Manca' ('Son of the Sun').

MADNESS OR MENTAL CHILDHOOD?

Max Müller seriously suggested that the "savage and irrational" element in myth arose out of a "period of temporary

---

[1] "The myth is not dependent upon the text in which it appears for the first time. That text as we have it was not written down by contemporary or nearly contemporary authority. Before it had become a written document it had lived long as oral tradition." (Gomme, *op. cit.*, p. 125.)

[2] When myth is 'renovated,' cleansed, cast into literary form, or in any way subjected to alteration, it is known as 'secondary' myth—that is, it exists in a secondary state.

madness through which the human mind had to pass." "Was it," he asks, "a madness identically the same in the south of India and the north of Iceland?" The state of mind, the mental attitude, was and is, of course, very much the same among savages or barbarians from Cape Horn to Novaia Zemlia; but no 'madness' is mingled with the mental equipment of primitive man, although he is irrational. What Professor Müller mistook for 'madness' was the child-like propensity of the savage or barbarian, or even the uncultured person, to delusion, ignorance, and distortion of facts and experiences. The imbecility of savage theories and stories is due to a scanty stock of acquired ideas and lack of experience in wielding the higher powers of reason. In short, savage or primitive man, although highly observant, explains such facts as come within his range of view by employing imagination rather than reason.[1] He is in a condition of mental childhood, when imagination is very much more powerful than reason. Thus he imagines that all other physical entities in nature are, like himself, gifted with powers of speech, volition, and thought. This is called 'animism'—*i.e.* the bestowal of a soul (Lat. *anima*) upon all objects.[2] The winds and the waters speak and obviously travel; the trees are articulate; the lower animals he regards as his equals. He does not bring reason, as we understand it, to bear upon his experience. The 'wonders' in these tales are no marvels to him; the brutalities of savage life recounted in them, the barbarian atmosphere and colour, are his everyday experiences.[3] He hands the tale on; but his descendants fail to comprehend its meaning and

---

[1] "In this class of tradition we are in touch with the struggles of the earliest ancestors of man to learn about the unknown." (Gomme, *op. cit.*, p. 130.)

[2] "All the knowledge they possess is that based upon their own material senses, and therefore when they apply that knowledge to subjects outside their own personality they deal with them in terms of their own personality." (Gomme, *op. cit.*, p. 132.)

[3] Some modern writers believe animism to be a relatively late manifestation in the religious history of mankind. It seems to me to occur spontaneously wherever and whenever the mind of man is discovered in a condition sufficiently primitive to receive it, and as it is the original mental characteristic of all children, whether savage or civilized, I fail to recognize its significance as a later demonstration of human thought.

aim ; its almost animal savagery repels them, and at length more advanced generations, shocked at what seems to them blasphemous nonsense, discard it altogether, or so cleanse and refine it as not infrequently to render its original meaning entirely undiscoverable.

SAVAGERY IN GREEK MYTH

As an example of how the savage element displays itself in the mythic tales of such a refined and poetically gifted people as the Greeks, the myth of the birth of Zeus may be instanced. When Cronus had displaced Uranus, the first monarch of Olympus, he took to wife Rhea, one of the Titan race. Gæa, his mother, however, prophesied that as he had overthrown Uranus, he himself would be overthrown by one of his own children. So uneasy did he become in consequence of this prediction that whenever a child was born to him he tore it from its mother's arms and swallowed it whole. Five children did he swallow in this manner, greatly to the grief of Rhea, who, lamenting to Gæa the loss of her offspring, was advised by her next time she had a child to take a stone and wrap it in swaddling-clothes and give it to Cronus to swallow as if it were the infant, at the same time carefully concealing the real child in some secluded place until it reached maturity. This Rhea did, and Cronus duly swallowed the stone she gave him, imagining it to be one of his own children and therefore his possible future destroyer. But Rhea hid the child in a cave in the island of Crete, where the goat Amalthea nourished him with her milk. There were placed in the infant's vicinity armed men, who, whenever he cried, performed a war-dance, clashing their spears and shields to drown his wailing ; and so within a year the boy grew to full manhood. At length Gæa gave Cronus a draught which made him vomit up the stone he had swallowed, together with the five children previously devoured—two gods and three goddesses. These young gods made war upon the elder deities, and after a ten years' struggle were victorious over them, banishing them to the dismal region of Tartarus.

In this myth the savage element is strikingly apparent.

INTRODUCTORY

Through the mists of allegory we seem to discern (1) the replacement of one tribal head by another ; (2) the prediction of the tribal prophetess or crone ; (3) a condition of cannibalism ; (4) a reminiscence of fetishistic stone-worship in a stone being mistaken for a young god ; (5) the nurture of a child by a goat, perhaps a primitive form of nursing ; (6) a war-dance by armed savages ; (7) the younger men of the tribe banishing the older men to a less desirable spot ; (8) the primitive right of the youngest son to succeed the father.

Now we find numerous myths similar to this in all quarters of the world. "Bushmen tell of *Kwai Hemm*, the devourer, who swallows that great god, the mantis insect, and disgorges him alive with all the other persons and animals engulphed in the course of a long and voracious career. The moon in Australia, while he lived on earth, was very greedy, and swallowed the eagle-god, whom he had to disgorge. Mr Im Thurn found similar tales among the Indians of Guiana. The swallowing and disgorging of Heracles by the monster that was to slay Hesione is well known. Scotch peasants tell of the same feats, but localize the myth on the banks of the Ken in Galloway. Basutos', Eskimos', Zulus', and European fairy tales all possess this incident, the swallowing of many persons by a being from whose maw they return alive and in good case." [1]

Many circumstances of myth go to illustrate its primitive and barbaric origin. The tales of gods who masquerade as animals are probably reminiscent of a time when they were worshipped in animal form.[2] The Greek mysteries, which were merely acted myths, conserved the savage rite of daubing the initiate with clay, a practice common among African, Australian, South American, and Papuan uncivilized peoples. They also retained from primitive times the use of the 'bull-roarer,' two flattened pieces of wood attached to a string, which on being swung produces a mysterious humming noise, a device employed by many savage folk to keep away women and the profane from the performance of their rites and ceremonies. Early

---

[1] Lang, *Myth, Ritual, and Religion* (4th ed.), vol. i, p. 295.
[2] See remarks on totemism, p. 28.

man, engaged in ceaseless strife, regarded his gods as in constant conflict with giants or with each other. They abduct each other's wives, they are cowardly, gluttonous, immoral, and given to magic, just as is savage man himself.

SAVAGERY IN THE VEDAS AND BRAHMANAS

Although the Vedas of India are 'sacred' works, principally repositories of devotional hymns, they bear traces of this barbarism which permeates all mythology. We find the deities in their pages comporting themselves as one might expect the lowest savages to do, although the whole religious sentiment of the work is opposed to these acts. The later Brahmanas, treatises on the intricacies of ritual compiled by a priestly caste of fairly exalted character, also teem with myths in which barbaric thought is encountered. Their pages, indeed, are the meeting-place of savagery and semi-civilization. In one myth the mother of Indra is a cow, Indra being represented as a drunkard who intoxicates himself with *soma*, and as a murderer who actually kills a priest. These circumstances in his myth are relics of an age when he was, although a god, regarded as man-like, and a savage man at that. This is due to the religious instinct called 'anthropomorphism.'

Nearly all the Greek peoples worshipped stones, some named after the gods[1]—a relic of fetishism—and their later religion kept much of savage practice. Homer speaks of Athene as 'owl-eyed.' Was she once worshipped as an owl? The deities in the *Iliad* are extraordinarily human, not to say barbarous, in their propensities, and have a knack of transforming themselves into animal shapes when pursued or pursuing, loving or hating. They reflect the Greek idea of Homer's day, yet they are even older.

MYTH AND EARLY SCIENCE

Enough has been said to illustrate the existence of the savage element in primitive myth. Not only do later myths account for the religious element in the more primitive examples,

---

[1] Gill, *Myths and Songs from the South Pacific*, p. 60.

but they explain, or attempt to explain, primitive scientific notions as well.[1]

The desire to know the 'reason why' early creates a thirst for knowledge, an intellectual appetite. "When the attention of a man in the myth-making stage of intellect is drawn to any phenomenon or custom which has to him no obvious reason, he invents and tells a story to account for it."[2] The character of most primitive myths amply justifies this statement. They are mostly explanations of intellectual difficulties, answers to such questions as, What is the origin of or reason for this or that phenomenon or custom? How came the world and man to be formed as they are? In what manner were the heavenly bodies so placed and directed in their courses? Why is the lily white, the robin's breast splashed with red? How came into force this sacrificial custom, this especial ritualistic attitude, the detail of this rite? The early replies to these questions partake not only of the nature of myth, but of science—primitive science, but science nevertheless—for one of the first functions of science is to enlighten man concerning the nature of the objects and forces by which he finds himself surrounded, and their causes and effects. These replies are none the less scientific because they take the shape of stories. Their very existence proves that the above questions, to clear up which they were invented, were asked. They cannot be accounted for without the previous existence of these questions. Mythology is the savage's science, his manner of explaining the universe in which he lives and moves. Says Lang: "They frame their stories generally in harmony with their general theory of things, by what may be called 'savage metaphysics.'" Of course they did not think on the lines of a well-informed modern scholar. Müller remarks in an illuminating passage:

[1] "Primitive science was also primitive belief." (Gomme, op. cit., p. 140.) Again (p. 132): "Where savages ask themselves, as they certainly do ask themselves, whence the sky, whence the winds, the sun, moon, stars, sea, rivers, mountains, and other natural objects, they reply in terms of good logic applied to deficient knowledge." Again (p. 130): "Our own research in the realms of the unknown we dignify by the name and glories of science. The research of our remote ancestors was of like kind. . . . It was primitive science."

[2] Tylor, Primitive Culture, vol. i, p. 369.

INTRODUCTION TO MYTHOLOGY

"Early man not only did not think as we think, but did not think as we suppose he ought to have thought."

One of the chief differences between the outlook of the primitive savage and that of civilized man is the great extension in the mind of the former of the theory of personality, an outlook we have already called 'animism.' Everything possesses a 'soul,' or at any rate will-power, in the judgment of the savage. But not only are sun, sky, river, lightning, beast, tree, persons among primitive or backward peoples; they are savage persons.

ANIMISM : A FOSSIL FAITH

Research and travel combine to prove that earliest man and the lowest savages cannot be found without myths, which, as we have seen, are both religion and science. The first recognized stage in man's mental experience is animism, so that the earliest myths must have been 'animistic.'[1] Roughly, animism is the belief that everything has a soul or at least a personality, but no race has yet been discovered possessing purely animistic beliefs. Even the lowest races we know have developed these considerably, and so we are only acquainted with animism in its pure form theoretically,[2] as a phase of religious experience through which man must at one time have passed. It is, in fact, a fossil faith. But just as fossil animals and plants have their living representatives to-day, so do ideas and conceptions representing this petrified form of religion and science still flourish in our present-day superstitions and our present-day faiths.

Animistic myths naturally show primitive ideas regarding the soul. Animism will be dealt with more fully hereafter, but

[1] Animism has been defined by Dr Tylor as "the doctrine of spiritual beings, including human souls"; but the term is often extended to include *animatism*, "the doctrine that the great part if not the whole of the inanimate kingdom as well as all animated beings are endowed with reason, intelligence, and volition, identical with that of man."

[2] "We have no opportunity of observing historically man's development from blank unbelief into even the minimum or most rudimentary form of belief. We can only theorise and make more or less plausible conjectures as to the first rudiments of human faith in God and in spiritual beings. We find no race whose mind as to faith is a *tabula rasa*." (Lang, *The Making of Religion*, p. 53.)

INTRODUCTORY

In this introductory sketch we will cite one or two examples of animistic myth to illustrate what was, so far as we know, the earliest type of myth. Stories are found telling of journeys to the spirit land, of talking animals, of men metamorphosed into animals and trees, and these are all animistic or originate in animistic belief.[1] Modern folk-tales containing such stories possess a very great antiquity, or are merely very old myths partly obscured by a veneer of modernity. Spirit stories which have obviously a primitive setting or atmosphere are almost certainly animistic. Thus tales which describe the soul as a bird or a bee, flitting about when the body is asleep, are either direct relics of an animistic age, or have been inspired by earlier animistic stories handed down from that age. The tales of spirit journeys to the Otherworld, the provision of implements, weapons, shoes, and so forth, placed in the grave to assist the soul in its progress to the Land of Shadows, invariably point to an animistic stage of belief—the belief in a separable 'soul,' in an entity entirely different and apart from the 'tenement of clay' that has perished.

PRE-ANIMISTIC RELIGION

There are not wanting authorities of discernment who believe that even this early phase was not the primitive phase in the religious experience of man. Of these the most clear-sighted and perspicuous in argument is Dr Marett, reader in anthropology at Oxford University. In a pregnant chapter-preface in his highly suggestive book, *The Threshold of Religion*, Dr Marett says: "Psychologically, religion requires more than thought, namely, feeling and will as well; and may manifest itself on its emotional side, even when ideation is vague. The question, then, is, whether apart from ideas of spirit, ghost, soul, and the like, and before such ideas have become dominant factors

[1] Tylor supposes animism to have arisen from "two groups of biological problems present to the mind of early man :

"(1) What is it makes the difference between a living body and a dead one, what causes waking, sleep, trance, disease, and death?

"(2) What are those human shapes which appear in dreams and visions?" (*Primitive Culture*, vol. i, p. 428.)

23

in the constituent experience, a rudimentary religion can exist.
It will suffice to prove that supernaturalism, the attitude of
mind dictated by awe of the mysterious, which provides
religion with its raw material, may exist apart from animism,
and, further, may provide a basis on which an animistic doctrine
is subsequently constructed.   Objects towards which awe is
felt may be termed powers." He proceeds to say that startling
manifestations of nature may be treated as ' powers ' without any
assumption of spiritual intervention, that certain Australian
supreme beings appear to have evolved from the bull-roarer,[1]
and that the dead inspire awe.   This he calls ' supernaturalism,'
and regards it as a phase preceding animism.

FETISHISM

Very closely allied to and coexistent with animism, and
not to be very clearly distinguished from it, is fetishism.   This
word is derived from the Portuguese *feitiço*, a charm, ' something made by art,' and is applied to any object, large or
small, natural or artificial, regarded as possessing consciousness, volition, and supernatural qualities, especially magic
power.[2]

Briefly and roughly, the fetish is an object which the savage
all over the world, in Africa, Asia, America, Australia, and,
anciently, in Europe, believes to be inhabited by a spirit or
supernatural being.   Trees, water, stones, are in the ' animistic '
phase considered as the homes of such spirits, which, the savage
thinks, are often forced to quit their dwelling-places because
they are under the spell or potent enchantment of a more
powerful being.   The fetish may be a bone, a stone, a bundle of

[1] See p. 19.

[2] The term ' fetishism ' has been objected to upon the ground that " it has been
used in so many different and contradictory senses that it is very likely to be mis-
understood. . . . Even the word *fetish* should only be used in its historic sense, to
describe a limited class of magical objects in West Africa." (*Handbook of Folklore*,
p. 298.) This objection is scarcely a practical one, and to eliminate a word which has
rendered excellent service to anthropology and has been adopted by students in all
parts of the world to designate a definite class of religious objects and the especial
description of the cult which clusters round them savours of pedantic caprice, while
no equivalent is tendered for the word it is proposed to abolish.

feathers, a fossil, a necklace of shells, or any object of peculiar shape or appearance. Into this object the medicine-man may lure the wandering or banished spirit, which henceforth becomes his servant; or, again, the spirit may of its own will take up its residence there. It is not clear whether, once in residence or imprisonment, the spirit can quit the fetish, but specific instances would point to the belief that it could do so if permitted by its 'master.'[1]

We must discriminate sharply between a fetish-spirit and a god, although the fetish may develop into a godling or god. The basic difference between the fetish and the god is that whereas the god is the patron and is invoked by prayer, the fetish is a spirit subservient to an individual owner or tribe, and if it would gain the state of godhead it must do so by long or marvellous service as a luck-bringer. Offerings may be made to a fetish; it may even be invoked by prayer or spell; but on the other hand it may be severely castigated if it fail to respond to its owner's desires. Instances of the castigation of gods proper are of rare occurrence, and could scarcely happen when a deity was in the full flush of godhead, unless, indeed, the assault were directed by an alien hand.[2]

We have seen that the ancient Greeks had in their temples stones representing 'nameless gods' who seem to have been of fetish origin. Thus a fetish may almost seem an idol, and the line of demarcation between the great fetish and the idol is slender, the great fetish being a link between the smaller fetish and the complete god.

Myths showing fetishistic belief are few and obscure, but the writer recently unearthed, in the fishing village of Newhaven, near Edinburgh, one which is a good example of the survival of a fetish myth and of the rise of a fetish to godhead.

[1] The *jinn* inhabiting Aladdin's lamp and ring appear to have been fetishistic spirits of this type.

[2] Well-known instances of assault upon gods are : the overthrow of the discredited Russian god, Peroun, by his disillusioned worshippers; the profanation of Balder's grove by Frithjof (*Frithjof Saga*); the destruction of the idols of the Mexican gods, Uitzilopochtli and Tlaloc, by the Spanish conquerors. Other instances could be cited, nearly all acts of insanity, rashness, or hostility, rarely of disappointment.

INTRODUCTION TO MYTHOLOGY

FROM FETISH TO THUNDER-GOD

Perusing an old book entitled *Tales and Traditions of Leith*, the writer read of one Brounger, " an old fisherman who at one time resided at Newhaven, and who, when unable to go to sea himself, used to ask his neighbours for a few oysters or fish on their return from fishing," and curse those churlish enough to refuse. The curse was invariably effective, so that in the end the fishing community became anxious to propitiate an individual whose spoken word carried such weight, and regarded his demands in the light of an established claim. According to tradition, Brounger passed away, but his name remained a 'thing to conjure with'—literally. For a Newhaven fisherman to be told " Brounger's in your head-sheets " meant that the speaker cast on his vessel and all who sailed therein an evil spell, only to be broken by making the boat describe a circle in the water three separate times.

The student of myth will regard this 'old fisherman' with an eye of professional suspicion. Why should the mariners of Newhaven fear and mistrust the mere mention of one who in days more or less distant levied a petty toll of oysters or flounders from their fathers? He will find the scent grow hot when he is informed (and this is the point) that Brounger was 'a flint, and the son of a flint.' For the flint is the fetishistic emblem of the thunder-god, and Brounger was a deity of the storm.

Among many peoples the flint-stone symbolizes thunder, for from the flint comes fire. In America, for example, Tohil, who gave the Kiches of Central America fire, was represented by a flint-stone. Such a stone in the beginning of things fell from Heaven to earth, and broke into a myriad pieces, from each of which sprang a god—an ancient Mexican legend which shadows forth the subjection of all things to him who gathers the clouds together in thunder. This is the germ of the adoration of fetish stones as emblems of the fertilizing rains. The rain-charms of the Navaho Indians are hung round stones supposed to fall from the clouds when it thunders. With the Algonquin Indians a certain rain-god has a body of flint

26

INTRODUCTORY

which, broken, is changed into fruitful vines. The blood of Tawiscara, another Indian deity, turns to flint as it falls from his wounds. Hathor, the sky-goddess of Egypt, was the 'Lady of Turquoise,' as was the Mexican water-goddess. Is not the 'elf-arrow' (the flint arrow-head) a 'thunderbolt' to peasants of all countries, Britain not excepted? So we begin to see why Brounger was a 'flint,' and the 'son of a flint.' In days when the first Teutonic fishermen settled on the coast of Midlothian they brought with them a thunder-god, the root of whose name may perhaps be found in the old Gothic word *brinnan*, to burn; hence Brünger, 'the burner,' 'the devastator,' 'the wielder of lightnings,' worshipped in the flint and placated by gifts from that sea-harvest which he had power to give or to withhold.

From the Hebridean Isle of Fladdahuan comes a similar story. On the altar of the chapel of that isle, says Martin in his *Western Isles*, lay a round bluish stone, always moist. Wind-bound fishermen walked sunways round the chapel and then poured water on the stone, whereupon a powerful breeze was sure to spring up. Solemn oaths were also sworn upon the stone. A similar stone was possessed by the Isle of Arran, kept in the custody of a woman (the hereditary priestess of its cult?), and "wrapped up in fair linen cloth." In Inniskea, an island off the Irish coast, a stone wrapped up in flannel is brought out at certain periods to be adored by the inhabitants. It is kept in a private dwelling, and is called in the Irish Neevougi. It is prayed to in times of sickness and is requested to send wrecks upon the coast.[1] All this is within the ritual of rain-making, but Brounger, though a thunder- and rain-god, was requested *not* to visit his folk with tempest for the reason that their business lay in the furrows made by the keel and not in those of the plough.

One certain proof that Brounger was a supernatural being exists in a folk-poem to be found in the above-mentioned work on Leith traditions. A wedding ceremony is in progress, when Brounger glares through the window at the merrymakers. At

[1] See Gomme, *Ethnology in Folklore*, for several notable instances of stone-worship of this description.

once a cry arises that he must be placated. Sings one fisherman :

> " Let ilka body gie 'm a corse [copper piece],
> And Jock may gie him twa,
> An' the chiel will sune hae in his maut [drink],
> Syne he'll forget it a'.
> And when he's at the land o' Nod,
> To make the matter tight,
> I'll score the loon aboon the breath,
> An' syne we'll be a' richt."

To " score " a wizard (or witch) " aboon the breath," and thus procure some of his blood, rendered the possessors of it immune from the malice of the sorcerer. So we see that Brounger was at least no mere 'Longshoreman Billy,' earning a livelihood by terrorizing his brother salts, but ranked in some measure with the supernatural host. It is just possible, indeed, that he may possess a common origin with the Russian Perunu or Peroun, whose name also signified ' striker ' or ' lightning-wielder.'

TOTEMISM

Totemism is a phase of religion frequently encountered in myth. Briefly and crudely defined (and any brief definition of it must essentially be crude), the totem is an animal, plant, or inanimate object connected traditionally with a certain social group which takes its name from the totem or uses it as a symbol. The persons composing this 'group' suppose themselves to be descended from the totem animal or plant, or to be related to it. There is a magico-religious bond between the totem animal and themselves, and the totem may not be eaten by the members of the community of which it is the patron unless in a ceremonial manner and at stated seasons.

Examples of the totem in myth are, as has been said, frequent. In the Roman myth of Jupiter and Leda, for instance, we encounter Jupiter in the form of a swan ; many of the Egyptian animal-headed gods are totemic ; certain swine-gods of the ancient Britons were of the same class ; and we know that some of our ancestors would not eat geese, just as certain Red Indians will not eat beaver or racoon, because these animals represented, or represent, the beast-patron of their tribe.

INTRODUCTORY

About the beginning of the eighteenth century certain French missionaries—among them the Jesuit Lafitau—were struck with the importance of totemism in the religious and social life of the North American Indians. Lafitau saw more clearly than any of his colleagues the nature of this peculiar socio-religious condition, and was even led to apply what he saw among the Iroquois Indians to the interpretation of the Greek Chimæra! During the first part of the nineteenth century the facts concerning totemism began to reach Great Britain from missionaries and travellers in every part of the globe. Moreover, allusions to what were undoubtedly totemic conceptions could be traced in the authors of antiquity — Diodorus, Herodotus, Pausanias, Ælian, etc. In 1869 M'Lennan pointed out that many totemic customs and beliefs survived in various civilizations, ancient and modern. About 1885 Frazer and Robertson Smith approached the subject with a larger body of facts. Later, Tylor, Spencer, Lubbock, Lang, Jevons, Cook, and Grant Allen threw themselves into the study of this remarkable phase of socio-religious life.

POLYTHEISM

In this introduction we are dealing with the various divisions, more or less arbitrary, made by students of myth and comparative religion, and will not here attempt any description of the processes by which spirits of the animistic, fetishistic, and totemic types evolve into perfected deities. In a condition of polytheism we encounter the gods fully evolved, and often arranged in a hierarchy closely resembling the social polity of the tribe or people from whose religious imagination it has sprung.

Polytheism—a multiplicity of gods—is a condition arrived at by more than one route. Several great and powerful deities may shed a number of attributes and variants which themselves become personalized into gods. Egyptian mythology teems with examples of this, as almost all its principal gods absorbed or gave birth to several others in this manner. For example, from Horus was evolved Horus the Elder, Horus the Younger, Heru-an-Mut (a local god worshipped at Edfu),

29

Heru-Khenti-Khat (a god with a crocodile's head), the Horus of Khnemu ('Horus of the Two Horizons,' or the Harmachis of the Greeks, a form of Ra, the sun-god), Heru-Behudeti (who prevailed in the southern heavens at midday), and so forth. Gods belonging to certain towns or religious centres were collected and grouped, perhaps by priestly influence, into a pantheon in order of their importance.

Among semi-civilized people, then, the activities of the greater gods are constantly being enriched by new functions. Dialectical misunderstandings led to descriptive terms which brought about a change in divine names. The fortunes of kingdoms or royal races, migration and conquest, the contact of race with race through trade and travel, the adoption of foreign deities, all served to modify and expand the pantheons of the ancient world.

MONOTHEISM

Monotheism—the worship of one god—may emerge from polytheism in more ways than one. A certain god by dint of a miracle, because he is the deity of a conquering race, because of the enterprise of his priests, or by absorbing lesser gods, becomes the most powerful and popular deity in a state or neighbourhood. Or he may be the god of the reigning dynasty, a circumstance sufficient to secure for him at least a fashionable recognition so long as that dynasty survives. We usually find that such gods have vested in them the right to pardon sin, and they are indeed the founts of righteousness in virtue of their all-sufficing nature. But, apart from all the above considerations, the rise of moral feeling and a higher standard of conduct, order, and life were connected with the communal rise of monotheistic worship and the more exalted religious outlook it brings.

THE NATURE OF MYTHIC LAW

Tylor has stated that myth displays a regularity of development which cannot be accounted for by motiveless fancy and must be attributed to laws of growth. These laws, as has been seen, are practically universal in their application. But besides those forces which bring the myth into being—those demands of primitive man for explanation and intellectual satisfaction—there are other factors which begin to work upon myth at birth, and do not cease to act upon it, in succession, until perhaps it loses its earlier characteristics.

Thus we first find, going to work by analogy with certain contemporary savage examples and by induction, the purely animistic myth. As we have seen, this bestows personality and will-power upon inanimate objects, glorifies animals, and is practically without religious significance. Such a myth is found among the Chinook Indians of the north-west coast of America in the adventures of Blue Jay, a bird with human attributes who travels to the country of the Supernatural People and succeeds in defeating them in climbing, diving, whale-spearing, and archery. As we possess it, the myth has undoubtedly been influenced by successive waves of advancing native thought, but no sophistication by European influence is discernible. The impudence and effrontery of the Blue Jay bird led to its adoption as the central figure in many a tale, and, later, as the hero of the universal story of the 'Harrying of Hell,' in which a supernatural being traverses the country of the dead and brings defeat and disgrace upon its inhabitants in order to show the savage mind that it was possible to conquer death and Hell. Thus we have emanating from an animistic idea (1) the bird as person (in the myth a 'person' is spoken of as splitting wood with his beak); (2) the bird as tale-hero ; (3) the bird as vanquisher of death and Hell. Further elaborations of the myth, had social and tribal circumstances permitted of its growth, might well have shown us Blue Jay as the winged god, the principle of 'evil,' or perhaps in an even more exalted mythic capacity. Had the Chinooks remained undiscovered in their own environment and been capable of the evolution of a literature, who shall say to what heights of sanctity the conception of Blue Jay might not have risen ?

FROM BIRD- TO MAN-GOD

Lest the reader unaccustomed to the developments of mythic law think such a statement exaggerated, he shall be shown the valuable 'test of recurrence,' frequently employed by the rational experimentalist in myth, a test which, conversely, is his undoing if his conclusions are ill founded. The myth of the Aztec war-god Uitzilopochtli is similar to that of Blue Jay. It recounts how Uitzilopochtli, guided by a bird, led the Aztecs from the Underworld (?) country of Aztlan to the valley of Mexico by means of a peculiar call. Later he appears in Mexican myth in the full panoply of the national god of war, the most important figure, save one, in the Aztec pantheon. To him human sacrifice was rendered, and the greatest temple in the land was erected. His cult boasted an exclusive high priest, and in all respects he was regarded as the national god of the Aztec race. Yet he never resigned certain of his bird-like characteristics—a circumstance from which he derived his name, signifying 'Humming-bird Wizard,' and denoting that he was a bird before he took human shape.[1] Paste images of him were eaten at certain festivals by way of a communion rite.

The personalized bird is to be met with not only in American myth, but in European and Asiatic story as well. The Romano-Greek winged Mercury was originally almost certainly such a figure as Blue Jay. Like the Chinook god, he was sprightly, vivid, fond of practical joking, and a notorious thief. Picus, the Latin war-god, was a woodpecker, whose picture adorned the banners of his devotees. The god, in human form, wore a woodpecker on his head. Instead of becoming a national deity like Uitzilopochtli, Blue Jay might, in the hands of a people of equal imaginative capacity to the Greeks, have evolved into a mere messenger of the gods, or under the more sober influences of Judaism have become a cherub or an archangel—such are the diversities of racial character and its effect upon religious development.

Myth is hedged round and protected from change by the spirit of sanctity, but it may fall a prey to the religious spirit when more fully evolved, for what is sanctity to one age is

---

[1] The author has shown that Uitzilopochtli was originally the agave plant, and that the humming-bird, which nests therein, was regarded as the spirit animating that plant (see *Discovery* for June 1920).

often blasphemy to its successor, and that which appears worthy of retention to religious conservatives and priests at one period may well be regarded as an abomination by their official descendants. Thus we find the philosophers of Greece almost to a man attempting to purge the myths of their race from the grossness of barbaric ideas ; we note, too, the strivings of the Egyptian and Babylonian priests to combine rival myths and to bring older religious story into line with more modern theological ideas—in a word, to modify the traditional myths of the race so that the old scientific and religious explanations of the universe—the myths—took quite a new shape.

The Causes of Mythic Change

The question then arises, What are the true causes of mythic change? If the conclusions previously presented be correct, these are :

(1) The evolution, growth, and advance of theological ideas. Thus a myth acceptable in 'animistic' times might not prove so under a monotheistic or even polytheistic *régime*. The myth which would apply to a bird- or animal- or tree-god might not be applicable to a man-like deity.

(2) The growth and development of the idea of the sacred and of ethical ideas. The barbarities and abominations of early totemic and other animistic myth, apart altogether from shocking the religious sensibilities of people in later ages shocked their moral feelings as well, and this resulted in more or less drastic changes, which, however, do not altogether disguise the original story.

(3) Adventitious circumstances, such as racial feeling and idiosyncrasy, the deliberate or accidental fusion of two or more myths by a priesthood or by force of popular belief or acquiescence.

(4) The circumstances in which myth survives the religion or living faith with which it was originally connected. Thus on the official demise of a religion it may continue to be celebrated secretly, and this secret celebration may degenerate into magic and its myths change into folk-tale.

It follows from these premises that practically all myth is

of extreme antiquity,[1] and once a myth becomes established it may, for many reasons, undergo considerable alteration by successive generations. Its character of an early human 'explanation' of the universe is lost in the passage of generations, and it comes to require explanation. Thus it is understood, more or less correctly, in later times to refer to a genuine historical occurrence, or as an allegory upon natural phenomena, as it is unlikely that the upholders of a religion with fixed tenets would deliberately manufacture myths, however they might purify or combine those with which their theological system was connected. The difficulty in popular acceptance of a newly forged religious story, the manifest impiety of the proceeding and its necessary character, are all too apparent. Apparent, too, is the sufficiency of the mere alteration or 'editing' of myths to account for such minor theological differences as arose, even under a polytheistic *régime* of the least advanced type. With very few exceptions, the polytheistic systems of antiquity contained so many added and alien deities that slight alteration would suffice for the full adoption of the new-comer into the pantheon. This process must not be mistaken for religious laxity, as the alien god was almost invariably identified with one or other of the national deities, and the myth would merely be altered so far as necessary.

THE 'EDITING' OF MYTH

Instances occur in which myths of exceedingly ancient origin have received a wholesale 'editing' at the hands of later scribes. One of the most striking instances of such a process is that of the Babylonian creation myth, which recounts the famous combat between the god Bel-Merodach and Tiawath, the terrible dragon of the abyss. In the myth in question the ancient Accadian concept of the fathomless deep and the Babylonian idea of the abyss, respectively entitled Apsu and Tiawath, are represented as husband and wife, an example of mythic amalgamation common enough. But from an attribute of Tiawath is formed a third god, named Mummu, who is

---

[1] As will be shown farther on, the author believes that the majority of mythic plots possess an animistic basis.

34

described as the son of the two original deities. In such an innovation we can assuredly trace the hand of the later mythographer, who, with less skill and greater levity than is usual, has ventured to evolve an entire trinity from one concept—that of the primeval abyss. Thus from the Babylonian and Accadian concept of 'the deep,' essentially one, has arisen an entire trinity of evil. A further addition is made to this infernal band in the shape of Kingu, whom Tiawath calls her 'only husband'; but as he enters the mythic field Apsu and Mummu leave it, and are heard of no more in the course of the tale. It may be that at this point the story was taken up by a new scribe, who did not approve of the action of his predecessor in describing the hostile trinity, originally one conception, as three separate deities—but that is merely conjecture. The Babylonian cosmogony as we possess it is presented in purely epical form, and it is practically certain that in this shape it differed greatly from the originally accepted myth upon the same subject. Indeed, the inclusion in it of later gods proves it to be a good example of myth which has undergone transformation more than once.

THE CLASSIFICATION OF MYTH

It has been said that the chief divisions of myth correspond to the chief problems which the universe presents to the curiosity of untutored man. Thus we find that most myths will fall under such heads as the origin of the world, the origin of man, the origin of the arts of life, star myths, sun and moon myths, myths of death, myths of fire-stealing, hero myths (including tales of the adventures of demigods), myths regarding taboo, beast myths, myths of journeys through the Underworld or Otherworld, myths to account for customs or rites, and other less important varieties.

THE DISTRIBUTION OF MYTH

This is a good place to discuss the vexed question whether all myths have sprung from one common centre, or whether each one is the spontaneous creation of man's brain in separate parts of the world.

Both theories possess a measure of truth, for certain tales have undoubtedly been widely disseminated, some of them being altered by foreign influence, while certain others are obviously of spontaneous growth. Examples of widely disseminated stories are readily encountered. The solar hero, who as son of the sun comes to earth to instruct men in the arts of life, and after a strenuous mundane career returns to his father's bright kingdom, is common to Greeks, Celts, Teutons, and Red Indians. Flood myths, again, are as widely spread as any variety of tale.

Those who uphold the theory of the origin of myth in one centre and its wide dissemination have not so far explained fully how myths became so widespread. Of course the purchase or capture of slaves, intermarriage with alien women, intercourse with alien peoples, trade and commerce, may account for many similarities,[1] but the question yet awaits reply, "Can myths 'drift' across many thousands of miles of sea-water?" The complete isolation of Australia throughout the ages, and the similar situation of America, two continents which possess, as a late distinguished student of myth was wont to say, "the whole bag of tricks" of mythology as found elsewhere, show that the answer is not a simple one. In any case, if there be any genealogical connexion between the myths of the Old World and the New, the myths of Asia and Australia, it must be of extreme antiquity, dating from before the remote geological period when all communication was cut off between America, Australia, and the rest of the globe. That may not have been so very long ago, comparatively speaking, for America, but for Australia it must have been "at a time so remote as to permit of no traditions. No record, no folk-tales, as in the case of the Maoris of New Zealand, are preserved by the Australians . . . nothing, as A. W. Howitt points out, that can be twisted into referring even indirectly to their first arrival."[2]

[1] The school originated by Professor Elliot Smith has much to recommend it; but its hypotheses need further elucidation, a greater amount of evidence to buttress them, and—it is spoken in all friendliness—it lacks a spirit of tolerant and serious consideration for the views of its opponents; all of which it will gain in good time.

[2] Channing Arnold in article "Australia," *Ency. Brit.* (11th ed.).

INTRODUCTORY

Dr Klaatsch of Heidelberg says that the Australians are "a generalized, not a specialized, type of humanity—that is to say, they are a very primitive people, with more of the common undeveloped characteristics of man, and less of the qualities of the specialized races of civilization." It is likely, however, that they are closely related to the Dravidians of the Indian Deccan, and that they are not so low in the scale as Klaatsch believes. Even so, the very distant date at which they arrived in the Australian continent precludes the likelihood of their carrying with them any form of religious belief that was not of an even more archaic character than those we are studying.[1]

Flood myths possess an almost world-wide similarity. We find the story of the man and woman who escape the universal deluge in a cunningly contrived boat or chest in Greece, Assyria, Palestine, Mexico, and other countries. In such stories we have good examples of myths apparently disseminated from one original tale or event; but that resemblances between myths are no criterion of a common origin is proved by widespread examples in which circumstances of time and geography forbid all possibility of borrowing. The belief that once the soul had partaken of the food of the Underworld it might not return to earth is common to ancient Greeks, Finns, and Red Indians, and if any original conception gave rise to the notion in these widely separated countries it must be sought in an altogether archaic and prehistoric era.

SOPHISTICATED MYTHS

Myths generally become altered or 'sophisticated' by contact with a higher civilization than that of the people which originally developed them. The myth of Joskeha and Tawiscara given on p. 191 is a notable instance in this connexion. Some barbarous mythic systems have become coloured by Biblical narrative, but it is not safe to conclude so because of a surface resemblance. The rule holds good, generally speaking, that myths found current among primitive people and

---

[1] It would be very unjust to Professor Elliot Smith and his school, however, if it were not stated that they possess many good arguments against this, for which see the publications issued by the University of Manchester.

having marked ethical characteristics in which 'good' and 'evil' are sharply contrasted almost certainly show sophistication by the agents of a superior civilization. But if the rule were to be ruthlessly adhered to it would not admit the evolution of religious belief or the heightening of the ethical standard among the lower races, who must pass through such phases of development as those through which our fathers passed, with this exception, of course, that the process is quickened in their case by contact with races possessing a much higher standard of general culture.

By a process of interaction all mythic systems of uncivilized peoples are probably at the present day highly sophisticated, so that to encounter a truly spontaneous myth uncoloured by alien belief or priestly conception is probably impossible. At the same time it is a characteristic of myth and folk-tale that no matter how greatly cultural surroundings alter them they tend to keep the basic elements of which they were originally compounded. We all know that matters of fact as they pass from one individual to another become greatly distorted. Strangely enough, this is not the case with myth and folk-tale. The reason is hard to discover, but the fact is certain. The writer has observed among children a prompt indignation at the 'mis-telling' of a traditional tale. Once the terms of a story become fixed he will be bold who will attempt to alter them when recounting them to children or savages. In short, where the circumstances of a story are well authenticated a barrier exists against the tendency, shown in gossip, to adorn the original plot, to add or subtract from it. This appears to be due to a strong conservative instinct in the childish and savage mind.

"To generalize," said Blake, "is to be an idiot," but to generalize is one of the functions of science. In a general sense, then, the more simple and archaic the characteristics of a myth, and the more it reflects an early state of society, the greater the antiquity it is naturally likely to possess. The more 'literary,' the more embellished it is by the graces of art, and the more cunning it displays in the business of story-telling, the later it will be. Many myths have, of course, been built up by slow degrees only, the myth of Osiris being an admirable example. It grew with the importance of the god himself, who perhaps from a mere local spirit came to be the great deity of the dead.

Proof of the authenticity of myth—that is, the proof by which it is known as the genuine aboriginal product of a primitive folk—is obtained by what Tylor has called "the test of recurrence." That is, if we discover a tale possessing the same elements in several different parts of the world "we cannot set down the coincidence to chance or fraud." This is practically a 'law,' and is one of the most valuable conclusions which has as yet enriched mythological science.

An outline—and merely an outline—of the principal questions with which students of myth are at present chiefly concerned has now been furnished. These, as has been said, will be amplified in succeeding chapters, the purpose of this introduction having been served if the reader is enabled by its perusal to follow intelligently the subsequent examination, on a more extensive scale, of the subjects indicated.

CHAPTER II
THE PROGRESS OF MYTHIC SCIENCE

MANY are the hypotheses and systems advanced to account for the origin and existence of myth. It will greatly assist our comprehension of these and our ability to discern those most worthy of consideration if we examine them chronologically as well as critically. If we begin our review with the gropings of the first far-off thinkers who attempted an analysis of myth, and put to themselves the question " What is myth, its origin and its meaning?" and advance through the centuries until we encounter present-day theories, then we should be well equipped to pursue our course without fear of the pitfalls encountered by early writers on tradition, or, let us hope, of falling into the grave errors inevitable when mythological data were less plentiful than at the present time.

It must be clearly understood that this sketch does not deal with the *makers* or restorers of myth, but with the views and notions of critics who have sought to discover its nature and meaning. Again, we would remind the reader that we are not dealing with religious science, but with such mythological notions as have come down to us from early times to the present.[1]

The first critic of myth was Xenophanes of Colophon (*fl.* 540–500 B.C.), an Ionian exile in Sicily, afterward living at Elea, in Southern Italy. He supported himself by travelling from

---

[1] It follows that neither is this a sketch of the history of the science of folklore. The Greeks of Pausanias' day may have possessed the elements of a folklore. He flourished before the State recognition of Christianity, but Greek myth in his day was breaking down. In any case, such questions are foreign to our inquiry, which deals with myth as defined by us and with that alone. The great students of folklore are alluded to in this sketch for what they have written on myth, and for nothing else. The present condition of the science demands explicit statement in this respect, and this must be our excuse in making it.

place to place and reciting his own poems. The important part of his writings for us is that in which he attacks the polytheism prevalent in his day. Xenophanes did not accept the mythical idea of man-like deities then current. "There is one God, greatest among gods and men," he writes, "neither in shape nor in thought like unto mortals . . . yet men imagine gods to be born and to have raiment and voice and body, like themselves. . . . Even so oxen, lions, and horses, if they had hands to grave images, would fashion gods after their own shapes and make them bodies like to their own." Again he says: "The rainbow, which men call Iris,[1] is a cloud." Xenophanes appears by his writings to have taken up the position of a theologian protesting not against polytheism, but against the idea that the gods possessed human appearance and attributes. Besides the one great god he seems to have recognized a plurality of minor divinities who govern portions of the universe. He stigmatized anthropomorphic myths as "the fables of men of old."

Theagenes of Rhegium was the founder of a very popular system of mythology. He pleaded for an allegorical rather than a literal reading of myth. For example, as we have already mentioned, he considered the battle of the gods 'unbecoming,' and attempted to show that in reality it was an allegorical rendering of the war of the elements. According to his view, Hephæstus and Apollo personified fire; Hera, wife of Zeus, was air; Poseidon, the sea-god, represented water; Artemis was the moon, and so on. Other gods, he attempted to show by an examination of their names, were personifications of moral or intellectual qualities.

Pherecydes of Syros (*fl.* sixth century B.C.) wrote a treatise, in which myth, allegory, and science were blended, on nature and the gods. He contended that the elements of fire, air, and water sprang from Cronus, the principle of time, and that from these elements later gods emerged. Zeus is called the 'principle of life,' so that we have in Pherecydes' interpretation of myth a pseudo-scientific idea that time was the originator of

---

[1] Iris, daughter of Thaumas and the ocean nymph Electra, was the personification of the rainbow and messenger of the Greek gods, especially of Zeus and Hera.

INTRODUCTION TO MYTHOLOGY

the elements, from which in turn the gods had their being—a very daring hypothesis for the sixth century B.C.!

Hecatæus of Miletus (*c.* 550–476 B.C.) was probably the first critic to distinguish myth from historic fact. Socrates (*c.* 471–399 B.C.) attempted to show that the nature of divine beings could be discovered by an analysis of their names. Prodicus (born *c.* 465 B.C.) is noteworthy for the 'modern' character of his outlook. First of all, he says, arose such great powers as benefit mankind (for example, the Nile), then deified men, who rendered services to humanity.

Pherecydes of Leros (*fl. c.* 454 B.C.) modified the myths of Greece in order to adjust them to popular belief, so that it is scarcely correct to class him as a critic of myth. Ephorus (*c.* 400–330 B.C.) treated myths as historical episodes. "By straining after this fancied history he was prevented from searching into the genuine import of the legends."[1]

EUHEMERUS

The system of Euhemerus (fourth century B.C.), who lived under King Cassander of Macedonia, deserves more than passing mention. Like Ephorus, he considered that myth is history in disguise. The gods were men, and mists of time and later phantasy had so magnified and distorted their figures as to make them appear divine. In short, they were great men deified by later generations. The dead are magnified into gods in many countries, so Euhemerus' theory possesses a good deal of truth, but every god was not once a man, nor have all gods been evolved from the worship of the dead. The truth is that the myths of many gods have passed through a phase and have been coloured by an environment in which ancestor-worship has prevailed. Graves of gods are shown in many lands, and probably portions of legends relating to real men have been attracted into the myths of certain gods. Euhemerus' system of interpretation is known as 'euhemerism,' and was adopted by Vossius, the Abbé Banier, Huet Bishop of Avranches, Clavier, Sainte-Croix, Rochette, Hoffman, and to some extent by Herbert Spencer. Ennius popularized his

[1] Müller, *A Scientific System of Mythology*, 1838.

42

system in ancient Rome. Leclerc, one of Euhemerus' later disciples, actually proposed the theory that Greek mythology consisted of the diaries of old merchantmen and seamen!

Some Stoics and Platonists, such as Plutarch, endeavoured to render myths more intelligible by explaining them 'pragmatically,' and this system too saw in the gods of Greece kings or merely men. Another system, the 'Psychic,' believed myth to be explanatory of the various stages through which the soul must pass. Other Stoics, again, saw in myths reference to natural phenomena. Thus the first school, the 'Pragmatic,' would see in the figure of Pallas Athene a transfigured mortal queen; the second, the 'Psychic,' would explain her as the 'understanding,' and the third, the 'Stoic,' as the thicker air between moon and earth.

Driven to the wall by Christianity, the remaining believers in Greek myth attempted to justify it by the allegorical system of interpretation. The early Christian fathers like St Augustine (A.D. 354–430) applauded the system of Euhemerus, in which they beheld the abhorred mythology abandoned by one himself a pagan. Porphyry (A.D. 233–304), however, considered that there might be a moral meaning in myth, and others thought it possible that it concealed a germ of religious truth.

MEDIEVAL MYTHOLOGY

The Middle Ages produced no criticism of myth worthy of attention. Popular belief in medieval times regarded the gods and goddesses of antiquity as of diabolic origin, or at least as 'pagans' who had been relegated to Hell on the advent of Christianity. This view was, of course, sedulously supported by the priesthood, as may be seen in the medieval legend of Tannhäuser. Prior to the Renaissance period, with its revival of classical studies, the gods of Greece and Rome were frequently confused or identified with other pagan deities and even with religious leaders like Mohammed, as, for instance, in the phrase 'Mahound and Termagent,' which alludes to the pairing of Mohammed and Tyr, or Tyr Magus, a Scandinavian divinity. In *The King of Tars*, an English romance, probably of the fourteenth century, we read how the Sultan of Damascus destroyed his idols, " with sterne strokes and with grete, on Jovyn and Plotoun, on Astrot and sire Jovyn." Here Roman and Semitic deities are mingled in "hideous ruin," like the wicked angels of Milton, whose poem, by the way, encouraged a later belief that the Arch-fiend and his associates were no other than the gods of the elder faiths, Beelzebub, Belial, and, among others,

Osiris, Isis, Orus and their train.

An old Scots piece, entitled *Sir John Rowll's Cursing*, dating perhaps from the last quarter of the fifteenth century, and in all probability written by a priest of Corstorphine, near Edinburgh, contains several interesting allusions which show the condition of mythological knowledge at that day. It is directed against certain persons who have rifled the priest's poultry-yard. Sir John is powerful in anathema, and his thunders must have caused trepidation among the more superstitious of his parishioners, but the only lines of his rhymed 'Billingsgate' apposite here are those containing the names of demons, because these show us how the mythic characters of antiquity were regarded in his time. He says that the pilferers of his hen-roosts will be hanged and given to the fiend, and continues:

> . . . and Cerberus thair banis sall knaw
> For thair dispyt of the Kirkis law,
> Gog and Magog and grym Garog,
> The Devill of hell the theif Harog,
> Sym Skynar and St Garnega,
> Julius appostata,
> Prince Pluto and quene Cokatrice,
> Devetinus the devill that maid the dyce,
> Cokadame and Semiamis,
> Fyremouth and Tutivillus,
> And Browny als that can play kow [1]
> Behind the claith wt mony mow.[2]
> All this about the beir salbe [3]
> Singand ane dolorous dergie.

Let us try to identify some of these figures. We may pass over Cerberus, and Gog Magog, who has by this date evidently

---

[1] Cow. A 'shelly-coat cow' was, in Scots parlance, a bogy. It is thought that the shells on such an animal are a reminiscence of the scale armour of the vikings, whose memory was a terror to the Scottish peasantry. To 'cow' is, of course, much the same as to 'bully.'

[2] Grimace.　　　　[3] That is, "These shall surround the bier."

resolved himself into two separate individuals. In Harog we probably see that 'Old Harry' who is so frequently apostrophized, perhaps a variant of the Norse god Odin. In Sym Skynar we may have Skrymir, the Norse giant in whose glove Thor found shelter from an earthquake, and who sadly fooled him and his companions. Skrymir was, of course, one of the Jötunn, or Norse Titans, and probably one of the powers of winter; and he may have received the popular name of 'Sym' in the same manner as we speak of 'Jack' Frost. Julius the Apostate, Pluto, and the Cokatrice are easily identified. Semiamis is, of course, Semiramis, and it was quite possible that the Babylonian queen bulked in the popular imagination as an Eastern goddess, fit companion for Mahound or Mohammed.

EIGHTEENTH-CENTURY MYTHOLOGERS

The study of myth can hardly be considered scientific in our modern sense until nearly the end of the eighteenth century. During the seventeenth century and the early portion of the eighteenth works were published from time to time which professed to give an outline of the myths of Greece and Rome, but in these the critical spirit was almost entirely absent. Francis Bacon (1561–1626) leaned to the allegorical interpretation of myth. Thus, Narcissus was self-love, Dionysus passion, and the Sphinx science. Natalis Comes (*d.* 1582) saw in myth allegories of natural and moral philosophy. The first writer to strike upon the true line of interpretation was De Brosses (1709–1777), who in 1760 published a work, *Du culte des dieux fétiches, ou parallèle de l'ancienne religion de l'Egypte avec la religion actuelle de Nigritie*. De Brosses showed that animal-worship in ancient Egypt was a survival of practices such as existed among modern savages. Lafitau (in 1724) also pointed out the savage element surviving in Greek myth, for which he found many parallels in his experience as a Jesuit missionary among the Indians of North America. But all writers on myth were not so rational as these. Thus the Abbé Banier in his *La mythologie et les fables expliquées par l'histoire* (Paris, 1738) traced (as the title of the book indicates) all myths to an historical basis.

INTRODUCTION TO MYTHOLOGY

Bryant (1715–1804) in 1774 published *A New System, or an Analysis of Ancient Mythology*, in which he traced all mythologies to Biblical sources. Thomas Taylor (1758–1835) in his translation of Pausanias regarded all myth as allegory.

Friedrich Schelling (1775–1854) was the first to see a connexion between the formation of myth and national development. Without possessing the orderly and logical mind so necessary to the student of tradition, he was able to seize spasmodically upon truths or facts which strongly buttressed his theory. Creuzer in his *Symbolik und Mythologie* (Leipzig, 1810–1812) laid stress on the religious character of myth. According to his view, myth is of the nature of religious teaching, proceeding from an original revelation, and carefully handed down in symbolic form by priestly schools. This secret wisdom passed from the Orient to Greece and became the kernel of all myths, which therefore contain the wisdom of antiquity in an allegorical form. To unriddle this is the task of the mythologist, who can only succeed in doing so by intuition. The mythologist is, like the poet, born not made, according to Creuzer.

Although the symbolic method is nowadays as dead as the dodo, and in any case could only apply to very late myths which were the work of poets or philosophers, it still holds good that the elucidation of myth is not a matter of pure mental induction, but that it frequently results from intuition; and who can doubt, with the brilliant examples of Lang, Gomme, Marett, Saussaye, Hubert and Mauss, Reinach, Rendel Harris, and Elliot Smith before them, the proud assertion that great students of tradition *are* "born not made"?

With K. O. Müller's (1797–1840) *Prolegomena zu einer wissenschaftlicher Mythologie* (1825; Eng. trans. by Leitch, 1844) the truly scientific treatment of myth begins. He saw clearly that the true laws underlying the confusion of mythic science as he found it were not to be approached by one but by many ways. The explanation of a myth, he said, must be the explanation of its origin. A knowledge of the popular life of antiquity he regarded as indispensable, and he drew a distinction between the actual, original myth and the myth as sophisticated

46

by poets and philosophers. Mythic materials, he argued, must be resolved into their original elements. His dicta are landmarks, almost laws—if the term 'law' may be applied to a science where at present all is rather nebulous.

THE PHILOLOGICAL SCHOOL

The comparative study of language did much to reawaken both interest and industry in the study of myth, and the philological method of explaining mythic phenomena arose. This system has been called 'comparative mythology.' The appellation is scarcely correct from a scientific standpoint, as, strictly speaking, the term 'comparative mythology' implies the comparison of the details of one myth with those of another, in an attempt to prove the universality of the nature of myth, or by 'the test of recurrence' to show that widely distributed myths are related, and that fragments found only in one 'fit' the other. This comparative mythology implied the comparison of mythic names in various Indo-European languages with a view to showing that what was dark and seemingly inexplicable in one language might be made clear by comparison with the known mythic appellations in another language.[1]

The leader of this school, the history of which is important for the proper comprehension of the evolution of mythic science, was Professor Max Müller[2] (1823–1900), who, coming from Germany to Oxford at the age of twenty-three to undertake the translation of the ancient religious books of India on behalf of the East India Company, rapidly made a position for himself in English scientific circles by his sound scholarship, indefatigable energy, and wide general culture. The deep study of comparative philology led him to apply its results to myth. He regarded language as a necessary condition of thought, not its arbitrary expression, and considered that words, therefore, contain the key to thoughts. If language is determined by thought, thought is also determined by language. Mythology, according to Müller, is properly a form of thought

---

[1] Thus, according to Müller, the name Athene, unintelligible in its Greek form, at once becomes explicable when compared with the Sanskrit Ahana, 'the dawn.'

[2] His views will be found stated in *Selected Essays* and *Lectures upon Language*.

so essentially determined by language that it may be described as 'a disease of language.' Its origin must be looked for in a stage of human development in which intuition or instinct almost predominates, while abstract thought is unknown. Thus mythical terms precede mythical thought, and the peculiarities of language which lead to the formation of myth are the gender of words, polyonymy (numerous meanings attached to one word), synonymy (the possession of similar meanings by two or more words), poetical metaphor, and so forth. But the entire Müllerian conception of mythic science must not be taken as being contained only in the expression that myth is a 'disease of language.' Myth, according to Müller, is to be comprehended principally through language, but not through language only. By reference to language many but not *all* mythic phenomena may be understood. Just as certain rash disciples of Darwin did much to stultify their leader's evolutionary theory by their applications of it, in the same manner some of Müller's followers so distorted and exaggerated his views on myth as to hamper him greatly.

Müller was not the first to apply the methods of comparative philology to myth, but he was by far the most distinguished exponent of the system. Before him G. Herman and others attempted to explain myths by etymology, but they restricted their efforts to the Greek language only. It was not until the researches of Franz Bopp [1] (1791–1867) and others laid the foundations of the science of comparative philology that the way was clear for the study of myth on a linguistic basis. These studies succeeded in establishing the relationship of the 'Indo-Germanic' languages, and, working with these proven facts behind him, Müller boldly applied them to mythic phenomena. For example, he brought forward a comparative formula of the name of Zeus or Jupiter which he stated thus:

Diaush-Pitar = Zeus Pater = Jupiter = Tyr.

Thus, according to him, the name Diaush-Pitar in Sanskrit was equivalent to Zeus Pater in Greek, Jupiter in Latin, and

[1] See his *Comparative Grammar*, English translation by Eastwick (3rd ed.), 1862.

PROGRESS OF MYTHIC SCIENCE

Tyr in old Teutonic.[1] This etymological result is sufficiently scientific in character for acceptance by even a severe critic of the system. But scarcely had Müller's method acquired vogue— and its recognition was of the widest—than a small army of critics arose whose determined opposition had to be reckoned with. Many of their objections, it is now clear, were due to misunderstandings. Wherever they lit upon a paradox or were enabled to confuse the issue by any ambiguity or slackness in Müller's phraseology, they too often took more than a full advantage of the chance to score. Indeed, so unsparing was the criticism to which his conclusions were subjected, and so great was his irritation thereat, that at length he accused certain of his adversaries of an attempt to traduce his moral character by charging him with mendacity.

MÜLLER'S CONTEMPORARY CRITICS

But if his critics were unfair, they had legitimate grounds for a certain opposition to his system. Many of his propositions, as well as those of his followers, were doubtful; the method was often pushed to extremes which just escaped being ludicrous; and the somewhat ponderous erudition behind it seemed only to heighten the absurdity of some of its conclusions, although the charm and usual clarity of Müller's literary style were not to be denied. The combat waxed fierce, and both sides brought up all their forces. Linguistic science, it was said, is an uncertain medium for determining the substance and nature of thought. The linguistic and etymological methods had been discarded by philosophy, only to make an unwelcome reappearance in mythology. The original meaning of a word is often totally at variance with its later use. Again, similar mythic conceptions are found with totally different names, and divergent ones with the same names. These were serious objections, but they do not destroy the strictly verifiable conclusions of the philological school. At present the school is in

[1] See "The Lesson of Jupiter," *Nineteenth Century* for October 1885: "To understand the origin and meaning of the names of the Greek gods and to enter into the original intention of the fables told of each, we must take into account the collateral evidence supplied by Latin, German, Sanskrit, and Zend philology." See also *Lectures on Language*, 2nd ser., p. 406.

the deepest discredit; indeed, it may be said to possess scarcely a single follower; but that its methods are applicable to certain classes of mythic phenomena no mythologist of experience would deny.

MÜLLERIAN INTERPRETATIONS

Examples which illustrate the Müllerian interpretation or misinterpretation of myth are his treatment of the tale of Cephalus, Aurora (Eos), and Procris. Cephalus was the sun, the son of Herse, the dew; therefore he represented the sun rising over dewy fields. Eos, as the word implies, is the dawn. Procris comes from a Sanskrit root *park*, meaning to sprinkle, and is also the dew; therefore it is the equivalent of Herse, the meaning of which may be found in a Sanskrit root *vrish*, ' to sprinkle.' The myth is then interpreted: Cephalus loves Procris—that is, the sun kisses the morning dew; Eos loves Cephalus—that is, the dawn loves the sun. Procris is faithless, but her new lover turns out to be the sun in another guise —that is, the dewdrops reflect the sun in manifold colours. Procris is slain by Cephalus—that is, the dew is absorbed by the sun. Thus natural phenomena lurk behind the names of gods and heroes.

The philological school had its internal divisions also. Its arbitrary interpretations made for schism, and there was considerable diversity of opinion regarding myths and mythic personages. Two sub-schools arose, the solar and the meteorological. The first, headed by Müller himself, " saw sun-gods everywhere," in myth, folklore, and legend. Perhaps its most zealous disciple was the Rev. Sir George William Cox (1827–1902), author of *The Mythology of the Aryan Nations* (1870) and *An Introduction to Mythology and Folklore* (1881), two works of great erudition and charm, powerfully advocating the universality of the sun myth and based upon a truly scientific investigation of a large number of myths and tales. Cox did not insist upon the philological interpretation of myths so much as on their solar character, and he is " fully aware of the dangers involved in attempts to explain Teutonic, or Greek, or Latin, or Scandinavian myths solely from Aryan sources."

He also admits the existence of nature myths other than solar, but to his mind most of those which are not solar are stellar or nebular.

The founders of the meteorological school saw in all myths the phenomena of the thunder and lightning. Dragons and similar monsters guard treasures and fair maidens in a celestial stronghold till the arrival of the hero-god, who slays the monsters and rescues the maiden. Thus, said they, the dark and threatening thunder-clouds imprison the light of heaven until the coming of the god, who dissipates them. The chief supporters of this theory were Kuhn (1812–1881) and Darmesteter (1849–1894). Laestrin too attempted to interpret myths from nebular phenomena which he had observed on the Alps.[1]

Few perfectly certain results were achieved by the philological school. Of convincing certainty at the first blush, a more searching examination reveals difficulties, and shows that the theories do not fit the myth with any degree of exactitude; but philology has rendered and will render real service to mythology, and this young mythologists would do well to bear in mind.[2]

THE ANTHROPOLOGICAL SCHOOL

But the final blow to the pretensions of the philological method as a 'universal solvent' of mythic problems was dealt by the anthropological school of mythologists. This school accounts for the "wild and senseless" element in myth by replying that such "wild and senseless" conceptions can occur only in a savage and primitive state of society, and that therefore when such elements are found in the myths of civilized and cultured peoples they must necessarily be a legacy from a savage past—survivals of savage belief. But ere we proceed further in our investigation of the work of the anthropological

---

[1] See his *Nebelsagen* (1879) and *Das Räthsel der Sphinx* (1889).

[2] Apart from its philological efforts, the work of Müller and his disciples is of permanent value, and his critics undoubtedly did a disservice to mythological science when they condemned it root and branch. The training of no student of mythology can be complete if it lacks a consideration of Müller's works, which, of course, must be perused in the light of the comparative failure of his linguistic hypotheses.

school, let us see by what arguments it finally divested the philologists of all authority in the sphere of mythology.

It held, then, that Max Müller's system was a result of the discovery of the basic unity of the Aryan languages, and was founded on an analysis of these languages, but it showed that precisely similar myths exist among Eskimos, Red Indians, South Sea Islanders, Maoris, Bushmen, and other savage races. "The facts being identical, an identical explanation should be sought; and as the languages in which the myths exist are essentially different, an explanation founded upon the Aryan language is likely to prove too narrow." [1] Again, although we may discover the original meaning of a god's name, it does not assist us to understand the myths connected with him, for a striking figure in myth collects around it many age-old stories and mythic incidents which have originally no connexion whatsoever with it, just as barnacles are collected by a vessel in harbour. "Therefore, though we may ascertain that Zeus means 'sky,' and Agni 'fire,' we cannot assert with Max Müller that all the myths about Agni and Zeus were originally told of fire and sky. When these gods became popular they would inevitably inherit any current exploits of earlier heroes or gods." [2] So that if these were credited to them it would be erroneously. Names derived from natural phenomena too, such as sky, clouds, dawn, and sun, are habitually assigned by savage peoples to living persons. Thus a tale told of a real man or woman bearing one of these names might easily become mingled or confused with myths about the real sky, cloud, sun, dawn, etc. For such reasons the philological analysis of names is bound to be uncertain in its results. Moreover, when primitive or savage people think of natural phenomena and celestial bodies, they have no such ideas in their minds concerning them as have civilized people. They usually think of them as human beings with like passions to themselves—in fact, in an 'animistic' way. Müller held that it was gender-terminations that led later ages to the belief that natural phenomena possessed personalities, whereas the

[1] Lang in *Ency. Brit.* (11th ed.), art. "Mythology."
[2] *Ibid.*

anthropological school retorted that *au contraire* "gender-terminations were survivals from an early stage of thought in which personal characteristics, including sex, had been attributed to all phenomena." This stage of thought is to be observed among savages and young children, who habitually regard inanimate objects as alive.

MANNHARDT

The defection of Mannhardt, who had long been a pillar of the philological school, was a further blow to its failing prestige. In a work published shortly before his death (*Antike Wald- und Feldkulte*, 1877) he explains the growth of his views, and states that "the assured gains" of the philological school "shrink into very few divine names such as Dyaus = Zeus = Tuis; Parjany = Perkunas; Bhaga = Bug; Varuna = Uranus, etc." Many of the other equations of divine names he regards as mere *jeux d'esprit*. "To the principle of Max Müller," he says, "I can only assign a very limited value, if any value at all" (*op. cit.*, p. 20). And again: "Taken all in all, I consider the greater part of the results hitherto obtained in the field of Indo-Germanic comparative mythology to be, as yet, a failure, premature or incomplete, my own efforts in *German Myths* (1858) included." In an essay on Demeter published somewhat later he further insisted upon the weakness of the philological method. Moreover, he disapproved of finding celestial phenomena in myths of terrestrial happenings. To this standpoint he was brought by his own experience of how easy (and fatal) it is to become the victim of a 'mythological habit'—that is, the interpretation of myths by one method and by that alone. Writing to his friend Müllenhoff in 1876, he said that he had become uneasy "at the extent which sun myths threaten to assume in my comparisons." Mannhardt was a wise man and an honest one. He saw clearly that there is no universal solvent for myth, no single philosopher's stone by which it may be made to yield its secrets, no royal road to its elucidation.

At the same time he adhered to the truth that "a portion of the older myths arose from nature poetry which is no longer directly intelligible to us, but has to be interpreted by means of analogies. . . . Of these nature myths, some have reference to the life and circumstances of the sun." As Lang has said of him:[1] "Like every sensible person, he knew that there are numerous real, obvious, confessed solar myths *not* derived from a disease of language. These arise from (1) the impulse to account for the doings of the sun by telling a story about him as if he were a person; (2) from the natural poetry of the human mind. What we think they are *not* shown to arise from is forgetfulness of meanings of old words, which, *ex hypothesi*, have become proper names." And again: "It is a popular delusion that the anthropological mythologists deny the existence of solar myths, or of nature myths in general. These are extremely common. What we demur to is the explanation of divine and heroic myths at large as solar or elemental, when the original sense has been lost by the ancient narrators, and when the elemental explanation rests on conjectural and conflicting etymologies and interpretations of old proper names—Athene, Hera, Artemis, and the rest."

Mannhardt's method was more that of the folklorist than the philologist. He closely examined peasant custom and rite in the hope of discovering survivals of paganism. Indeed, his work may be said to be the foundation upon which Sir James George Frazer (whose work will be fully reviewed later) built his imposing edifices of research, *The Golden Bough* and other works.

THE ANTHROPOLOGICAL POSITION

The anthropological creed might, broadly, be stated as follows, with, of course, small divergences caused by internal division:

(1) The savage and irrational element in 'civilized' myth is composed of primitive survivals in more civilized times.

(2) The comparison of civilized with savage myth—that is, of later with earlier myth—frequently throws light upon the character of the latter.

(3) The comparison of similar myths among widely divergent

[1] *Modern Mythology*, pp. 55, 63.

peoples frequently illuminates their primitive character and meaning.

Broadly speaking, too, the anthropological school accepts such views as have been laid down in the introductory chapter concerning animism, fetishism, and totemism ; and when we come to deal with authorities who diverge in any way from these views we shall show how they differ.

SIR E. B. TYLOR

Sir E. B. Tylor, the virtual founder of the anthropological school, in his *Researches into the Early History of Mankind* (1865) and *Primitive Culture* (1871), first laid down the anthropological position with clearness and accuracy.

In a statement which appeared in his epoch-making work, *Primitive Culture*, Tylor briefly reviews the conceptions of the early commentators regarding myth, and shows how necessary breadth of knowledge and handling is for mythological work. The scientific interpretation of myth is strengthened and assisted by the comparison of examples. There are groups of myths, and the greater the number which can be grouped together, the more evidence is provided for the formation of a true science of mythology. Few and simple are the principles which underlie a solid system of interpretation. " The treatment of similar myths from different regions, by arranging them in large compared groups, makes it possible to trace in mythology the operation of imaginative processes recurring with the evident regularity of mental law ; and thus stories of which a single instance would have been a mere isolated curiosity take their place among well-marked and consistent structures of the human mind. Evidence like this will again and again drive us to admit that even as 'truth is stranger than fiction,' so myth may be more uniform than history." [1]

The work is limited to the consideration of well-authenticated mythic ideas of almost universal occurrence. " The general thesis maintained is that myth arose in the savage condition prevalent in remote ages among the whole human race, that it remains comparatively unchanged among the

[1] *Primitive Culture* (London, 1871), p. 282.

modern rude tribes who have departed least from these primitive conditions, while even higher and later grades of civilisation, partly by retaining its actual principles, and partly by carrying on its inherited results in the form of ancestral tradition, have continued it not merely in toleration but in honour." [1]

IMPORTANCE OF SAVAGE MYTH

The evolutionary character of myth necessitates that its study should be commenced among races of low culture. " If savage races, as the nearest modern representatives of primeval culture, show in the most distinct and unchanged state the rudimentary mythic conceptions thence to be traced onward in the course of civilisation, then it is reasonable for students to begin, so far as may be, at the beginning. Savage mythology may be taken as a basis, and then the myths of more civilised races may be displayed as compositions sprung from like origin, though more advanced in art. This mode of treatment proves satisfactory through almost all the branches of the enquiry, and eminently so in investigating those most beautiful of poetic fictions to which may be given the title of Nature Myths." [2]

The nature of personalism in myth is debated, as is the share of language in its formation, and here it will be seen that Tylor has not the extreme hostility of certain of his followers to the Müllerian doctrine. He says : " Language, no doubt, has had a great share in the formation of myth. The mere fact of its individualising in words such notions as winter and summer, cold and heat, war and peace, vice and virtue, gives the myth-maker the means of imagining these thoughts as personal beings. Language not only acts in thorough unison with the imagination whose product it expresses, but it goes on producing of itself, and thus, by the side of the mythic conceptions in which language has followed imagination, we have others in which language has led, and imagination has followed in the track. These two actions coincide too closely for their effects to be thoroughly separated, but they should be distinguished as far as possible. For

---

[1] *Primitive Culture* (London, 1871), pp. 283, 284.
[2] *Ibid.*, p. 284.

myself, I am disposed to think (differing here in some measure from Professor Max Müller's view of the subject) that the mythology of the lower races rests especially on a basis of real and sensible analogy, and that the great expansion of verbal metaphor into myth belongs to more advanced periods of civilisation. In a word, I take material myth to be the primary, and verbal myth to be the secondary, formation. But whether this opinion be historically sound or not, the difference in nature between myth founded on fact and myth founded on word is sufficiently manifest. The want of reality in verbal metaphor cannot be effectually hidden by the utmost stretch of imagination. In spite of this essential weakness, however, the habit of realising everything that words can describe is one which has grown and flourished in the world. Descriptive names become personal, the notion of personality stretches to take in even the most abstract notions to which a name may be applied, and realised name, epithet, and metaphor pass into interminable mythic growths by the process which Max Müller has so aptly characterised as 'a disease of language.' It would be difficult indeed to define the exact thought lying at the root of every mythic conception, but in easy cases the course of formation can be quite well followed." [1]

The student of myth must possess the ability to transport himself into the imaginative atmosphere of the untutored mind. The inspection of 'nature mythology' helps to show that much myth is related to natural phenomena. "In interpreting heroic legend as based on nature-myth," says Tylor, "circumstantial analogy must be very cautiously appealed to, and at any rate there is need of evidence more cogent than vague likenesses between human and cosmic life. Now such evidence is forthcoming at its strongest in a crowd of myths, whose open meaning it would be wanton incredulity to doubt, so little do they disguise, in name or sense, the familiar aspects of nature which they figure as scenes of personal life. Even where the tellers of legend may have altered or forgotten its earlier mythic meaning, there are often sufficient grounds for an attempt to restore it. In spite of change and corruption,

[1] *Primitive Culture* (London, 1871), p. 320.

myths are slow to lose all consciousness of their first origin." [1]
And "the etymology of names, moreover, is at once the guide
and safeguard of the mythologist [p. 321]. There was no
disputing the obvious fact that Helios (Sol) was the sun, and
Selene the moon." He examines groups of myths "produced
from that craving to know causes and reasons which ever
besets mankind" (p. 392). Allegory is then treated of. It
"cannot maintain the large place often claimed for it [p. 408],
yet it cannot be passed over by the mythologist. A number
of fanciful myths are of the nature of allegory, as that of
Pandora in Hesiod, or Herakles choosing between the paths
of pleasure and virtue." In concluding his chapters on
myth, Tylor remarks in a passage of profound insight: "The
investigation of these intricate and devious operations has
brought ever more and more broadly into view two principles
of mythologic science. The first is that legend, when classified
on a sufficient scale, displays a regularity of development
which the notion of motiveless fancy quite fails to account for,
and which must be attributed to laws of formation whereby
every story, old and new, has arisen from its definite origin
and sufficient cause. So uniform indeed is such development
that it becomes possible to treat myth as an organic product
of mankind at large, in which individual, national, and even
racial distinctions stand subordinate to universal qualities of
the human mind. The second principle concerns the relation
of myth to history. It is true that the search for mutilated
and mystified traditions of real events, which formed so main
a part of old mythological researches, seems to grow more
hopeless the further the study of legend extends. . . . Yet
unconsciously, and as it were in spite of themselves, the shapers
and transmitters of poetic legend have preserved for us masses
of sound historical evidence." [2]

TYLOR'S ANIMISTIC THEORY

The widely accepted theory of animism which has already
been described (p. 22) was promulgated by Tylor in this

---

[1] *Primitive Culture* (London, 1871), p. 320.
[2] *Ibid.*, pp. 415, 416.

58

work. Man, he thinks, first attained to the idea of spirit by reflection on various experiences such as sleep, dreams, trances, shadows, hallucinations, breath, and death, and by degrees extended the conception of soul or ghost until he peopled all nature with spirits. From among these spirits one is finally supreme, if the process of evolution is continued. This theory discounts the early connexion between religion and ethics, and Tylor believed that primitive man had no notion of religion or ethics.

JOHN FERGUSON M'LENNAN

John Ferguson M'Lennan (1827–1881), author of *Primitive Marriage* (1865) and *Studies in Ancient History* (1876), threw much light upon the origin and rise of the family and, incidentally, of totemism. Although he treats the subject from a sociological point of view, his work is of great value to students of myth because of its illustrations of totemism. His principal writings on totemism first appeared in the *Fortnightly Review* of 1869–1870.

HERBERT SPENCER

Herbert Spencer (1820–1903) explained his system of mythology in *Principles of Sociology*. The mental condition of man when he animates and personifies all phenomena is accounted for by degeneration, as in Spencer's view it is not primary but the result of misconception. Language is only one cause of this misconception : statements which had originally a different significance are, he thinks, misinterpreted, as are names of human beings, so that primitive races are gradually led to a belief in personalized phenomena. The defect in early speech, the "lack of words free from implication of vitality," is one of the causes which favour personalization. But in making this statement he appears to overlook the circumstance that such words as "imply vitality" do so because they reflect the thought of the men who use them before misconception can arise through their prolonged use. In any case, the misconstructions of language which he believes to have brought about the idea of personality are in his system "different in kind" from those of the philological school, "and the erroneous course of thought is opposite in direction." He believes the names of human beings in early society to be derived from incidents of the moment, the period of the day, or the condition of the weather. In certain tribes we discover persons named Dawn, Dark Cloud, Sun, etc. Spencer thinks that if a story exists concerning people so named, in process of time it will be transferred to the object or event, which will thereby become personalized. It is clear, however, that few such stories could be apposite, and that their occurrence would be rare.

Traditions of persons coming from the neighbourhood of some mountain or river may grow into belief in actual birth from it. For example, should tradition state that a man's parents came "from the rising sun," he will believe himself a descendant of the luminary, which thus becomes personalized. Holding as he does that ancestor-worship is the first form of religion, and that persons with such names as Sun, Wind, or Cloud may be thus worshipped, Spencer believed that nature myths are a kind of worship of ancestors. Implicit belief in the statements of forefathers is a further cause of personalizing. He explains the idea of descent from beast ancestors by the ancestor of the stock or tribe possessing an animal name, such as Wolf, Tiger, and so forth, and being confounded by his descendants with a real wolf or tiger. Spencer never saw that ancestral memory in savages is extremely short and rarely survives more than three generations. Nor is the savage at a loss to understand the custom of bestowing animal or nature names upon persons. He calls his own child Dawn or Wolf, and therefore he is not tempted to believe that his ancestor was really a tiger or the dawn. The animal descent almost invariably comes through the female line, and the mother's totem-kin name is adopted, yet savages do not worship their ancestresses. The theory, as Lang has said, requires "as a necessary condition a singular amount of memory on the one hand and of forgetfulness on the other.'

PROGRESS OF MYTHIC SCIENCE

WILLIAM ROBERTSON SMITH

One of the first and most remarkable upholders of the anthropological school was William Robertson Smith (1846–1894) a professor of Hebrew in the Free Church College, Aberdeen. The heterodox character of an encyclopædia article on the Bible led to his prosecution for heresy, of which charge, however, he was acquitted. But a further article upon "Hebrew Language and Literature" in the *Encyclopædia Britannica* (1880) led to his removal from the professoriate of the college. In 1881 he assisted Professor Baynes in editing the *Encyclopædia Britannica*, and in 1887 succeeded him as editor-in-chief. He was appointed Lord Almoner's Professor of Arabic at Cambridge in 1883, and Adams Professor of Arabic in 1889.

Robertson Smith's most remarkable work—that to which every modern student of comparative religion owes so much—is his celebrated *Religion of the Semites*, originally delivered as a series of lectures at Aberdeen in the three years from October 1888 to October 1891.

It is of course only this author's views on mythology that we have here to take into account.

Robertson Smith points out that in all ancient religious systems mythology takes the place of dogma. The sacred lore of a race assumes the form of stories about the gods, and these tales offer the sole explanation of religious precept and ritual act, but as myth had no sacred sanction and no binding force on the worshippers, it was not an essential part of religion. Myths "connected with individual sanctuaries and ceremonies were merely part of the apparatus of the worship; they served to excite the fancy and sustain the interest of the worshipper; but he was often offered a choice of several accounts of the same thing, and, provided that he fulfilled the ritual with accuracy, no one cared what he believed about its origin. Belief in a certain series of myths was neither obligatory as a part of true religion, nor was it supposed that, by believing, a man acquired religious merit and conciliated the favour of the gods. What was obligatory or meritorious was the exact performance of certain sacred acts prescribed by religious tradition. This being so, it follows that mythology ought not to take the prominent place that is too often assigned to it in the scientific study of ancient faiths."

Robertson Smith thought that in almost every case the myth was derived from the ritual, not the ritual from the myth. Ritual was fixed, and myth was variable. The one was obligatory, the other at the discretion of the worshipper. " Now by far the largest part of the myths of antique religions is connected with the ritual of particular shrines, or with the religious observances of particular tribes and districts. In all such cases it is probable, in most cases it is certain, that the myth is merely the explanation of a religious usage; and ordinarily it is such an explanation as could not have arisen till the original sense of the usage had more or less fallen into oblivion. As a rule the myth is no explanation of the origin of the ritual to any one who does not believe it to be a narrative of real occurrences, and the boldest mythologist will not believe that. But if it be not true, the myth itself requires to be explained, and every principle of philosophy and common sense demands that the explanation be sought, not in arbitrary allegorical theories, but in the actual facts of ritual or religious custom to which the myth attaches. The conclusion is that in the study of ancient religions we must begin, not with myth, but with ritual and traditional usage."

Myths which do not merely explain traditional practices, but "exhibit the beginnings of larger religious speculation," Robertson Smith also regards as secondary in character. They may be primitive philosophy or political attempts to unite religious groups, originally distinct, or perhaps due to the play of epic imagination. In the later stages of ancient religions mythology became increasingly important. " Myth interpreted by the aid of allegory became the favourite means of infusing a new significance into ancient forms. But the theories thus developed are the falsest of false guides as to the original meaning of the old religions. On the other hand, the ancient myths, taken in their natural sense, without allegorical gloss, are plainly of great importance as testimonies to the views of the nature of the gods that were prevalent when they were formed."

In the third lecture or chapter the author propounds the theory of animism in much the same terms as Tylor, and, speaking generally, the remainder of the work is occupied with considerations regarding the religious life of the Semitic peoples, their holy places, their ritual and sacrifice.

THEOBIOGRAPHY

Robertson Smith is undoubtedly correct in his statement that myth takes the place of dogma in primitive religion—that "the sacred lore of priests and people . . . assumes the form of stories about the gods." But having thus connected theo-biography[1] with religion and the religious spirit, it is difficult to discover why he denies a religious character to myth. "These stories," he says (p. 17), "afford the only explanation that is offered of the precepts of religion and the prescribed rules of ritual." If that be the case, surely the group of myths which detail the deeds of the chief deities is of prime importance to religion. The 'story' of a religion is its most precious asset. It is from the 'story' of their faith that the majority of people receive their ideas concerning it. What would Mohammedanism be without the story of the Prophet? What Buddhism without the tale of Gautama? What Christianity without the life of Christ? And if the argument applies to the higher forms of religion, it may surely be applied, and more so, to primitive faiths. Among savage or barbarous peoples the myth, the body of tales which circles round the gods, is universal tribal property. It takes the place of written scripture, it infuses all poetry and epic, it is represented in sacred drama, it is recited by the neophytes for the priesthood, it underlies the most sacred mysteries. The contention that myth was "no essential part of ancient religion" is based upon a fundamental misconception of the spoken or written story of the gods. In the present writer's view myth is a most

---

[1] This appears to the author a suitable term for those bodies of myth which deal exclusively with the lives and adventures of the gods, and differ therefore so strikingly from all other classes of myth.

important element of primitive religion ; for whereas ritual often impresses an alien people as magical and therefore inimical, and is not so readily borrowed, the wide transmission of myth proves that it not only impresses the imagination of the races among whom it has origin, but that it is able to take hold of neighbouring and even distant peoples as well.

Akin to the first error is Robertson Smith's further fallacy that ritual is prior in origin to myth in primitive religion. " It may be affirmed with confidence," he says, " that the myth was derived from the ritual, not the ritual from the myth." Therefore the savage sacrifices with much involved ceremonial to something concerning which he knows and has invented nothing !

THE CONSERVATISM OF CHILDHOOD

That myth is sacred may be seen, if our conclusions are correct, in a fact already employed to explain the fixed and unchangeable character of the folk-tale. Children, it is observed, listening to a traditional story do not approve of any alteration in its plot or circumstances. Is this dislike—one might almost say horror—of alteration in folk-tale a legacy of the religious dread of any attempt to tamper with the tales of the gods? If so, such a sentiment would only be likely to arise in an environment where the idea of the sacred had already made considerable headway.

This argument does not claim an ethical character for myth, nor for ritual or the other elements of religion, which did not originally know of or possess any ethical spirit, but had to acquire it painfully. The argument that belief in myth was not " obligatory as a part of true religion " is futile. It was not obligatory because it was natural and general. That one could not acquire religious merit by knowing it is also untrue. Intimate acquaintance with the religious story is in many civilized modern communities (Mohammedans, Hindus, British rural folk) the measure of piety, and among savages and the peoples of antiquity (Egyptians, Greeks, Australians, etc.) the religious story is the nucleus of the most sacred mysteries of the faith.

PROGRESS OF MYTHIC SCIENCE

CORNELIUS PETRUS TIELE

Cornelius Petrus Tiele (1830–1902), a professor of the history of religions at Leyden, although claimed as an ally by Max Müller, was much more inclined toward fellowship with the anthropological school. In his *Revue de l'Histoire des Religions* (1876, trans. 1878, xii, 250) he says: "I am an ally, much more than an adversary, of the new school, whether styled ethnological or anthropological. It is true that all the ideas advanced by its partisans are not so new as they seem. Some of us—I mean among those who, without being vassals of the old school, were formed by it—had not only remarked already the defects of the reigning method, but had perceived the direction in which researches should be made ; they had even begun to say so. This does not prevent the young school from enjoying the great merit of having first formulated with precision, and with the energy of conviction, that which had hitherto been but imperfectly pointed out. If henceforth mythological science marches with a firmer foot, and loses much of its hypothetical character, it will in part owe this to the stimulus of the new school."

Again he says (*op. cit.*, p. 253): "If I were reduced to choose between this method and that of comparative philology, I would prefer the former without the slightest hesitation. This method alone enables us to explain the fact, such a frequent cause of surprise, that the Greeks, like the Germans, . . . could attribute to their gods all manner of cruel, cowardly, and dissolute actions. This method alone reveals the cause of all the strange metamorphoses of gods into animals, plants, and even stones. . . . In fact, this method teaches us to recognize in all these oddities the survivals of an age of barbarism long over-past, but lingering into later times, under the form of religious legends, the most persistent of all traditions. . . . This method, then, can alone help us to account for the genesis of myths, because it devotes itself to studying them in their rudest and most primitive shape." At the same time, Tiele thought that the anthropological method "cannot answer all the questions which the science of mythology must solve, or at least must study." He also states that the anthropological school is "not entirely wrong" in claiming him as an ally, and goes on to say: "But I must protest in the name of mythological science, and of the exactness as necessary to her as to any of the other sciences, against a method which only glides over questions of the first importance and which to most questions can only reply, with a smile, *C'est chercher raison où il n'y en a pas.*"

Tiele also considered the anthropological school "too exclusive," and thought that it might have ignorant camp-followers. In the latter fear he was justified, as writers who saw totems and fetishes everywhere were at that time rife; and there are not wanting popular writers of the present day just as extravagant, who, while highly enthusiastic over the achievements of the school, only dimly appreciate the anthropological standpoint.

ANDREW LANG

Perhaps the greatest binding force, and certainly the greatest popularity, was given to the anthropological school by Andrew Lang (1844–1913), whose works *Myth, Ritual, and Religion* (1887), *Modern Mythology* (1897), and *The Making of Religion* (1898), contain originality, great dialectic ability, and keen insight. Waxing autobiographical in the second work, Lang wrote concerning his own position: "Like other inquiring undergraduates in the sixties, I read such works on mythology as Mr Max Müller had then given to the world; I read them with interest, but without conviction. The argument, the logic, seemed to evade one; it was purely, with me, a question of logic, for I was of course prepared to accept all of Mr Max Müller's dicta on questions of etymologies. Even now I never venture to impugn them, only, as I observe that other scholars very frequently differ, *toto cælo*, from him and from each other in essential questions, I preserve a just balance of doubt; I wait till these gentlemen shall be at one among themselves. After taking my degree in 1868, I had leisure to read a good deal of mythology in the legends of all races, and found my distrust of Mr Max Müller's reasoning increase upon me. The main cause was that whereas Mr Max Müller explained Greek myths by etymologies of words in the Aryan languages, chiefly Greek, Latin, Slavonic, and Sanskrit, I kept finding myths very closely resembling those of Greece among Red Indians, Kaffirs, Eskimo, Samoyeds, Kamilaroi, Maoris, and Cahrocs. Now if Aryan myths arose from a 'disease' of Aryan languages, it certainly did seem an odd thing that myths so similar to these abounded where non-Aryan languages alone prevailed. Did a kind of linguistic measles affect all tongues alike, from Sanskrit to Choctaw, and everywhere produce the same ugly scars in religion and myth? The ugly scars were the problem ! A civilised fancy is not puzzled for a moment by a beautiful beneficent Sun-god, or even by his beholding the daughters of men that they are fair. But a civilised fancy *is* puzzled when the beautiful Sun-god makes love in the shape of a dog. To me, and indeed to Mr Max Müller, the ugly scars were the problem."

Lang's first work on myth, *Myth, Ritual, and Religion*, after briefly reviewing the various systems of mythic interpretation prior to and current in his time, lays stress upon the difference between religion and myth, in which he sees two distinct human moods, the one sacred, the other wholly frivolous in origin. This conflict is present in all religions. The two moods, we are told (p. 5), are conspicuous even in Christianity, in prayers, hymns, and "the dim religious light" of cathedrals on the one hand, and on the other in the buffoonery of miracle plays and the uncouth blasphemies of folk-tales. Backward peoples too make a distinction between their religion and their mythology. The 'wild' element of mythic story is then explained as a survival from the savage state, the mental condition of savages is described in its bearing upon primitive fiction, and its outstanding types are outlined, as are some of the world's chief mythic systems—all to illustrate the anthropological standpoint of the author. Incidentally is developed the 'All-Father' theory, which will be dealt with later.

'ERRATIC FANCY' IN MYTH

In this work we have, perhaps, the most valuable statement of the anthropological case extant, but in it Lang insists too much upon a fundamental difference between myth and religion. He says (*loc. cit.*) : " For the present we can only say that the religious conception uprises from the human intellect in one mood, that of earnest contemplation and submission : while the mythical ideas uprise from another mood, that of playful and erratic fancy." Absurd and unholy stories of the gods are common, but all myths are not of this kind, and many were and are employed as ritual by various peoples, who recite them frequently as the histories of the gods they worship. Again, Lang's contention that myth is not 'religious' would seem to be defeated by his own just argument that myth containing 'wild' elements dates from primitive times. He accounts for its 'wildness' by its primitiveness ; it was blasphemous because savage. But although blasphemous to the civilized man, it may not be so to the uncultured barbarian, and to him may be even religious. Elsewhere Lang cites Australian myth to prove that one tale is told to "unimportant persons," such as women and boys, another to the initiated.[1] The first is of the nature of myth, the second religious in character. We can discern a measure of truth in what he advocates, but a hard and fast line cannot be drawn between myth and religion, as no one can say where myth ends and religion begins. They overlap ; and when we read of the pranks of the Greek Zeus or the Chinook Blue Jay we may say to ourselves : " Thus the gods figure in the imagination of the savage, in whom the religious sense is faint. Once myth emerges from the animistic, totemistic, and barbarous state it rises in character." But—and this is important—there still cling to it the age-long tales of the gods as savages, barbaric, bloodthirsty, absurd, in no way to be cleansed or 'edited' or rendered 'decent.' They are regarded by men as sacred because they are old.

[1] It seems to me that a small proportion only of myth as we know it can owe its origin to the intention of the males to conceal matters from the women and boys. Most written myth is certainly the work of priesthoods, and as it often accompanies ritual, the immobile character of the latter is a guarantee of its genuineness. Again, it frequently appears as pseudo-history, and could therefore scarcely be designed to screen anything more esoteric. The myths enacted in Hellenic mystery plays do not appear to have differed much in plot from the stories of popular acceptance, and the same may be said concerning those American myths which are danced out in the secrecy of male mystic societies.

PROGRESS OF MYTHIC SCIENCE

The arguments against Lang's conception of myth as the ribald brother of religion are as follows: (1) The majority of ancient myths are not absurd, obscene, or blasphemous in essence, as is proved by the circumstances of their invention. (2) Other myths which appear blasphemous to the civilized mind do not necessarily seem so to the savage mind. The strange sense of humour peculiar to savages is not taken into consideration by Lang, nor that most of the absurdities and obscenities arise from totemic sources *and are therefore necessarily animal in their characteristics.* (3) The preservation and recital of myths by priests proves their sacred character.[1]

Therefore, although a difference exists between myth and dogma, it is one of degree only, not of kind. In all ages the ribald mind has concocted scandalous stories concerning the gods, but most primitive myth is not to be classed as 'ribald,' as a careful perusal of it will show.

LANG'S GENERAL THESIS

Lang states his general thesis clearly on p. 8. He says: "Before going further, it is desirable to set forth what our aim is, and to what extent we are seeking an interpretation of mythology. It is not our purpose to explain every detail of every ancient legend, either as a distorted historical fact or as the result of this or that confusion of thought caused by forgetfulness of the meanings of language, or in any other way; nay, we must constantly protest against the excursions of too venturesome ingenuity. Myth is so ancient, so complex, so full of elements, that it is vain labour to seek a cause for every phenomenon. We are chiefly occupied with the quest for an historical condition of the human intellect to which the element in myths, regarded by us as irrational, shall seem rational enough. If we can prove that such a state of mind widely exists among men, and has existed, that state of mind may be provisionally considered as the fount and *origin* of the myths which have always perplexed men in a reasonable modern mental condition."

The irrational element in myth, to which we have already

---

[1] Extensive correspondence with students of myth has helped to convince me of the partial breakdown of Lang's argument.

given some consideration, is then discussed by Lang, and as our manner of dealing with it is founded upon his, it is unnecessary to recapitulate his arguments. It must be remarked, however, that he lays down (vol. i, p. 22) the conclusion that "All interpretations of myth have been formed in accordance with the ideas prevalent in the time of the interpreters." He states that his theory naturally attaches itself to the general system of evolution, and through it we are enabled to examine myth as "a thing of gradual development and of slow and manifold modifications." Thus we find that much of ancient myth is a thing of great complexity, composed of the savage 'explanation,' the civilized and poetic modification thereof, and the later popular idea of the original tale. "A critical study of these three stages in myth is in accordance with the recognised practice of science. Indeed, the whole system is only an application to this particular province, mythology, of the method by which the development either of organisms or of human institutions is traced. As the anomalies and apparently useless and accidental features in the human or in other animal organisms may be explained as stunted or rudimentary survivals of organs useful in a previous stage of life, so the anomalous and irrational myths of civilised races may be explained as survivals of stories which, in an earlier state of thought and knowledge, seemed natural enough. The persistence of the myths is accounted for by the well-known conservatism of the religious sentiment—a conservatism noticed even by Eusebius."

DIFFUSION OF IDENTICAL MYTHS

The diffusion of identical myths, Lang argues, is due to the universal prevalence of similar mental habits and ideas at one time or another, but he admits that this argument may be pressed too far, and that it will "scarcely account for the world-wide distribution of long and intricate mythical *plots*." The diffusion of mythic fiction would, in the judgment of the present writer, justify the opinion that in many instances borrowing and transmission take place ; but all cases should be examined on their individual merits.

PROGRESS OF MYTHIC SCIENCE

Lang proceeds to examine the mental condition of savages, in accordance with the views in our introductory chapter, and with special reference to totemism and magic. The animistic hypothesis is examined. His chapters relating to cosmogony may be passed over as containing no very original criticism. The author's 'All-Father' theory, as outlined in our notice of his book *The Making of Religion*, is set forth, and the remainder of that work is occupied with a description of the greater mythological systems of the world, regarding some of which he was not sufficiently well informed to speak with authority.[1]

"MODERN MYTHOLOGY"

In *Modern Mythology* (1897) Lang shows why the anthropological school in England was obliged to challenge Professor Max Müller. After pointing out the inconveniences of Müller's method in controversy, the author proves that Tiele leans more in the direction of his school than to that of Müller. He then reviews Mannhardt's position, which he shows to be also anti-Müllerian. He touches upon Müller's misunderstandings regarding totemism and reviews "the value of anthropological evidence." He points out that the past of savages must have been "a very long past," and insists upon the value of Tylor's "test of undesigned coincidence in testimony" (the famous 'test of recurrence') as a criterion of the value of myth. "The philological method in anthropology" is discussed. Says Lang: "Given Dr Hahn's book on Hottentot manners and religion: the anthropologist compares the Hottentot rites, beliefs, social habits, and general ideas with those of other races known to him, savage or civilised. A Hottentot custom, which has a meaning among Hottentots, may exist where its meaning is lost, among Greeks or other 'Aryans.' A story of a Hottentot god, quite a natural sort of tale for a Hottentot to tell, may be told about a god in Greece, where it is contrary to the Greek spirit. We infer that the Greeks perhaps inherited it from savage ancestors, or borrowed

[1] For example, on America, like Frazer, he bungles sadly, and seems to have betaken himself for information to the wrong authority in almost every instance, and especially when he desires to illustrate an argument.

71

it from savages. This is the method, and if we can also get a scholar to analyse the *names* of Hottentot gods, we are all the luckier—that is, if his processes and inferences are *logical*. May we not decide on the *logic* of scholars? But, just as Mr Max Müller points out to us the dangers attending our evidence, we point out to him the dangers attending his method. In Dr Hahn's book, the doctor analyses the meaning of the names Tsuni-Goam and other names, discovers their original sense, and from that sense explains the myths about Hottentot divine beings. Here we anthropologists first ask Mr Max Müller, before accepting Dr Hahn's etymologies, to listen to other scholars about the perils and difficulties of the philological analysis of divine names even in Aryan languages. I have already quoted his 'defender' Dr Tiele. 'The philological method is inadequate and misleading, when it is a question of (1) discovering the origin of a myth, or (2) the physical explanation of the oldest myths, or (3) of accounting for the rude and obscene element in the divine legends of civilised races.' To the two former purposes Dr Hahn applies the philological method in the case of Tsuni-Goam. Other scholars agree with Dr Tiele. Mannhardt, as we said, held that Mr Max Müller's favourite etymological 'equations' (Sarameya = Hermeias; Saranyu = Demeter Erinnys; Kentauros = Gandharvas, and others) would not stand criticism. 'The method in its practical working shows a lack of the historical sense,' said Mannhardt. Curtius—a scholar, as Mr Max Müller declares—says, 'It is especially difficult to conjecture the meaning of proper names, and above all of local and mythical names.' I do not see that it is easier when these names are not Greek, but Hottentot, or Algonquin!"

Then follows a review of the contending methods of the philological and anthropological schools in the explanation of various myths and ritualistic customs, and the method of the latter school is clearly vindicated.

LANG'S ANTI-ANIMISTIC HYPOTHESIS

The thesis of the first portion of Lang's *The Making of Religion* (London, 1898) is that the abnormal phenomena believed in by savages and later civilized peoples assisted them to evolve the idea of godhead. Lang holds that "the savage beliefs, however erroneous, however darkened by fraud and fancy, repose on a basis of real observation of actual phenomena." With such a contention, however ingenious, anthropology can scarcely concern itself, as our knowledge of the supernatural is by no means sufficient to permit us to apply it to anthropology.

The arguments put forward in the second part of the book are: (1) "That the conception of a separable surviving soul of a dead man was not only not essential to the savage's idea of his supreme god . . . but would have been wholly inconsistent with that conception." (2) That the original idea of god among primitive peoples was not animistic and did not evolve from the idea of the existence of spirit, but came first in order of evolution and was that of a "magnified non-natural man" (anthropomorphic and monotheistic). "He existed before death came into the world and he still exists." Moreover, such cults contained ethical and moral ideas not usually discovered in 'animistic' religions. Lang illustrates this theory by examples taken from Australian, Fuegian, Andamanese, Zulu, and other races of low culture.

As regards the first part of his contention, whatever may have been the case with primitive man (concerning whose religious ideas we can only theorize), it does not hold good of savages of the present day, when animistic ideas are universally in the transition state. The second argument is very much open to criticism, because the religious ideas of the races alluded to by Lang as monotheistic may have been modified by the theology of missionaries, Christian or Mohammedan. This criticism Lang himself held not to be justified by facts, and there are grounds for believing that his theory possesses a certain amount of truth. Before, however, it can be discussed in its entirety, the religious ideas of the peoples to which he alludes and those of other races similarly environed will require to be much more fully and rigorously examined and a much larger body of data collected. If Lang's conclusions could be justified, they would revolutionize the whole study of comparative religion. It would perhaps mean that such gods as Yahweh in Israel and Tezcatlipoca in Mexico, instead of being gradually evolved from lower spiritual forms, were survivals of very early conceptions of non-spiritual forms of deity. But Lang's data show that the early monotheistic, or the 'All-Father' idea, as he calls it, disappears because of the adoption of animistic ideas. Yahweh and Tezcatlipoca, we know, flourished side by side with and in an atmosphere of animism. It would be strange if the Hebrews, a branch of a race typically polytheistic (and therefore animistic), had not at one time been given to a similar worship, and everything seems to prove that they were originally polytheistic. If Yahweh was, as Lang suggested, an original 'All-Father,' it is strange that Noldeke should have been able to trace his name through the form *Shaddai* to *Shedi* ('my demon'), a name sufficiently animistic. This would appear to be a test of Lang's theory, but the question, as he stated, " can only be settled by specialists." He was right. He himself failed entirely to realize the weight and abundance of the evidence for early polytheism and animism among the Israelites. Again, when in Mexico we observe the rise of Tezcatlipoca from the obsidian stone, we must repeat that further special study alone can throw light on the question. Lang called his examination of the subject " a 'sketch'—not an exhaustive survey," but the thoughtful student of comparative religion will admit that it is a sketch raising questions of the greatest import to the science he explores.[1]

---

[1] Lang's 'All-Father' deities forcibly suggest evolution from the old 'sky-god,' if, indeed, they were not that deity without much alteration. The 'Sky-Father' in opposition, or at least in contradistinction, to the 'Earth-Mother' was merely the sky personalized as a 'magnified non-natural man.' Let us enumerate his attributes, given by Lang in the *Encyclopædia Britannica*:

    (1) His home is in the sky.
    (2) He is the maker of things.
    (3) Mankind are his disobedient progeny, whom he casts out of heaven.

This specification can allude to no type other than sky-gods, which are wholly 'animistic' in origin. If Lang had chanced to think of this resemblance himself, he would probably have been the first to admit the correctness of such a statement. His *The Making of Religion* bears proof of its obviousness on every page. The 'All-Father' idea certainly evolves from the personalization of the sky. He quotes

PROGRESS OF MYTHIC SCIENCE

SIR JAMES GEORGE FRAZER

One of the greatest modern names in primitive religious science is that of Sir James George Frazer, the world-famous author of *The Golden Bough*. Founded to some extent upon the principles of Mannhardt, Sir J. G. Frazer's mythological studies relate chiefly to vegetation and the deities connected therewith. Indeed, it has been said that he has seen gods of vegetation everywhere, just as the Müller school saw sun-gods everywhere.

Perhaps the most acute criticism upon Sir J. G. Frazer's great work is to be found in Lang's *Magic and Religion*, in the essay "The Ghastly Priest." The first critical paragraph of this makes amusing reading : " Still, the new school of mythology does work the vegetable element in mythology hard ; nearly as hard as the solar element used to be worked. Aphrodite, as the female mate of Adonis, gets mixed up with plant life. So does Attis with Cybele, so does Balder, so does Death, so does Dionysus with undoubted propriety ; so does Eabani, so does Gilgamesh, so does Haman, so does Hera, so does Iasion with Demeter, so does Isis, so does Jack-in-the-Green, so does Kupalo, so do Linus and Lityerses, so does Mamurius Veturius, so does Merodach or Marduk (if he represents Eabani or Gilgamesh), so does Mars, so does Osiris, so, I think, does Semiramis, so does Tammuz, so does Virbius, so does Zeus, probably ; so does a great multitude of cattle, cats, horses, bulls, goats, cocks, with plenty of other beasts. The solar mythologists did not spare heroes like Achilles ; they too were the sun. But the vegetable school, the Covent Garden school of mythologists, mixes up real human beings with vegetation."

FRAZER'S MAIN CONTENTION

Frazer's main contention is that the priest of the sanctuary of Diana Nemorensis, near the modern Nemi, in Italy (a priest

the Zuñi Indian god Awonawilona as an ' All-Father ' ; Awonawilona is a Sky-Father pure and simple, as his myth shows ; and practically all his other examples may be traced back in the same manner.

who was invariably a murderer, and who only held office until another murderer dispossessed and slew him, after plucking a bough from the tree under which he sheltered), has numerous parallels in other, ancient and modern, barbarian priesthoods. He says : " If we can show that a barbarous custom, like that of the priesthood of Nemi, has existed elsewhere ; if we can detect the motives which led to its institution ; if we can prove that these motives have operated widely, perhaps universally, in human society, producing in varied circumstances a variety of institutions specifically different but generally alike ; if we can show, lastly, that these very motives, with some of their derivative institutions, were actually at work in classical antiquity ; then we may fairly infer that at a remoter age the same motives gave birth to the priesthood of Nemi. Such an inference, in default of direct evidence as to how the priesthood did actually arise, can never amount to demonstration. But it will be more or less probable according to the degree of completeness with which it fulfils the conditions indicated above. The object of this book is, by meeting these conditions, to offer a fairly probable explanation of the priesthood of Nemi."

According to Frazer, too, the priest of Nemi was of a class regarded as divine. He says (vol. i, p. 231): "Thus the cult of the Arician grove was essentially that of a tree-spirit or sylvan deity. But our examination of European folk-custom demonstrated that a tree-spirit is frequently represented by a living person, who is regarded as an embodiment of the tree-spirit and possessed of its fertilising powers ; and our previous survey of primitive belief proved that this conception of a god incarnate in a living man is common among rude races. Further, we have seen that the living person who is believed to embody in himself the tree-spirit is often called a king, in which respect, again, he strictly represents the tree-spirit. For the sacred cedar of the Gilgit tribes is called, as we have seen, 'the Dreadful King'; and the chief forest god of the Finns, by name Tapio, represented as an old man with a brown beard, a high hat of fir-cones, and a coat of tree-moss, was styled the Wood King, Lord of the Woodland, Golden King of the Wood. May not then the King of the Wood in the Arician grove have been, like the King of May, the Leaf King, the Grass King, and the like, an incarnation of the tree-spirit or spirit of vegetation? His title, his sacred office, and his residence in the grove all point to this conclusion, which is confirmed by his relation to the Golden Bough. For since the King of the Wood could only be assailed by him who had plucked the Golden Bough, his life was safe from assault so long as the bough, or the tree on which it grew, remained uninjured. In a sense, therefore, his life was bound up with that of the tree; and thus to some extent he stood to the tree in the same relation in which the incorporate or immanent tree-spirit stands to it."

LANG'S CRITICISM OF FRAZER'S THESIS

But Lang controverts these premises. He does not regard the priest of the Arician grove as a likely representative of a god of vegetation. "First," he says (I quote at length because of the importance of the passage), "let us ask what we know about this ghastly priest. Let us begin with the evidence of Virgil, in the Sixth Book of the *Æneid* (line 136 and so onwards). Virgil says nothing about the ghastly priest, or, in this place, about Diana, or the grove near Aricia. Virgil, indeed, tells us much about a bough of a tree, a golden branch, but as to the singular priest, nothing. But some four hundred years after Virgil's date (say A.D. 370), a commentator on Virgil, Servius, tried to illustrate the passage cited from the *Æneid*. He obviously knows nothing about Virgil's mystic golden bough, but he tells us that, in his own time, 'public opinion' (*publica opinio*) placed the habitat of Virgil's bough in the grove haunted by the ghastly priest, near Aricia. It is, in fact, not known whether Virgil invented his bough, with its extraordinary attributes, or took it from his rich store of antiquarian learning. It may have been a folklore belief, like *Le Rameau d'Or* of Madame d'Aulnoy's fairy-tale. Virgil's bough, as we shall see, has one folklore attribute in common with a mystic sword in the Arthurian cycle of romances, and in the *Volsunga Saga*. I think that Mr Frazer has failed to comment on this point. If I might hazard a guess as to Virgil's branch, it is that, of old, suppliants approached gods or kings with boughs in their hands. He who would approach Proserpine carried, in Virgil, a bough of pure gold, which only the favoured and predestined suppliant could obtain, as shall be shown.

"In the four centuries between Virgil and Servius the meaning and source of Virgil's branch of gold were forgotten. But people, and Servius himself, knew of another bough, near Aricia, and located (conjecturally?) Virgil's branch of gold in that district. Servius, then, in his commentary on the *Æneid*, after the manner of annotators in all ages, talks much about the boughs of a certain tree in a certain grove, concerning which Virgil makes no remark. Virgil, as we shall see, was writing about a golden branch of very peculiar character. Knowing, like the public opinion of his age, something about quite other branches, and nothing about Virgil's branch, Servius tells us that, in the grove of Diana at Aricia, there grew a tree from which it was unlawful (*non licebat*) to break a bough. If any fugitive slave, however, could break a branch from this tree, he might fight the priest, taking his office if successful. In the opinion of Servius the temple was founded by Orestes, to the barbaric Diana of the Chersonese, whence he had fled after a homicide. *That* Diana received human sacrifices of all strangers who landed on her coasts. The rite of human sacrifice was, in Italy, commuted, Servius thinks, for the duel between the priest and the fugitive slave, Orestes having himself been a fugitive. The process is, first a Greek wanderer on a barbarous coast is in danger of being offered, as all outlanders were offered, to the local goddess. This rite was a form of *xenelasia*, an anti-immigrant statute. Compare China, the Transvaal, the agitation against pauper immigrants. Having escaped being sacrificed, and having killed the king in an unfriendly land, Orestes flies to Italy and appeases the cruel Diana by erecting her fane at Aricia. But, instead of sacrificing immigrants, he, or his successors, establishes a duel between the priest and any other fugitive slave. Servius then, not observing this, goes off into an allegorising interpretation of Virgil's branch, as worthless as all such interpretations always are.

PROGRESS OF MYTHIC SCIENCE

"The story about Orestes appears to myself to be a late 'ætiological myth,' a story invented to explain the slaying of the slayer—which it does not do; in short, it is an hypothesis. The priesthood is open not to men flying the blood feud like Orestes, but only to runaway slaves. The custom introduced by Orestes was the sacrifice of outlanders, not of priests. The story has a *doublette* in Pausanias. According to Pausanias, Hippolytus was raised from the dead, and, in hatred of his father, and being a fugitive, he went and reigned at the Arician grove of the goddess.

THE GHASTLY PRIEST

"For these reasons, apparently, Statius calls the Arician grove *profugis regibus aptum*, a sanctuary of exiled princes, Orestes and Hippolytus. From Suetonius we learn that the ghastly priest was styled *Rex Nemorensis*, King of the Wood, and that the envious Caligula, thinking the priest had held office long enough, set another athlete to kill him. The title of 'king,' borne by a priest, suggests, of course, the sacrificial king at Rome. Also Mr Frazer adduces African kings of fire and water, credited with miraculous powers over the elements. They kill nobody and nobody kills them. Then we have Jack-in-the-Green = May-tree = the Spirit of Vegetation—the May *King* and the *Queen* of the May. 'These titles,' as Mannhardt observes, 'imply that the spirit incorporate in vegetation is a ruler, whose creative power extends far and wide.' Possibly so. Now, the King of the Wood, the ghastly priest, lived in the grove of Diana, who (among other things) has the attributes of a tree-spirit. 'May not, then, the King of the Wood, in the Arician grove, have been, like the King of the May . . . an incarnation of the tree-spirit, or spirit of vegetation?' Given a female tree-spirit, we should rather expect a *Queen* of the Wood; and we assuredly do not expect a priest of Diana to represent the supreme Aryan god, nay to incarnate him. But this Mr Frazer thinks probable. Again, 'since the King of the Wood could only be assailed by him who had plucked the Golden Bough, his life was safe from assault so long as the bough, or the tree on which it grew, remained uninjured.'

79

INTRODUCTION TO MYTHOLOGY

WHAT IS THE 'GOLDEN BOUGH'?

"Here we remark the nimbleness of Mr Frazer's method. In vol. i, 4, he had said : 'Tradition averred that the fatal branch ' (in the grove near Aricia) 'was that golden bough which, at the Sibyl's bidding, Æneas plucked before he assayed the perilous journey to the world of the dead.' But I have tried to show that, according to Servius, this identification of two absolutely distinct boughs, neither similar nor similarly situated, was the conjecture of 'public opinion' in an age divided from Virgil's date by four hundred years.

"In the space between vol. i, 4, and i, 231, the averment of tradition, as Mr Frazer calls it, the inference of the curious, as I suppose, to the effect that Virgil's golden branch and the Arician branch were identical, has become matter of fact for Mr Frazer. 'Since the King of the Wood could only be assailed by him who had plucked the Golden Bough,' he says; with what follows.

"But who has told us anything about the breaking, by a fugitive slave, near Aricia, of a *golden* bough? Nobody, as far as I am aware, has mentioned the circumstance. After an interval of four hundred years, the golden bough of Virgil is only brought by Servius into connection with the wood at Aricia, because Servius, and the public opinion of his age, knew about a branch there, and did not know anything about Virgil's branch of gold.

" *That* branch is a safe passport to Hades. It is sacred, not to a tree-spirit named Diana, but to Infernal Juno, or Proserpine. It cannot be broken by a fugitive slave, or anybody else; no, nor can it be cut with edge of iron. None but he whom the Fates call can break it. It yields at a touch of the predestined man, and another golden branch grows instantly in its place.

> " Primo avolso non deficit alter
> Aureus. . . .
> . . . Ipse volens facilisque sequetur,
> Si te fata vocant.

"Virgil's bough thus answers to the magical sword set in a stone in the Arthurian legends, in a tree-trunk in the *Volsunga*

Saga, as Mr H. S. C. Everard reminds me. All the knights may tug vainly at the sword, but you can draw it lightly, *si te fata vocant*, if you are the predestined king, if you are Arthur or Sigmund. When Æneas bears *this* bough, Charon recognises the old familiar passport. Other living men, in the strength of this talisman, have already entered the land of the dead.

> " Ille admirans venerabile donum
> Fatalis virgæ, longo post tempore visum.

"I have collected all these extraordinary attributes of Virgil's bough (in origin, a suppliant's bough, perhaps), because, as far as I notice, Mr Frazer lays no stress on the many peculiarities which differentiate Virgil's bough from any casual branch of the tree at Aricia, and connect it with the mystic sword. The 'general reader' (who seldom knows Latin) needs, I think, to be told precisely what Virgil's bough was. Nothing can be more unlike a branch, any accessible branch, of the Arician tree, than is Virgil's golden bough. It does not grow at Aricia. It is golden. It is not connected with a tree-spirit, but is dear to Proserpine. (I easily see, of course, that Proserpine may be identified with a tree-spirit.) Virgil's branch is not to be plucked by fugitive slaves. It is not a challenge, but a talismanic passport to Hades, recognised by Charon, who has not seen a specimen for ever so long. It is instantly succeeded, if plucked, by another branch of gold, which the Arician twig is not. So I really do not understand how Mr Frazer can identify Virgil's golden bough with an ordinary branch of a tree at Aricia, which anybody could break, though only runaway slaves, strongly built, had an interest in so doing." [1]

FARNELL'S CRITICISM OF " THE GOLDEN BOUGH "

The Golden Bough is an exhaustive repository of mythic and anthropological fact. It has been criticized [2] as leaning too much to the side of the 'stratification' theory—that is, the belief in the existence of certain fixed religious conditions at different epochs of man's experience and the labelling of these by such names as 'animism,' 'totemism,' and the like. At least,

[1] *Magic and Religion*, pp. 207 *sqq.*
[2] See review by Lewis Farnell in the *Quarterly Review* for April 1915.

Thus says the *Quarterly*,
So savage and Tartarly.

The present writer cannot subscribe to such criticism. It should be plain that in the earliest times the animistic and pre-animistic types of religious experience must have held single and undisputed sway among the whole of mankind. 'Totemism' and 'fetishism' are merely animism in another form, and in effect there are only two great types of primitive religious belief, the animistic and the polytheistic, the latter differing from the former merely because animism, or personalization of all phenomena, animal or vegetable, developed into anthropo-morphism, which saw man's nature in the gods. It is admitted that the lesser stages of animism overlap each other in numerous instances, but one outstanding type gives shape to most systems of belief capable of classification, lesser types serving only to throw the one great one into relief. Thus Greek religion was unquestionably an anthropomorphic polytheism; the Mexican a polytheism with survivals of totemism and fetishism; and so on. But although the great central type permits us to give a broad classification to any religion, it is the lesser attributes which help us to pigeon-hole it properly. Thus we might class the majority of American religions as polytheisms newly emerged or emerging from animistic influences; but such a general definition would be imperfect because the combination of the bird-and-serpent myth has provided America with many outstanding divine forms in some measure different from gods evolved elsewhere. Monotheism is a religious condition so rare that it may be altogether discounted in classifying primitive religion. These conclusions hedge between the Frazerian view that religious experience is capable of more or less concrete classification, and the bewildering, chaotic opinion that classi-fication should be entirely discountenanced in religious science. While we may hesitate to speak with Sir James Frazer of such hard and fast periods as an " age of magic " or an " age of religion," we can subscribe to " anthropomorphism superimposed upon a previous theriomorphism or theriolatry," a description at which Sir James Frazer's reviewer cavils. He would doubtless tell us that many religious types coexisted in that age. Quite so; but were they as distinctive, as widespread, and as illustrative of prevailing conditions in such-and-such a region at such-and-such a period as the above?

THE 'ADJACENT' METHOD

Sir James Frazer is further accused of employing the universal comparative method at the expense of the 'adjacent' method, the method which studies the religion of a certain people in its own sphere. It is often pretended nowadays that more merit accrues to the pursuit of this form of anthropological science than to the comparative method. We do not deny that a very considerable degree of training, experience, and erudition is required to achieve success in it, but the assumption that it in any way approaches in magnitude the task which the comparative student proposes to himself is absurd. The greatest mythological studies are comparative in character. True, many works on particular mythologies are of outstanding excellence and charm; but students of comparative religion still await a work dealing with an isolated mythology of the calibre of *The Golden Bough*, mistaken as are many of its premises, Payne's *New World called America*, or Lang's *Myth, Ritual, and Religion*, unless it be, perhaps, Robertson Smith's *Religion of the Semites*.

It is, further, scarcely criticism to label Sir James Frazer's great work 'second-hand.' In works dealing with comparative mythology the facts collated must of necessity be gleaned from the writings of others. This cry is surely unsuitable to mythological debate!

The criticism that Sir James Frazer is unable to pursue to their logical ends the problems he proposes to himself is better founded, as is the charge of discursiveness. It is true, too, that he possesses the faculty of seeing resemblances but not differences when dealing with analogies, and that, consequently, he lumps too many diverse facts together. Lastly he is tacitly charged with perversion of evidence![1]

His definition of magic will be dealt with elsewhere.

---

[1] The implication is frivolous and crude. I observe, as a specialist in Mexican mythology, that Sir James habitually and most unfortunately makes use of the wrong authorities to substantiate his claims when dealing with this province of tradition;

INTRODUCTION TO MYTHOLOGY

The Golden Bough has served the passing and the present generations of mythologists and folklorists well as a great compendium of mythic and anthropological fact. From its far-flung influence none can escape. It is a body of learning to which the searcher must return again and yet again.

E. J. PAYNE

Edward John Payne, in his *History of the New World called America*, a work of surprising erudition too little known, applied the anthropological conception of myth to the mythologies of Mexico and Peru, but although his reading on these subjects was wide and his treatment marked by care and insight, he does not appear to have been closely acquainted with the *pinturas* or manuscript remains of the Mexican peoples, a knowledge of which is essential to all students of the subject. Instead of specializing upon any one department of American aboriginal civilization, he took the whole of it for his province and applied the anthropological method to all the conditions of American life, social, linguistic, agricultural, and religious; and he produced a work truly monumental in spirit, not surpassed by any kindred effort of his generation, in spite of the defect mentioned above.

SALOMON REINACH

Salomon Reinach has done good service to the science of comparative religion in France. After a distinguished archæo-

but that a scholar of his standing would descend to such depths there is not a shadow of proof. The science of tradition at the present time is in much the same state as was that of chemistry in the hands of the medieval alchemists—*i.e.*, a large degree of experiment must enter into its composition—and where all are beginners who dare cast the first stone, especially if it be against a man who has rendered such services to mythology and folklore as must be remembered with gratitude and even affection by all the workers in our common vineyard? Has he not taught us

> "To hope, till hope creates
> From its own wreck the thing it contemplates"?

I differ from him in many points *toto cælo*; but is not endeavour the most precious thing in a new science? May we not say in mythology as in literature, *Fax mentis incendium gloriæ*? The very circumstance that a man carries such a torch as is borne by Sir James entitles him to our highest esteem, even if, as in my own case, we only partially agree with his notions, or almost wholly dissent from them, as Mr Farnell seems to do.

84

logical career he interested himself in the study of religious science. In 1905 he began his *Cultes, mythes, et religions*,[1] and in 1909 he published a general sketch of the history of religions under the title *Orpheus*. In his preface to *Cultes, mythes, et religions* M. Reinach makes some lively and amusing remarks concerning the ignorance in France of later developments of religious science. Speaking of new theories, he says: "As a matter of fact, I do not exactly know who made the discoveries. The names of Tylor, M'Lennan, Lang, Smith, Frazer, and Jevons suggest themselves; but the one thing certain is that it was not myself. Mine has been a lowlier part—to grasp the ideas of my betters, and to diffuse them as widely as I might, first in my lectures at the École du Louvre, then in the Académie des Inscriptions, and again in many popular and scientific reviews. In France, when I began my excursions into these fields, the whole subject was so absolutely a sealed book that M. Charles Richet had to ask me to explain the word *totemism*, before I dealt with that group of phenomena in the *Revue Scientifique*. At the Académie des Inscriptions in 1900 the only members who did not doubt my sanity when I read some lucubrations on the Biblical taboos and the totemism of the Celts were MM. Maspero and Hamy. The German scholars whom I saw about the same time, Mommsen among the rest, had never heard of a totem.[2] The taboos and totems of the Bible, a question underlying those alimentary interdictions which ignorance regards as hygienic precepts, brought the Jewish theologians into the lists. One of them dealt faithfully with me as an anti-Semite, an epithet already hurled at me by my distinguished friend Victor Bérard, because I had ventured to impugn, in the pages of the *Mirage Oriental*, the antiquity and omnipresence of Phœnician commerce. To-day the voice of ignorance is a little less heard in the land. Thanks to the diffusion of the English works which have inspired me, thanks to the labours of the lamented Marillier and the editors of the *Année Sociologique*—thanks perhaps, in

[1] English translation by Elizabeth Frost, London, 1912.
[2] This deals an effective blow to more than one Teutonic claim to priority in this field.

some degree, to my own missionary efforts, which, with the ardour of the neophyte, I have carried into the very precincts of the popular universities—those who once kicked most obstinately against the pricks now acknowledge that the system of anthropological exegesis is 'the fashion,' and that 'something may be said for' totems and taboos."

DR F. B. JEVONS

Dr F. B. Jevons in his *Introduction to the History of Religion* avows himself a disciple of Lang so far as his views upon myth are concerned. He too believes that the religious feeling in myth is conspicuously absent, but that the consideration of myth cannot be excluded from the history of religion. He says (p. 250): "Myths are not like psalms or hymns, lyrical expressions of religious emotion ; they are not like creeds or dogmas, statements of things which must be believed : they are narratives. They are not history, they are tales told about gods and heroes, and they all have two characteristics : on the one hand, they are to us obviously or demonstrably untrue and often irrational; on the other hand, they were to their first audience so reasonable as to appear truths which were self-evident." Some myths, he thinks, " explain nothing and point no moral ; they are tales told for the sake of telling and repeated for the pleasure of hearing, like fairy-tales." What, then, he asks, is the difference between myths that 'explain' phenomena and those which obviously do not ? He considers that totems aroused curiosity and necessitated explanations, and that when the beliefs were dead and forgotten the stories invented to account for them would appear no longer as reasons or explanations, but as statements of facts which occurred 'once upon a time.' These stories were often appropriated to the wrong persons, and we have also yet to learn why they were grouped together, a point Dr Jevons considers as of first-rate importance, because "they would not have survived if they had not been combined together. We cannot suppose that they were first dissevered from the beliefs on which they originally depended for their existence, and then were subsequently combined so as to obtain a renewed existence, because they would probably have perished in the interval. We must therefore suppose that they were combined into tales ere yet the beliefs or institutions which gave them their first lease of life had perished. This means that the various parts of one institution, for instance, must have had each its separate explanation, and that these explanations were combined into one whole, the unity of which corresponded to the unity of the institution." (P. 254.) These contentions are confirmed, Jevons thinks, by certain ceremonies obviously representing the details of certain myths. "They afford instances of myths which from the beginning were tales and not merely single incidents; a single rite might consist of a series of acts, each of which demanded its own explanation; and the unity of the rite might produce a unity of interest and action in the resulting myth." (P. 254.) Stories designed to explain phenomena would provide a groundwork for a rich embroidery of incidents. The person who could remember these and could tell them effectively would not have to seek an audience, and semi-consciously he might substitute for part of the story an analogous incident.[1] "Tales with a permanent human interest would easily spread beyond the limits of the original audience." Myth is not religion; it is not the source of religion, it is "one of the spheres of human activity in which religion may manifest itself, one of the departments of human reason which religion may penetrate, suffuse, and inspire." The religious consciousness rejected the repugnant elements of myth, and perhaps the whole primitive hypothesis upon which myth was based. "The result would be twofold: the imagination would be more and more excluded from the region of speculation which produced the ordinary myths of early peoples; and more and more restricted to the path of religious meditation." (P. 266.) These are all conclusions which we cannot admit. Myth is not any less religious in character because associated with an early instead of a later form of religion, or because it was discarded in later times! In an important passage Dr Jevons declares with a great deal of truth that: "The extraordinary

[1] We have shown above that the conservatism of the savage, like that of the child, would not permit this.

notion that mythology is religion is the outcome of the erroneous and misleading practice of reading modern ideas into ancient religions. It is but one form of the fallacy that mythology was to the antique religions what dogma is to the modern—with the superadded fallacy that dogma is the source, instead of the expression, of religious conviction. Mythology is primitive science, primitive philosophy, an important constituent of primitive history, the source of primitive poetry, but it is not primitive religion. It is not necessarily or usually even religious. It is not the proper or even the ordinary vehicle for the expression of the religious spirit." Where the sensitiveness of the religious spirit "was great only those pieces of primitive science survived which were capable of being informed " by it.

THE RELIGIOUS INFLUENCE OF MYTH

Jevons' conception of the nature of myth, however, does not take into consideration that at least one class of myth—that which deals with the gods—has probably more influence upon the popular acceptance and spread of religious ideas of a primitive type than either dogma or ritual. Those myths which furnish accounts of the deeds and adventures of the gods are as much religion as are ritual or dogma. No religion can exist without an explanation of a god or the gods, their nature, their attitude toward men, and their divine environment; and such an explanation was myth. Although savage and primitive, myths furnished a suitable account of the gods to their primitive worshippers, whose habits they almost certainly reflected.

DR R. R. MARETT

Dr R. R. Marett, in an admirable and suggestive volume, *The Threshold of Religion* (1909), has, as we already know, distinguished between animism and the forms which preceded it. Regarding mythology proper and its " quality of religiousness," and speaking in connexion with religious observances, he says : " Meanwhile, whatever view be taken of the parts respectively played by animism, mythology, animatism, or what not, in investing these observances with meaning and colour, my main point is that the quality of religiousness attaches to them far less in virtue of any one of these ideal constructions, than in virtue of that basic feeling of awe which drives a man, ere he can think or theorize upon it, into personal relations with the supernatural."

Regarding 'explanatory' myths, Dr Marett says (p. 149): "What the learned know as 'ætiological myths' and juvenile readers of Mr Kipling as 'Just So Stories' undoubtedly tend to arise in connection with human institutions no less than in connection with the rest of the more perplexing or amazing facts and circumstances of life. It is the 'nature of man' (as it is of the child, the father of the man) to ask 'Why?' and further to accept any answer as more satisfactory than none at all. Again, it is sound method in dealing with myth as associated with ritual at the stage of rudimentary religion to assume that for the most part it is the ritual that generates the myth, and not the myth the ritual."[1]

THE EUROPEAN 'SKY-GOD'

Professor A. B. Cook of Cambridge has collected a wealth of material to prove the existence throughout the length and breadth of Europe of a sky-god worshipped by both Celt and Teuton; but he elevates this cult into something resembling a state mythology, and we have no record of any such state religion. Early Celtic and Teutonic religions must have been incipient only, and far from possessing any such organization and unity.

THE GRIMMS

Having concluded our review of the ideas and hypotheses of the great mythologists proper, we will glance at what has been

[1] It must of course be clear to the 'meanest intelligence' that it is quite possible for myths to be created to explain ritual, but such myths must, almost of necessity, be late in origin and can only arise when the original myth which gave rise to the ritualistic practice has been lost. For what reason, it may be asked, is ritual invented and originated? Surely it presupposes a divine being, and if it does, it creates a myth; unless, of course, ritual was originally a magical act, an attempt to use some occult force, such as *mana*. One can understand that in the latter circumstances a myth may ultimately arise from ritual, otherwise I am unable to comprehend the contention, so often made in works dealing with mythology, that ritual is prior to myth. Nor do I consider magical ritual 'religious' but pseudo-scientific in nature, as magic is invariably pseudo-scientific and not religious at all.

said by the great students of folklore. Jakob Ludwig Karl Grimm (1785–1863) along with his brother Wilhelm Karl (1786–1859) published in 1816–1818 *Deutsche Sagen*, an analysis and criticism of the old German epic traditions, and in 1812–1815 *Kinder- und Hausmärchen*. Their first volume of the Eddaic songs of Iceland saw the light in 1815, and the *Deutsche Mythologie* in 1835. The last-named work traces the myths of Germany from a period as remote as is permitted by the evidence down to the time when they became merged in popular tradition. Folklore is indebted to the Grimms, who originally discerned its importance, but they did not in any way connect the stories themselves with custom or superstition. They were inimical to the allegorical method and decidedly trended toward the later position of Mannhardt and his school.

SIR G. L. GOMME

Few names are more distinguished in folklore than that of the late Sir George Laurence Gomme. His standpoint on myth is to be found in his able and liberal-minded treatise upon *Folklore as an Historical Science*, on p. 101 of which he says: " They [the mythologists] have entirely denied or ignored all history contained in the folk-tale, and they have proceeded on the assumption, the bald assumption not accompanied by any kind of proof, that the folk-tale contains nothing but the remnants of a once prevalent system of mythology. . . . It is not, however, upon the mistakes of other inquirers that the mythologists may rest a good claim for their own view. The *Historia Britonum* of Geoffrey of Monmouth disposes of neither the myths nor the history of the Celts. It shows myth in its secondary position, in the handling of those who would make it all history, just as now there are scholars who would make it all myth. In front of the legends attaching to persons and places is the history of these persons and places. Behind these legends lies the domain of the unattached and primitive folk-tale."

There should not be much doubt concerning which tales are of the nature of myth and those which enshrine historic fact. Does the tale bear a strong resemblance in more than one of its circumstances to any other tradition or group of traditions? If so, it should be a comparatively simple matter to judge to which group it belongs, although the student requires to be constantly on his guard. The transition from fact or surmise to myth, myth to pseudo-history, or from history to myth, and then perhaps to history again; from legend to history, from history to legend, or from folk-tale to history— these metamorphoses must be searched for diligently. Our 'test of recurrence' is not always sufficient, for occasionally myth will be seen to group with folklore and legend and *vice versa*.

On p. 125 of his admirable book Sir George says: "The traditional narrative, the myth, the folk-tale, or the legend, is not dependent upon the text in which it appears for the first time. That text as we have it was not written down by contemporary or nearly contemporary authority. Before it had become a written document it had lived long as oral tradition. In some cases the written document is itself centuries old, the record of some early chronicler or early writer who did not make the record for tradition's sake. In other cases the written document is quite modern, the record of a professed lover of tradition. This unequal method of recording tradition is the main source of the difficulty in the way of those who cannot accept tradition as a record of fact. In all cases the test of its value and the interpretation of its testimony are matters which need special study and examination before the exact value of each tradition is capable of being determined. The date when and the circumstances in which a tradition is first reduced to literary form are important factors in the evidence as to the credibility of the particular form in which the tradition is preserved; but they are not all the factors, nor do they of themselves afford better evidence when they are comparatively ancient than forms of much later date and of circumstances far different. It cannot be too often impressed upon the student of tradition that the tradition itself affords the chief if not the only sure evidence of its age, its origin, and its meaning; for the preservation of tradition is due to such varied influences that the mere fact of preservation or the method or particular date of preservation cannot be relied upon to give the necessary authority for the authenticity of the tradition. Tradition can never assume the position of written history, because it does not owe its origin, but only its preservation, to writing."

Dealing with the relations of myth to history, Sir George says (p. 128): "Because mythic tradition has been found to include many traditions which of late years have been claimed to belong to a definitely historical race of people, it must not be identified with history. This claim is based upon two facts, the presence of myth in the shape of the folk-tale and the preservation of much mythic tradition beyond the stage of thought to which it properly belongs by becoming attached to an historical event or series of events, or to an historical personage, and in this way carrying on its life into historic periods and among historic peoples. The first position has resulted in an appropriation of the folk-tale to the cause of the mythologists; the second position has hitherto resulted either in a disastrous appropriation of the entire tradition to mythology, or in a still more disastrous rejection both of the tradition and the historical event round which it clusters. Historians doubting the myth doubt too the history; mythologists doubting the history reject the myth from all consideration, and in this way much is lost to history which properly belongs to it, and something is lost to myth."

Sir George subscribes to Robertson Smith's statement that "Mythology was no essential part of ancient religion, for it had no sacred sanction and no binding force on the worshippers." Yet on the next page (p. 148) he says: "Myths constitute a part of the *serious life* of the people." He also speaks of myth (p. 149) as being told "in the hushed sanctity of a great wonder," of primitive myth being "preserved in a special manner and for *religious purposes*" (p. 150), and (on the same page) he alludes to its "sacredness." Yet it had "no sacred sanction and no binding force"!

Mr Sidney Hartland

Mr Sidney Hartland in his *Science of Fairy Tales* (1890) has applied "the principles and methods which guide investigators into popular traditions to a few of the most remarkable stories embodying the fairy superstitions of the Celtic and Teutonic peoples." The unity of human imagination is pleaded for. "Man's imagination," writes Mr Hartland, "like every other known power, works by fixed laws, the existence and operation of which it is possible to trace ; and it works upon the same material—the external universe, the mental and moral constitution of man, and his social relations. Hence diverse as may seem at first sight the results among the cultured Europeans and the debased Hottentots, the philosophical Hindoos and the Red Indians of the Far West, they present, on a close examination, features absolutely identical. . . . The incidents [of story-plots] . . . are not merely alike; they are often indistinguishable." Further, the anthropological standpoint is upheld. In *The Legend of Perseus* (1894–1896) the author has attempted to show "the dependence of the folk-tale upon custom and superstition, and to determine the place of origin of one world-famous tale."

Dr Rendel Harris

Dr Rendel Harris of Manchester has in several works propounded mythological views of startling novelty, with a wealth of illustration and argument which do credit alike to his scholarship and his didactical skill. In his latest work, *The Ascent of Olympus*, which it is incumbent upon all students of myth to study, he explains the cults of Dionysus, Apollo, Artemis, and Aphrodite. In Dr Harris's view the cults of these gods are respectively cults of the ivy, the apple, the mugwort, and the mandrake, of which plants the deities in question were personifications. Early Greek religion is thus evolved from the witch-doctor's garden, and, *a fortiori*, Olympus itself is a later development of the *hortus siccus* of the medicine-man. I will not attempt to advance any criticism of Dr Harris's thesis in this place, as I freely confess that his iconoclastic conclusions stun me. He triumphs in argument, and I live in fear and trembling that in his next book he may prove that Hephæstus was evolved from a tenpenny nail, or Poseidon from a lobster. As he is strong, let us beg him to be merciful also, for if he further depreciates our old mythological stock, those of us who are professional mythologists will be forced to dispose of it and begin life over again as his apprentices.

As proof of his masterly presentment of the astounding conclusions he has advanced, I quote the following summing-up from his *Ascent of Olympus* (p. 57):

"Let us refresh our memory as to the method we pursued and the results which we obtained in the case of the cults of Dionysos and Apollo. It will be remembered that we started from the sanctity of the oak as the animistic repository of the thunder, and in that sense the dwelling-place of Zeus; it was assumed that the oak was taboo and all that belonged to it; that the woodpecker who nested in it or hammered at its bark was none other than Zeus himself, and it may turn out that Athena, who sprang from the head of the thunder-oak, was the owl that lived in one of its hollows. Even the bees who lived underneath its bark were almost divine animals, and had duties to perform to Zeus himself. The question having been raised as to the sanctity of the creepers upon the oak, it was easy to show that the ivy (with the smilax and the vine) was a sacred plant, and that it was the original cult-symbol of Dionysos, who thus appeared as a lesser Zeus projected from the ivy, just as Zeus himself, in one point of view, was a projection from the oak. Dionysos, whose thunder-birth could be established by the well-known Greek tradition concerning Semele and Zeus, was the ivy on the oak, and after that became an ivy fire-stick in the ritual for the making of fire. From Dionysos to Apollo was the next step: it was suggested in the first instance by the remarkable confraternity of the two gods in question. They were shown to exchange titles, to share sanctuaries, and to have remarkable cult-parallelisms, such as the chewing of the sacred laurel by the Pythian priestess, and the chewing of the sacred ivy by the Mænads: and since it was discovered that the Delphic laurel was a surrogate for a previously existing oak, it was natural to inquire whether in any way Apollo, as well as Dionysos, was linked to the life of Zeus through the life of the oak. The inquiry was very fruitful in results: the undoubted solar elements in the Apolline cult were shown to be capable of explanation by an identification of Apollo with the mistletoe, and it was found that Apollo was actually worshipped at one centre in Rhodes as the Mistletoe Apollo, just as Dionysos was worshipped as the Ivy Dionysos at Acharnai. Further inquiry led to the conclusion that the sanctity of the oak had been transferred by the mistletoe from the oak to the apple tree, and that the cult betrayed a close connection between the god and the apple-tree, as, for instance, in the bestowal of sacred apples from the god's own garden upon the winners of the Pythian games. In this way it came to be seen that Apollo was really the mistletoe upon the apple-tree for the greater part of the development of the cult, just as Dionysos was the ivy, not detached as some had imagined, but actually upon the oak-tree. It was next discovered that the garden at Delphi was a reproduction of another Apolline garden in the far north, among the Hyperboreans, the garden to which Boreas had carried off Orithyia, and to which (or to another adjacent garden) at a later date the sons of Asklepios were transferred for the purpose of medical training. . . . Apollo came from the North as a medicine-man, a herbalist, and brought his simples with him. His character of a god of healing was due, in the first instance, to the fact that the mistletoe, which he represented, was the All-heal of antiquity. . . . An attempt was then made to show that the very name of Apollo was in its early form Apellon, a loan-word from the North, disguising in the thinnest way his connection with the apple-tree. The apple had come into Greece from the North, perhaps from Teutonic peoples, just as it appears to have come into Western Italy from either Teutons or Celts, giving its name in the one case to the great god of healing, and in the other to the city of Abella in Campania, through the Celtic word *Aball*."

PROFESSOR ELLIOT SMITH

Professor George Elliot Smith, of University College, London, has brought to the problems of archæology a mental freshness and originality of outlook that have placed him in the front rank of the science in a surprisingly short space of time. He is the chief supporter of the theory that by slow

95

degrees the civilization of ancient Egypt spread itself over the habitable globe, even to far America. His sledge-hammer logic and array of excellent if rather limited illustrations are capable of daunting the most doughty opponent. In his recent book, *The Evolution of the Dragon*, he probes as deeply into the basic mysteries of mythology as Dr Rendel Harris, of whose work he says : " Our genial friend has been cultivating his garden on the slopes of Olympus, and has been plucking the rich fruits of his ripe scholarship and nimble wit. At the same time, with rougher implements and cruder methods, I have been burrowing in the depths of the earth, trying to recover information concerning the habits and thoughts of mankind many centuries before Dionysus and Apollo and Artemis and Aphrodite were dreamt of. In the course of these subterranean gropings no one was more surprised than I was to discover that I was getting entangled in the roots of the same plants whose golden fruit Dr Rendel Harris was gathering from his Olympian heights. But the contrast in our respective points of view was perhaps responsible for the different appearance the growths assumed. To drop the metaphor, while he was searching for the origins of the deities a few centuries before the Christian era began, I was finding their more or less larval forms flourishing more than twenty centuries before the commencement of his story. For the gods and goddesses of his narrative were only the thinly disguised representatives of much more ancient deities decked out in the sumptuous habiliments of Greek culture."

The Evolution of the Dragon contains three essays, " Incense and Libations," " Dragons and Rain-gods," and " The Birth of Aphrodite," all of which are of the first importance to students of mythic science, as illustrating the possibility of tracing evolved divine figures to their primitive forms. The first essay begins with Professor Smith's well-known hypothesis that the reasons for the adoption of custom are not " simple and obvious," and are not inspired by reason, but by tradition. Man is not an inventive animal, and two independent inventions of any custom, story, or article of utility are improbable. The part played by the ancient Egyptians in the development of certain arts and beliefs was a paramount one. The necessity for obtaining wood, spices, and gums for the mummification of the dead forced them to make long voyages; and consequently they became the missionary carriers of the religious customs and ideas they had evolved at home, disseminating these throughout the Mediterranean world. Professor Smith then traces the early idea of godhead to the apotheosized ruler or king, whose posthumous benevolence rendered the land fertile. He believes that animism received its definite form in Egypt, where it was fostered by the art of mummification, and spread thence broadcast. The development of animism was enormously complex. It received its first great impetus from an early Egyptian king who believed that he could restore the breath of life to the dead by means of the magic wand. Then the burning of incense before a body or statue was intended to convey to it the warmth, the sweat, and the colours of life. Mummification, indeed, "laid the foundation of the ideas which subsequently were built up into a theory of the soul : in fact, it was intimately connected with the birth of all those ideals and aspirations which are now included in the conception of religious belief and ritual." The development of animism, too, brought the supernatural idea of the properties and functions of water, an idea which had previously sprung up in connexion with agriculture, into a more definite form. It was a factor in the development of the paraphernalia of the gods and of current popular belief, of the temple and its ritual, and led to a definite formulation of the conception of deities.

The second essay, "Dragons and Rain-gods," is the longest of the three. The dragon legend, says Professor Smith, is the history of the search for the elixir of life. "The original dragon was a beneficent creature, the personification of water, and was identified with kings and gods." "The dragon myth, however, did not really begin to develop until an ageing king refused to be slain, and called upon the Great Mother as the giver of life to rejuvenate him. Her only elixir was human blood ; and to obtain it she was compelled to make a human sacrifice. Her murderous act led to her being compared and ultimately identified with a man-slaying lioness or a cobra.

The story of the slaying of the dragon is a much-distorted rumour of this incident ; and in the process of elaboration the incidents were subjected to every kind of interpretation, and also confusion with the legendary account of the conflict between Horus and Set." Thus the Great Mother became confused with Horus as the avenger of the god, and legendary complications caused Horus to be regarded as her son. But the infamy of her deeds of destruction seems to have led to her being further confused with the rebellious followers of Set. " Thus an evil dragon emerged from this blend of the attributes of the Great Mother and Set."

It seems to me that this theory is much too complicated and multiplies difficulties, as will be seen if we ponder for a moment the history of the Mother-goddess in Mexico. In Mexican myth the earth is represented as a monster, Cipactli, the pictures of which suggest a crocodile, a swordfish, or a dragon, probably a dragon, that great earth-monster common to the mythologies of many races and most conveniently called the ' earth-dragon.' The sign ' Cipactli ' became the first in the calendar, and with it are connected the creative deities and the Earth-Mother or Great Mother. Circumstances exist which lend colour to the idea that, as in other countries, the Mexican Mother was at one time regarded as forming the earth, the soil. At the terrible and picturesque festival of the Xalaquia (' She who is clothed with the soil ') a sacrificed virgin enriched and recruited with her blood the frame of the worn-out goddess, who had been, says Seler, " merged in the popular imagination with the all-nourisher, the all-begetter, the earth." Perhaps the best evidence that the Earth-Mother was evolved from the earth-dragon is the colossal stone figure which once towered above the entrance to the temple of Uitzilopochtli in Mexico and is now housed in the museum of that city. In this figure, as in a similar though less massive statue from Tehuacan, the characteristics of the Cipactli animal are reproduced in a wealth of scale, claw, and tusk. The direct descent of the Great Mother from the earth-animal, the personification of the earth-beast as a divine being, explains her savage wantonness and spares us the necessity for the elaborate genealogy

98

with which Professor Elliot Smith so ably dowers her. He cannot allege that Egypt had no earth-dragon, because Apep is alluded to in the *Book of Overthrowing Apep* as a crocodile and a serpent, and that he was developed from the earth-beast seems fairly clear. He might also say that the Mexican myth was a distorted echo of the Egyptian. But the evolutionary process is too apparent in Mexican art to permit of such an hypothesis.

The last paper, "The Birth of Aphrodite," traces that goddess, not to the mandrake, as Dr Harris does, but to the cowrie-shell. The cowrie was an amulet employed to increase the fertility of women, and in time came to be personified in statuettes. Hence arose the idea of a Great Mother, a giver of health, life, and good luck. "These beliefs," says the Professor, "had taken shape long before any definite ideas had been formulated as to the physiology of animal reproduction, and before agriculture was practised." It is impossible to quote more from the work of this most suggestive and stimulating of all modern writers on mythology, and I can only here warn my readers against the unwisdom of leaving his essays unread.

The great ability with which Professor Elliot Smith presents his thesis is as obvious as the probability of most of his ideas, but it seems to me that he regards them too much as proven facts, and that he fails to recognize the insecurity of hypotheses based upon the present inadequate data of early religious manifestations. These essays are the outcome of a brilliant mind impatient of the lumbering slowness of the mythological machine, and they show a kind of prophetic gift which pierces beyond proof, and may be accepted as infallible, if uncanny, or rejected as over-adventurous. For my part, I feel that Professor Smith is right in by far the greater number of his beliefs, but I can scarcely admit that he supplies me with sufficient proof. Rather would I say that his book affects me as a work of genuine theoretical inspiration and insight, and not as a cold catalogue of established facts. Professor Smith is the Galileo of mythology—a science which has brought forth many personalities of ponderous erudition, but few geniuses. This does not mean that he is illogical, or that his papers are not prepared with adequate and even meticulous care. It means that he is looking out of a casement through which he alone has the right of vision, and, seeing things so plainly as he does, he expects those who do not possess similar gifts to participate in his clairvoyance. His proofs, if few, are always apposite. The reviewer might wish that each of the essays occupied three portly volumes instead of a demy octavo book of 234 pages, and included a much larger number of confirmatory illustrations.

RECAPITULATION

The space allotted to this chapter would be greatly exceeded if we alluded to the numerous collectors of myth who have enriched the science with their labours. So far we have limited ourselves to the work of the great theorists, and we will now recapitulate their ideas, and draw therefrom our conclusions, accepting only what we believe to be correct and 'safe,' and adding our own inferences and deductions. Summarized, these ideas are as follows :

(1) The anthropological school showed that the identity between Aryan and savage myth could not be explained upon a linguistic basis.

(2) Tylor laid stress upon the value of the comparison of myth and the 'test of recurrence.' He did not entirely discount philological evidence, but denied the large place claimed for allegory.

(3) He showed that myth displayed a regularity of development not to be accounted for by motiveless fancy, but by laws of formation.

(4) The promulgation of the animistic hypothesis by Tylor is a landmark in mythic science.

(5) Robertson Smith showed that myth takes the place of dogma in primitive religions.

(6) Lang demonstrated the unsoundness of the 'disease of language' theory.

He laid stress on the irrational element in myth ;

Indicated the complexity of mythic development ;

Showed how the evolutionary theory may be applied to myth ;

Pointed out that the persistence of myth was accounted for by religious conservatism ;

Laid it down that the occurrence of identical myths may be accounted for by the universal prevalence of similar mental habits (this, however, will not account for long and intricate plots).

(7) Jevons points out the reflection of myth by ritual.

(8) The present writer believes :

(i) That myth is for the most part sacred in character.

(ii) That it is prior in origin to ritual and is not derived from it, except in a secondary sense.

(iii) That mythic conditions are capable of a more or less exact classification.

Having indicated our own attitude toward myth, we will now proceed to examine the manner in which the idea of the gods was evolved.

CHAPTER III

THE EVOLUTION OF THE GODS

THE evolution of the idea of godhead in the mind of man is in its later stages inalienably associated with the conception of spirit.[1]

As we have seen (pp. 58-59), Tylor considers that man first attained the idea of spirit by reflection on experiences such as sleep, dreams, trances, shadows, hallucinations, breath, and death, and by degrees extended this conception of soul or ghost until he peopled all nature with spirits, from among which one supreme being was finally raised above all.

An outline of the animistic conception has been provided in the introductory chapter. Here it is only necessary to apply it to the evolution of deity. The opinion of Marett, that in an early stage of human development pre-animistic 'powers' exist which do not partake of the nature of spirit, does not require to be restated, as it has but little bearing upon the question directly before us; and we will advance to that stage in human mental development when spirit has become fully recognized. The conception of simple personalization could not have lasted long at any epoch, as it would sooner or later be brought into contact with the idea of the separable soul. Thus if gods were regarded as 'magnified non-natural men' (the very phrase

[1] The general theory of this work, though, as already stated, eclectic, is, so far as its opinions upon the evolution of the idea of spirit or soul is concerned, in sympathy with the animistic hypothesis of Tylor, an hypothesis subjected to a certain amount of criticism from the younger generation of students of comparative religion. But as these students have not yet erected a worthy rival explanation of the evolution of godhead, and as what they have accomplished is of the most fragmentary nature, we will refrain from reviewing their work, and will content ourselves with an examination of the animistic idea, bringing to bear upon it only such criticism as seems really necessary.

'non-natural' is against the personalization idea), or physical objects or natural phenomena were worshipped or placated because of their peculiarities, the idea of spirit would undoubtedly infuse and alter these beliefs at a very early stage in their career. Thus no deity could well escape becoming spiritualized. Why should this be so? Why should spiritualization be necessary to deity? The point is important. If we admit that certain physical objects were worshipped because of their peculiarities, if we believe that the earth and sky, for example, were personalized and conceived as without spiritual attributes in the beginning, that only *what was seen* was worshipped, how comes it that among the most primitive races the god, as apart from his idol, is invisible—that is, spiritual? The idol may, of course, be a relic of the period when only what was beheld was worshipped, but that period must indeed have been brief, when one takes into consideration the probable early junction of the ideas of spirit and deity.

IDEA OF SPIRIT CONCEIVED EARLY

The conception of spirit must have been an early idea, contemporary, one would imagine, with the dawn of reason. Man, claiming for himself the possession of spirit, could scarcely deny it to a superior power, and if the fear of godhead agitated him when beheld in the convulsions of nature, as in the thunderstorm or earthquake, how much more would the half-heard mutterings of the *unseen* agencies dwelling in the whistling winds and darkling woods cause terror in his breast? Regarding the physical agencies he knew the worst, and could learn how to avoid or mitigate their terrors, but what chance had he against those agencies he could not perceive, and how much greater must have been his fear of them? Thus was born that dread of the invisible, the unseen, which even to-day chills the human heart and plays havoc with human imagination.

The idea of the separable soul thus evolved from visions and dreams and applied to godhead might assist in the making of several varying forms of deity, as in fetishism, totemism, or the worship of the dead—if, indeed, it did not originate in this latter form. The application of spirit to deity perhaps found its first illustration in the worship of ancestors—a low form of evolution in the line of godhead, as few gods evolved from ancestors survive more than several generations, and few of the great departmental deities of the higher early religions display signs of having evolved from ancestors. Moreover, where such signs are present they are of doubtful value. The religion of China is perhaps the only great example of the continuity of the worship of ancestors. But it is important to note that this form of deity *may* have been that to which the idea of spirit was first applied.

Fetishism forms an important link in the evolution of the mere animistic spirit into the god. Before examining the manner in which a fetish originates and rises to godhead, let us see exactly what class of spirit is supposed to inhabit it.

THE DEVELOPMENT OF THE FETISH

The fetish is pre-eminently a personal familiar—that is, a spirit which for certain reasons (the desire for shelter and food, or because a powerful spell has been laid upon it) becomes attached to a human being. It is acquired by a person or a family for luck, and in return requires a certain amount of worship or respect, sacrifice, and feasting. It may receive good or evil treatment according as it behaves to its votaries. It is by no means a tutelar deity, since it may be bought or sold, loaned or inherited. It generally has its home in some object, preferably of a peculiar shape or character, inhabiting a figure shaped in human or animal form, a stone, bone, necklace of fingers, a carved or painted stick, a curious fossil, a stuffed skin, the dried hand of an enemy—in short, anything that fancy or caprice may dictate.

The manner of making a fetish is almost universally the same. Says Mr Davenport Adams of the Samoyede image-makers[1]: "The bleak and lonely island of Waigatz is still, as in the days of the Dutch adventurer, Barentz, supposed to be the residence of the chief of these minor divinities. There a block of stone, pointed at the summit, bears a certain resemblance to a human head, having been wrought into this likeness

[1] *Curiosities of Superstition*, pp. 155, 156.

by a freak of nature. The Samoyede image-makers have taken it for their model, and multiplied it in wood and stone; and the idols thus easily manufactured they call *sjadaei*, because they wear a human (or semi-human) countenance (*sja*). They attire them in reindeer skins, and embellish them with innumerable coloured rags. In addition to the *sjadaei*, they adopt as idols any curiously contorted tree or irregularly shapen stone; and the household idol (*Hahe*) they carry about with them, carefully wrapped up, in a sledge reserved for the purpose, the *hahengan*. One of the said Penates is supposed to be the guardian of wedded happiness, another of the fishery, a third of the health of his worshippers, a fourth of their herds of reindeer. When his services are needed, the *Hahe* is removed from its resting-place, and erected in the tent or on the pasture-ground, in the wood, or on the river's bank. Then his mouth is smeared with oil or blood, and before him is set a dish of fish or flesh, in return for which repast it is expected that he will use his power on behalf of his entertainers. When his aid is no longer needed, he is returned to the *hahengan*."

PAYNE ON THE FETISH

Mr Payne in his *History of the New World called America* has an admirable passage about the fetish. He says: "The spirits, then, whom the savage believes to share the world with him, are considered to be substantial beings, consisting of flesh and blood like man himself; and like him nourished by food and drink. They are therefore not immortal: like man, they are liable to death by violence or starvation. They are also subject to that alternation of want and abundance which occupies so large a space in human experience. In this circumstance, coupled with the fact that some of these spirits are conceived as injurious or evil, others as benevolent or good, we have the key of primitive theology. Man seeks to keep the good or benevolent spirits alive, to satisfy their wants, and to give them pleasure, in the hope of interesting them by this means in the success of his own enterprises: and for this purpose he provides them with food and drink. Hunting peoples, who have no gods, occasionally sacrifice food to the spirits, in order to obtain success in the chase: thus the Veddah of Ceylon place on the ground offerings of blood and burnt flesh for the Vedde-Yakko (spirit of the chase), promising further offerings of the same kind when the game is caught. If the spirit accepts these offerings, he is understood to appear to them in dreams, telling them where to hunt. Some low agricultural and cattle-keeping tribes, who have not attained the conception of gods, place pieces of manioc-root and ears of maize on branches of trees, to propitiate the spirits. These sacrifices of the Veddah illustrate in its simplest form the principle which lies at the root of all. The spirits for whom they are intended are beings of animal nature, chiefly differing from other animals in that they are naturally invisible, but have the power of assuming various forms, and of moving swiftly through the air from place to place. Air, perhaps, rather than earth, is conceived to be their proper element: it is at any rate certain that food-offerings, in order to reach them, must be committed to the air. There are only two methods of doing this, libation and combustion: the former adapted to liquids, the latter to solids. Liquids are poured on the ground, on a stone, or into a bowl or other receptacle, and pass into the air by simple evaporation. Solids are burnt, and pass into the air in the form of smoke. In offering to the spirits food in the form of blood, the Veddah follows the universal logic of primitive savagery. Man once consumed his game warm and raw. Fatigued with the chase, emaciated perhaps by previous fasting, the savage slays his victim, drinks of the hot blood, feels himself at once invigorated, and makes his meal upon its flesh at leisure. The rest of the blood, spilled on the ground, quickly dries up. The savage, who has but one solution for most physical phenomena, concludes that the spirits have drunk it. Blood, therefore, is their natural food. In this, repugnant as it is to modern prejudices, the savage sees nothing revolting or unnatural. Blood, which is in truth only the material of flesh, is to him a perfectly natural food; scarcely less so, perhaps, than milk, which is nothing but blood filtered through a gland. Henceforth, a part of the blood of all animals that man slays, wild or domestic, will be poured out for the spirits, or for the gods who succeed them. Ultimately, when man abandons the practice, once universal, of feeding on blood, all the blood of a slaughtered animal is poured out as the share of the invisible powers. Sometimes, in a later stage, when sacrifice is more fully developed, clotted blood is collected when the carcase is cold, and wrapped in a cloth ; this is placed in a basket and suspended in the air. Such was the practice of the advanced Indians of Nicaragua, between the lake and the ocean, emigrants from Mexico, when sacrificing, after the chase, to the *teomazat* and *teotoste*, or gods of the deer and rabbit respectively. It is equally in accordance with primitive logic to offer to the spirits a portion of the flesh. The invisible powers must have their share of all that man delights in : at a later period offerings are made them of fermented liquors, narcotics, perfumes, and the material of clothing and ornaments. From the solid parts of the slain animal those are selected which are most easily volatilised. A portion of the fat, ultimately all the fat which adheres to the internal organs of the slain animal, is therefore burnt, and reaches the nostrils of the spirits in the form of a grateful savour. At a later period, when man depends for flesh food on domesticated animals, such offerings are reserved for gods of the first rank : and hence in Peru the chief deities, who alone were thus honoured, obtained the distinctive name of *huira-cocha* (fat sacrifices)."

THE 'SUCCESSFUL' FETISH

Such fetishes as are 'successful'—that is, such of them as survive the test of domestic use and prove luck-bringers—may by their miraculous acts or the power and policy of their immediate devotees become gods. But it must be borne in mind that a fetish-object is the place of imprisonment or residence, manufactured by human agency, of a spirit which has concluded a bargain with its devotees to act for their mutual benefit. Only a series of marvels of a protective or fortune-making nature can raise it to the rank of godhead, or, as has been said, the policy of its owners, who thus constitute themselves its priesthood. Says Mr Payne: "Before the gods are thus permanently established they have usually passed through a period of probation. Only the fittest survive: if the god proves useless for the purpose for which he exists, whether of securing success in the chase, abundant crops, or fortune in war, he is forthwith abandoned. Where game and fish abound, and agriculture remains in its rudiments, the gods are chiefly required to render assistance in hunting, fishing, and war, though some are employed to secure success in cultivation. Such was the condition of the tribes throughout the vast region of the Amazon river who had gods for each of these purposes. On an expedition of war one of the war-gods was placed in the prow of the boat; on a fishing expedition this place was occupied by a god holding a fish. When out of use the gods were stowed away in baskets; in case these expeditions proved unsuccessful the gods were thrown aside and replaced by others. But those which survive the test of experience are cherished in families as possessions of the highest value. These are the *t'raphim* of the Hebrews, the *penates* of the Latins, the *cconopa* of the Peruvians: words in each case meaning precisely the 'nourishers' or 'food-givers' of the household. According to the Biblical narrative, the daughter of an Aramæan sheikh considered herself entitled to take with her some of these family gods when she crossed the Euphrates with her Hebrew husband: an incident which recalls the Turcoman legend of Sekedschet, whose Chinese wife brought household gods with her as part of her dowry. These gods, it is clear, were regarded as mere chattels, existing for the benefit of their owners: in Bokhara, indeed, they were commonly bought and sold at markets or fairs. So long as man worshipped only these merely factitious gods, this essential instability obviously prevented his religious ideas from gaining force and permanence: qualities which first appear when he begins to worship the distinguished dead, and only become conspicuous when he adopts as objects of veneration the permanent objects and forces of nature."

TOTEMS AS GODS

A totem spirit achieves godhead in much the same way as the fetish. That the totem develops into the god is abundantly proven by the animal likenesses and attributes of many deities in lands widely separated. The animal-headed gods of Egypt, the bovine deities of Assyria, the animal gods of many pantheons are, very many of them, totemic in origin. These frequently attained a human semblance at a later stage of their history, but in many instances the original totem animal or a portion of its insignia remained. Thus the Grecian Pallas Athene was attended by an owl; Apollo was accompanied by a mouse ('Apollo Smintheus'); the Mexican god of war, Uitzilo-pochtli, was frequently disguised in a cloak made of humming-birds' feathers; and Prometheus must have possessed wings to enable him to steal the fire from heaven. Many gods, as Lang says, exhibit traces of "fur and feather," but all of these are not necessarily totemic. Where the act of devouring the deity symbolically by means of the substitution of an animal or man for the eponym or god is indulged in at certain stated intervals, the origin of the god so communed with is totemic, and this fact often serves to determine the nature of a deity.

Says Salomon Reinach (*Cultes, mythes, et religions*, p. 7): "The distribution of the clan totems among the tribal and national gods was not the work of a day: it must have been conditioned by a whole mass of circumstances—alliances, wars, local amalgamations—the clue to which is obviously lost forever. One factor of the first importance seems to have been the ritual of sacrifice; which, like all rituals, is eminently conserva-tive. Take the case of a clan owning the bull as its totem, and sacrificing it at intervals. In time the era of personal deities is ushered in; the bull is converted into an attribute of the chief god, and offered up to him in sacrifice: yet there lingers a more or less distinct recollection of the victim's own divinity."

It has been well said that man cannot realize the gods *as* gods until he becomes aware of his own humanity. Before that they must appear to him as what Marett calls 'powers.' That is where animism with its branches, totemism and fetishism, may be distinguished from the religions of the higher cultus, the polytheisms which possess definite pantheons, and the monotheisms. It is noticeable that in early myth *animals often take the place of gods*, a sure sign that the race which regarded the animal as occupying the place of a creator or hero had not yet 'found itself' as human, had not yet realized the enormous nature of the gulf which separates animal and human nature, was yet totally in the dark regarding the great things of which man was capable, his marvellous adaptability and wondrous destiny. When man realizes his superiority, then the totem-gods take on his own image, retaining only the symbols or insignia of the beast, or perhaps part of their ancient animal appearance. Thus the Egyptian sun-goddess, Bast, from being represented in early times as a cat pure and simple, was later figured as a woman having a cat's head. Uitzilopochtli, the Aztec war-god, evolved from humming-bird shape to man-like similitude, retaining, however, the colibri-feather cloak. The Mayan maize-spirit, when he attained god-like proportions, was represented as a young man wearing on his head-dress the graceful waving plumes of the maize-plant. These instances are illustrative of the different manner in which various peoples free their minds of the old beast-god ideas handed down for untold generations. Thus the strongly conservative Egyptians, probably because of fusion with other races, adopt the anthropomorphic form, but still retain the animal appearance in its most significant item—the head ; the symbol-loving Aztecs preserve the humming-bird's feathers on their war-god's dress, while the still more anthropomorphic Greeks content themselves with placing the animal image beside the man-like god, instead of in any way amalgamating the two conceptions.

Ancestor-Worship

The process of manufacturing a god from a dead man, although at first sight apparently less involved than that of the evolution of a deity through fetishistic or totemic media, is found on close examination to be even more complex. Among many primitive races, and some that are not primitive, it is the bounden duty of the dead man's son to see that his *manes*, his spirit, wants for nothing. Even as he cherished his son during the first years of the infant's life, so his heir is now bound by all he holds sacred to cherish his ghost and guard it against hunger, thirst, and cold. Woe betide the unfilial wretch who neglected the tomb of his father! Among the Egyptians, Assyrians, and Chinese such a dereliction of duty was regarded with the utmost abhorrence. Dreadful was the lot of the uncared-for dead. Says the Gilgamesh epic, the greatest literary product of ancient Babylonia:

> The man whose spirit has none to care for it—
> Thou and I have often seen such an one—
> The dregs of the vessel, the leavings of the feast,
> And that which is cast out upon the street are his food.

Great care was bestowed by Egyptian sons upon the *post-mortem* welfare of their parents, and the most solemn duty of a Chinaman is that of tending the spirits of his dead forefathers. This attention in course of time evolves into a very deep reverence, which greatly exalts the dead in the estimation of their descendants. In India and elsewhere critical observers have watched the progress of the evolution into godhead of innumerable dead men. A holy ascetic dies, famous throughout the neighbourhood for his piety and the rigour of his life. Miracles occur at his shrine. His surviving relatives foster the cult of his fame. His human "personality becomes misty, his origin grows mysterious, his career takes a legendary hue, his birth and death were both supernatural; in the next generation the names of the elder gods get introduced into the story, and so the marvellous tradition works itself into a myth, until nothing but a personal incarnation can account for such a series of prodigies. The man was an avatar of Vishnu or Siva; his supreme apotheosis is now complete, and the Brahmins feel warranted in providing for him a niche in the orthodox pantheon."[1]

This, of course, is an instance where the memory of his sanctity helps to turn a man into a god. No such idea enters into the earliest ancestor-worship. Among primitive savages the dead man would be worshipped because of the memory of his personal might when alive, the number of his clansmen and

[1] A. C. Lyall, *Asiatic Studies*, p. 19 (London, 1907).

adherents, and for similar reasons. But 'human' gods, ancestors and others, seldom reach any great altitude of deity.

THE COMPACT WITH THE GODS

At a very early epoch in the relations of man with the gods we find him entering into a tacit understanding which develops into a well-recognized pact. Even when the gods are in the fetish state we find the hunter smearing blood upon their mouths and imploring their assistance in return. It is a case, as the old proverb says, of 'Ka me, ka thee.' Man undoubtedly possesses an instinctive belief in the existence of a superior being or beings. He may twist this fundamental belief into any shape he pleases, but basically it remains the same. This belief in gods is not in itself religion. Inalienably possessing the idea of the existence of deity, and shaping it as his intelligence permits, man has yet to make religion, which consists in the worship and cult of supernatural beings, for his comfort, uplifting, assurance, and help. Man says to himself, "If He be with us who shall be against us?" and with the god for him feels secure against every adversary.

The 'comfort' derived from faith, of which all must have greater or less experience, the assurance that man is watched over, guided, and tended by a being to whom he is an object of solicitude, was probably experienced at a much earlier stage of human history than is generally admitted, but the bargain, the compact by which both man and god dwell together to mutual advantage, is obviously antecedent to these feelings, and is dictated by calculation as opposed to pure love. "Feed us, send us plenteous game, O Divine One, and we shall in turn maintain thee with sacrifice." Such is the compact. A similar bargain is made when man quits his hunter's life and begins to live an agricultural existence; nor does the nature of the pabulum offered to the gods differ with the adoption of an agricultural existence. Blood is the food of the gods when man sacrifices to them in his capacity of hunter, and continues to be so when he adopts cereals, although instances do occur of cereal and vegetable sacrifices. Vegetarian gods are few, and the majority of savages favour the cult of Abel, not that of the brother who angered Yahweh by the agricultural nature of his sacrifices. The most complete instance on record of a compact in which a markedly agricultural community rigidly maintained the blood-sacrifice to the gods is that of ancient Mexico, where thousands of prisoners of war were annually immolated, and where an annual strife between the states of Mexico and Tlaxcala was upheld for the purpose of furnishing the altars of one or other with human victims.

THE CORN-SPIRIT AS GOD

These considerations lead to the question : In what manner are the gods of the agricultural community evolved? Does the corn-spirit, the genius of the wheat or maize, triumph over and banish the older animistic deities of the chase? These certainly sink into a secondary position, although some gods of totemic origin continue to flourish, despite their new agricultural surroundings, and even survive and hold high positions in the pantheon, perhaps altered by later political and abstract ideas out of all semblance to their original condition. Old tribal gods, too, may become agricultural.

In what manner, then, does the triumphant corn-spirit evolve into the god? And, firstly, what is the nature of a corn-spirit? In animistic belief everything natural possesses life and so, probably, 'soul,' 'ghost,' or 'spirit,' the corn-plant no less than any other object. Representations of corn- and maize-gods almost invariably show them as symbolically decorated with the plant they were supposed to inhabit. The genius, spirit, or informing soul of the grain would in an agricultural community attain such prime importance that within a short time it would undoubtedly receive divine honours.

FROM CORN-SPIRIT TO GOD

The corn-spirit was capable of attaining a high rank of godhead, as we may see from the myth of the Egyptian god Osiris. Osiris was the first to instruct men how to plant the corn-seed, and his annual festival began with the tillage of the soil. In one of the chambers dedicated to him in the great temple of Isis at Philæ his dead body is represented with stalks of corn springing from it. These are being watered by a priest, and the accompanying inscription reads that this is "Osiris of the mysteries who springs from the returning waters" (of the Nile). Surely such a painting can only illustrate Osiris as a corn-deity. And were not, according to legend, his mangled remains scattered up and down the land of Egypt?— perhaps a mythical way of expressing the sowing or winnowing of the grain, an interpretation supported by the tale that Isis placed the severed limbs of Osiris on a corn-sieve.

Granted, then, that Osiris was a corn-spirit in one of his manifestations, we have now to judge from his tale how far it is possible for the corn-spirit to evolve in the line of godhead —to what altitude of deity it is possible for him to soar and what divine honours he is capable of reaching.

At an early stage of Egyptian history we find Osiris the deity of an agricultural religion, plainly the god of a grain-growing people. His cult persisted through all the exigencies and changes of Egyptian theology and occupied a prominent place in the affections of the people, who, although they acknowledged the worship of Ra and Amen at various epochs, continued faithful to Osiris. His worship by reason of its antiquity and popularity triumphed in the end over more aristocratic and perhaps alien forms. But the early conception of Osiris as the spirit of the corn-plant and afterward as a guardian deity of agriculture, although maintained in essence, was greatly modified and overshadowed by the attributes which were bestowed upon him at a later period. Thus, like Persephone and other corn-deities, he was regarded as a god of the Underworld, or place of the dead, and consequently as judge of the departed. In his history we observe the process of evolution from an animistic spirit inhabiting the corn-plant to a god embodying divine justice, and holding in his hands both reward and punishment.

A great deal has been written concerning the supposed non-ethical and non-moral character of mythological figures. In early times it is probable that the gods were no less savage and immoral than their worshippers ; but when we encounter well-known deities for the first time in the pages of classical authors, we have little difficulty in discovering that although the attributes of savagery still cling to them, they are also informed by a spirit of justice and wisdom, if not of mercy or compassion. Such qualities, indeed, as man desired in the gods, he endowed them with. Again, the existence of collegiate or monastic institutions in such countries as Egypt, India, Mexico, and Babylonia did much to foster contemplation and piety, and greatly assisted the evolution of the ethical spirit. When we first meet with Osiris, Ra, Thoth, Ptah, and other Egyptian gods, they are the repositories of justice and wisdom, if not of love and compassion. The same holds good of many Hindu deities, notably of Brahma. The Greek gods were, perhaps, unfortunate in the circumstance that the age of their first literary presentment preceded that of their ethical evolution. Accounts of the Spanish conquerors of Mexico lead us to believe that at least one Mexican deity, Tezcatlipoca, possessed a sense of justice, and that another, Tlazolteotl, forgave sin ; and the traditions of many modern savage peoples are not without god-like figures whose ethical standpoint is superior to that of their worshippers.

With the material now to our hand it is important that we fully employ every possible rational method of interpretation. The folly of adopting one key to open all mythological doors has been illustrated by the fate of such systems as attempted to interpret the nature of the gods by theories of a 'disease of language' or the solar nature of all deities. The 'vegetable' school, as Lang dubbed it, possesses almost as many pitfalls for the unwary. Let no method, linguistic, solar, anthropological, dominate our conclusions, but let none be absent from our counsels.

CHAPTER IV
THE VARIOUS TYPES OF DEITY

THERE are certain objections against giving 'departmental' names, such as 'god of fire,' 'god of wine,' to deities, but in certain stages of religious evolution these 'departmental deities' are found—gods of fire, water, earth, and air, hunting, thunder—deities connected with various crafts and even with certain qualities. It is, however, only in the higher stages of polytheism that such deities are finally stamped with the 'departmental' character.[1]

As has already been pointed out, there is more than one explanation of such gods. Fault has been found with the division of deities into agricultural and non-agricultural, but there is no doubt whatever that the change from nomadic to agricultural life and the consequent altered conditions gave birth to a completely new set of religious ideas. In the nomadic or hunting stage of existence, when man depends for subsistence upon the flesh of animals and such wild fruits as he can procure, he regards with veneration the supernatural beings he thinks help or hinder him in the chase. Thus among certain North American Indian tribes the barbarian hunter has a fetish shaped like a mountain-lion. After making it an offering, he places its carven nostrils to his own, believing that by so doing he inhales its courage. He then breathes out deeply, in order to spread the breath of the animal over a wide area and paralyse all the game in the neighbourhood. On slaying a deer he cuts out the liver and smears the blood thereof on the mouth of the fetish as a reward. Finally he prays

[1] Of course 'departmental' gods may possess many attributes, some of these entirely foreign to their character-in-chief, and drafted upon it by the circumstances of myth, politics, or amalgamation with other forms.

to the Great Deer, the mythical or magnified ancestor of the animal killed, not to seek vengeance against him for having taken the life of one of his children.

This is a picture of the utilitarian side of a savage hunter's religion, and it is a representative one. Thus we see with what simple religious elements the hunter has to do, and yet what an involved ritual these primitive ideas may bring in their train. He recognizes other supernatural beings than his own personal and tribal fetishes, the eponymous heads of the beast clans. For example, he fears and attempts to placate the being whom he deems to cause the thunder and lightning. Later he sees in this god a great hunter, the patron of his own craft of the chase, launching the fiery shaft from heaven.

The wind and the sun may appear to him to possess personality and even deity, as they symbolize the breath and heat of life; but he can scarcely adore them with the same fervour as that of the husbandman, who depends entirely for his sustenance on the good will of sun and wind.

The transition from the nomadic or hunting state to the agricultural may or may not be abrupt. It may depend on slow evolution or on the union of a hunting with an agricultural people, but whatever the cause of the adoption of more settled habits of existence, the gods of the chase do not all at once disappear into the background. Many of them hold their own until a later stage of polytheism is reached, and not a few supernatural forms of a primitive 'departmental' or 'animistic' type have achieved high rank in more than one later pantheon. Thus, as has already been shown, the Mexican Uitzilopochtli and the Latin Picus were evolved from bird totems which had led their respective tribesmen to battle in the days of old.

But the great measure of difference between the religions of nomadic and agricultural peoples is the compact which each makes with its gods. Adoration in the animistic stage is caused either by a sense of fear, by the indefinable feeling for the sacred, or because something is hoped for from the deity placated or worshipped. The contract between the hunter and the fetish which guides his actions with its advice or magic is of a low material type. He can scarcely have an agreement with a thunder-god or any such being, but with the gods which preside over vegetable growths the husbandman makes a very definite contract. An unpropitious season brings home to him the risk attending an agricultural existence, famine staring him in the face. Remembering the manner in which he placated the deities of his nomadic existence—by sacrifice—he proceeds by a like process[1] to placate the new deities upon whose goodwill the growth of his crops depends. The earth may be weary after bearing so much grain; therefore it must be drenched with blood in order that it may recover from the strain. The clouds may be absent, so that the corn becomes scorched and withered ; therefore a tithe of human life must be given to the water—in other words, victims must be drowned. The ever-present sun must be kept in good humour, for without his light and heat the grain would not germinate and human life would be destroyed ; therefore the steam of blood must arise to fill his nostrils. The contract is clear though unwritten : " Continue to feed us, O gods, and we shall feed you."

Thus the strictly departmental type of deity arises. At first he is a mere corn-spirit, maize-spirit, earth-spirit, water-, thunder-, sun-spirit, or what not—sun, water, grain, or earth personified—but as generations pass his fame grows and attracts wider reverence. His attributes become numerous, his ritual more involved ; and the wondrous sentiment of the sacred surrounds him with a mystic veil. Ethical ideas become attached to his worship ; he is regarded as a fount of righteousness ; and, from being non-moral and non-human, he comes to possess a sanctified human character as well as more than human powers. Let us examine a few ' departmental' types of godhead with the object of tracing them back to their original forms, if possible.

THE SUN-GOD

It will be well if we commence our inquiry with deities which are obviously of elemental origin.

One of the first to attract our attention is naturally the sun

---

[1] Of course these deities may have an animistic origin ; indeed, they certainly do have, so that the idea of sacrifice will not seem novel.

THE VARIOUS TYPES OF DEITY

himself. In all times and in most climates the great luminary has been regarded as the source of life. In nearly all the higher mythologies he occupies a distinguished place, if not the principal seat, in the pantheon. In the later stages of his god-head, also, his attributes themselves are deified ; but it is in his early career as a god that we must first deal with him here.

In the earliest animistic conception of the sun he is regarded as having life and volition at least equal, if not superior, to man. His character among a primitive people may be gauged from the utterance of the Peruvian monarch who cast doubts upon his godhead and told the solar priesthood that so far from possessing the attributes of deity, the sun was com-pelled by some force superior to himself to make the same journey daily over a fixed path. That this had not occurred to the solar worshippers of Peru shows that they gave no scientific interest, but merely a devout observation, to the luminary, and that, without bestowing any theological thought on the matter, they had merely adopted the old animistic idea of the sun as a living thing, little more or less.

When we come to examine later phases of sun-worship (and these cast light upon early solar religious ideas) we may discern that the original animistic idea of the sun as a living thing has evolved into, or given way before, a more purely anthropomorphic idea. This is a point of the first importance. Many writers on mythology appear to be under the impression that in later polytheistic times the sun was regarded itself as a personified god, and in some cases it may be so, but the idea was by no means universal, and it would seem that the sun-god was regarded more as a dweller in the house of the sun than as the sun himself.

Similarly the supernatural beings known as culture-heroes come to earth for a season, introduce the arts of civilization to men, and return once more to their bright abode, usually in a westerly direction. Such is the Greek Apollo, whereas another Greek god, Helios, is the sun himself. Apollo repre-sents the dusk-dispelling, civilizing agency of the orb of day, and with his golden arrows slays the Python, the serpent of night. In Egyptian mythology the sun is a boat in which several deities daily take ship to cross the heavens. Behind these anthropomorphic conceptions, however, lurked the older animistic idea, for we find that the Egyptians speak of the sun, the luminary itself, as *the* god, and that the Mexicans call it *the* teotl, the deity *par excellence*. Thus the animistic and anthropomorphic systems were in certain mythologies kept distinct. In others the animistic idea of the sun—that is, the sun itself, personified—remained to the end, as in the case of the Babylonian Merodach or the Japanese Ama-terasu. It is necessary, however, that the mythologist should distinguish between the anthropomorphic ' man of the sun ' and the merely animistic concept of the sun-god.

Having thus distinguished between earlier and later types of the sun as deity, let us attempt to discover first his attributes as a god, and secondly if any definite and universal type of myth attaches to him. A generation ago mythologists were prone to " see sun-gods everywhere," as Mannhardt expressed it ; but since that time the pendulum has swung too far in the other direction. Abundant criticism has been launched against the ' solar ' theory, but it is not always pertinent and in many cases it is merely futile. The theory suffered from the philological school with which it was unfortunately bound up, and neither critics nor readers seem to be able to judge it on its mythological merits alone. In our inquiries as to the attributes and mythical character of the sun-god we shall find that the one will cast light on the other, for as his almost universal myth becomes revealed to us his attributes will gradually unfold themselves. In disentangling solar myths, too, we must be careful to lift the veil of allegory often cast over them later.

A rough synopsis of the groundwork of solar myth might be given as follows. After the sun has risen from the mysterious darkness, and after he has forsaken his first love, the dawn, he pursues his course, gaining access of strength as he proceeds in his bark or fiery chariot until, having passed the zenith, he gradually declines in strength, and on the verge o the western heavens encounters the monster night, who fights with and devours him. He must then traverse the Underworld, with all its dangers and horrors, until he succeeds in emerging once more at the gates of morning.

THE VARIOUS TYPES OF DEITY

Let us take a typical myth of this description, from which we may be able to gauge the universality of the sun legend. Apollo was the offspring of Zeus and Leto, the sky and the darkness. The name of his mother, denoting the oblivion of night, reappears in 'Lethe,' the gloomy river of the Underworld, and in 'Latmos,' the 'Land of Shadows.' In the Ionian hymn which recounts the circumstances of his birth we read that Leto, when about to become his mother, could find no resting-place until she came to Delos. In that little stony island alone could she find repose, and so poor was it that she dreaded that her son, the great being about to be born, would spurn it into the sea. When Apollo was born the earth rejoiced and Delos became covered with flowers; but he was weak and helpless until Thetis touched his lips with the drink and food of the gods, when his swaddling-clothes, the white mists, fell off, and, seizing his lyre, he sang the praises of Zeus. His sojourn in Delos was short, and a second hymn tells us of his westward wanderings, of how he journeyed from land to land, always, however, returning to his native Delos. As soon as he cast from himself his swaddling-clothes, the white mists, he seized his quiver, the universal symbol of the sun-god, and, thus armed, went forth on his westward journey, until he came to the fountain of Telphussa, where he desired to remain, but Telphussa urged him to seek the more favoured land of Krisa. He then betook himself to Parnassus, where the two supernatural builders, Trophonius and Agamedes, raised a palace for him. It is at this point that he is confronted with the dragon which all sun-heroes meet and overcome.

Thus we see that Apollo is born of a mother whose name is darkness, that he casts from him the mists which enshroud him, and soars in the height of his glory over Parnassus, latterly overcoming the Python.[1]

A story with a similar groundwork is that of Beowulf

[1] As I have shown elsewhere (p. 95), Professor Rendel Harris has brought a good deal of proof in favour of a hypothesis that Apollo was the god of an apple cult; but it was not as such that he was known to the later Greeks, whatever he may have been originally—an instance, if such were needed, that the solar story finds its way into the myths of gods of all types.

in our earliest English saga. Betaking himself to the court of King Hrothgar of Jutland, whose realm was being devastated by the monster Grendel, he succeeded in slaying him, but later had to dive to the bottom of the sea to encounter Grendel's mother. Years afterward he fights with and conquers a dragon who guards a treasure, but in the combat is poisoned by its fangs. Beowulf came to land in the traditional sun-boat as a child. The Saxons called their harvest month *Beo* or *Bewod*, and Grendel is, of course, the water-provider. The later dragon typifies the continued contest between the sun-god and darkness, and the treasure it guards is, of course, the gold of the setting sun, or perhaps the elixir of life.

Similar stories are told regarding Indra, Cadmus, Horus, and lesser sun heroes, such as Hercules, Perseus, Bellerophon, Sigurd, Siegfried, and Rustem. The sun myth too has found its way into folklore. A good example is the folk-tale of King Arthur, which shows how in all ages the sun story has been interwoven with tales of local and even national heroes. A great obscurity rests upon Arthur's birth, but at manhood he springs into almost instant prominence and is hailed as rightful monarch of Britain. He slays not one dragon but several. He possesses the magic sword which all solar heroes wield. He kills his thousands and tens of thousands, and finally, when placed *hors de combat*, like other solar heroes, at Camelot, does not perish, but is wafted in a magical boat to the island of Avalon in the western sea. The sun myth has also attached itself to the stories of many of Arthur's knights, especially to that of Sir Tristram. May it not be that even the Round Table symbolizes the sun?

THUNDER-GODS

As a class, the deities usually called thunder-gods present a peculiarly involved mythological problem, as they almost invariably possess agricultural or military significance. The animistic conception of the thunder is instanced in such myths as those of the tribes of the Andes, who imagine the thunder to reside on the summit of a mountain, surrounded by clouds, through the canopy of which the fire-red limbs of the personified storm-spirits can ever and anon be seen. Other tribes symbolize the thunder as a bird, the flapping of whose pinions causes the reverberation of the storm, and this conception is found among primitive peoples both in the American and Australian continents. In passing it may be profitable to compare such a myth with the Greek tale of Prometheus, the Titan who stole fire from Heaven for human use. Regarding the original bird form of Prometheus there can be little doubt. Other forms of the myth, in America, Australia, and elsewhere, tell of a hero who in bird form stole the celestial fire, and it is obvious that to reach Heaven Prometheus must have been provided with the means of flight. There appears to be a distinct connexion between the fire-stealing myth and that of the thunder-bird. These animistic conceptions of the thunder prepared the way for an anthropomorphic presentation of the deity who wielded the bolts of Heaven, or launched the lightning spear; and if we examine the attributes of certain thunder-gods in the state of transition between the animal and the human form, we shall find that they retain evidences of their bird-like origin. Thus Uitzilopochtli, the great lightning- and war-god of the Aztecs, bears a name signifying that in primitive Aztec legend he was regarded as a bird pure and simple. Going farther afield in America, we find that Yetl, the thunder-god of the Thlinkeets, borrowed the wings of a supernatural crane, with which he flew about, as did Odin and Sin in Scandinavian and Haida in Indian myth. In Vancouver the thunder is represented by a bird, Tootah. The Hindu thunder-god, Indra, not only steals the heavenly liquor, as do many bird-gods, but in order to procure it he takes the shape of a quail. In other mythologies, in those of Greece and Scandinavia, for example, Zeus and Thor, who wield the thunder, have become too greatly humanized, if such a term may be employed, to display any original bird-like characteristics, if they ever possessed them. In passing it may be well to note briefly the apparatus of the thunder-god, the machinery by which he creates the noise of thunder. As has been said, the thunder-bird among the North American Indians effects this by the beating of his wings. Another American thunder-god causes the noise by beating a sheet of metal. The thunder of Thor is produced either by the blows of his mighty hammer or the rumbling of the wheels of his chariot drawn by goats. The reverberation of Jupiter's thunder proceeds from bolts forged for him by the Titans in the bowels of Mount Etna.

An important attribute which we may observe here is the thunder-god's lightning spear or arrow. This is the attribute of the Greek Apollo, of at least half a dozen American thunder-deities, of Indra, and of the Egyptian goddess Neith. En-lil, the thunder-god of Babylonia, was also a god of war. As patron of the chase and war, the thunder-god is often repre-sented with a spear or bow and arrow, as, for example, the Mexican god Mixcoatl, who is supposed to range far and wide in search of game. Often, too, the lightning flash is symbolized by the serpent; Uitzilopochtli's robe was interwoven with serpents, and he possessed a drum of serpent's skin, while 'Mixcoatl,' just cited, signifies 'Cloud-serpent.' Besides sym-bolizing the lightning flash, the serpent in its connexion with the thunder-god may typify the rain which invariably ac-companies thunder; and because of his character as a fertilizing agent and bearer of the rain which causes vegetable growth, the thunder-god is at times regarded as a deity of agriculture, even in his character of war-god. The Roman Mars so appears in the song of the Arval brethren, a sect whose duty it was to guard crops and herds, and as Mars Sylvanus he was invoked by the Roman farmer in the yearly lustration of his land. The Mexican Uitzilopochtli, too, was regarded as a patron of agriculture.

As we have seen in the myth of Brounger, the thunder-god might be connected in some manner with flint, from the circumstance that fire is capable of being struck from that mineral.

A word is necessary upon the connexion of the thunder-god with rain and with water generally. There are, of course, water-gods who have nothing whatever to do with thunder, but a good many thunder-gods possess power over not only the rain but the winds as well. Especially is this the case in America.

THE VARIOUS TYPES OF DEITY

MARINE DEITIES

Another striking example of the manner in which deities become departmental is the sea-god or goddess. As the corn-god presided over the harvest of the land, so does the sea-god preside over the harvest of the waste of waters. Later, when men build ships and go down to the sea in them, the powers and functions of these marine deities become greatly magnified. The circumstance that sea-gods or goddesses are almost invariably represented as having a fish's tail is accounted for in the same manner as the possession of animal characteristics by certain land deities is explained—that is, just as gods derived from eponymous or totemistic animals are sometimes represented as men with animal heads or animal attributes, so deities which were once eponymous fish are represented partly in anthropomorphic, partly in piscine form.

The following are instances of this. The coast Peruvians before the Spanish Conquest regarded the sea in much the same manner as many primitive peoples regard the land—that is, as a nourishing mother. Indeed they called it Mama-cocha, or Mother Sea, because it yielded the fish which formed so large a part of their subsistence. The whale was a general object of worship all along that coast, and the skate, sea-dog, dory, crab, and sardine, especially the last, were worshipped. It was not the individuals of those finny tribes which the Peruvian Indian adored, but the original eponymous fish which engendered all the others of the same species, and sent them periodically into the ocean, according to the season of each, to be food for man. All over North and South America the belief held good that animals, birds, and fish have eponymous counterparts who act as kings, chiefs, or even gods to the others of their species.[1] In course of time such fish-gods became anthropomorphic. In Peru, again, we find in connexion with the worship of the fish-bearing lake Tuncapata the adoration of an idol called Copacahuana, carven out of a bluish-green stone (obviously the symbol for water) and having the

---

[1] The study of these eponymous animal-gods will one day certainly throw a flood of light upon the obscure question of the origin of totemism.

body of a fish, surmounted by a rude human head. She was venerated as the giver of the fish with which the lake abounded. To come to classical examples, Poseidon and Neptune were usually represented as half man, half fish, bearded and grasping a trident. Oannes or Ea, the sea-god of Babylonia, is also figured as a man with a fish's tail, below which human feet peep out. Like many corn-gods or gods of the harvest, he was also a culture-god, and, according to Berosus, taught the natives of the Babylonian shore the arts of life. Thus, as the corn-plant itself, as we shall see, is capable of evolving into a god, so was the fish—so intimate and complete is the connexion between religious conceptions and the food supply. In one representation of a deity executed as a bas-relief on the walls of Nimrud, and on a signet from Nineveh, we notice that the head and shoulders of the deity are covered by the skin of a fish, remnant of his piscine origin, just as many anthropomorphic gods, once animal in form, have the skins of their animal prototypes cast about the upper parts of their statues.

It was probably not until men took to the sea that the god of the waters developed to the full his protective or destructive tendencies. Thus the raising or allaying of storms, the granting of favourable winds and prosperous voyages, would naturally vest in the sea-god, once navigation became general. His relation to the other gods would then become a mere matter of mythic rearrangement and a niche would be found for him in the pantheon. As the sun-god or wind-god was supreme in the sky, so was he supreme in the waters ; nor did his dominion stop with the sea alone, but every estuary, lake, river, or even brook, was beneath his sway and peopled by his subjects.

LUNAR GODS

The deity who presides over the moon is in most pantheons full of mythological interest. Primitive ideas of the luminary regarded it as equally the cause of vegetable growth with the sun ; the work which was accomplished by the sun through the day was, argued early man, continued by the moon at night. All primitive time-reckoning was calculated on a lunar basis, and as time-reckoning among savages assumes the character of science, this would assist in bestowing upon the spirit which presided over the moon a certain reputation for wisdom. Primary lunar spirits are not as a rule very high in the scale of god-like evolution.

As the moon is associated with the dampness and dews of night, an ancient and widespread belief connects her with water. Thus in folklore she is universally associated with rain ; but she has also an evil reputation as the distributer of miasmatic fogs and exhalations, because these more generally make their appearance during the hours of her reign. The Mexicans invariably confounded the words *citatli*, the moon, and *atl*, water. As representing water, the universal mother, the moon was regarded as the patroness of fertility. She is also often the goddess of love, ruling over the hours of night, generally sacred to courtship. With some of the more primitive peoples she is the mother of ghosts and all such nocturnal abominations.

Her connexion with wisdom has been touched upon. This is perhaps best instanced in the Egyptian moon-god Thoth, who, probably because he was supposed to keep the records of the Nile inundations, supposed to be under the influence of the moon, was also regarded as god of writing, and therefore, by inference, as god of wisdom. Diana, or Artemis, the chaste huntress of the Greeks and Romans, is, like many moon-goddesses, a patron of human fertility and love. But she is more ; as one of the ancient moon-goddesses, and therefore connected with the old lunar calendar, she was a deity of the harvest. Her character as a huntress is a little obscure. Some water-goddesses, like the Egyptian Neith, possess the lightning arrow, symbolical of the thunder-cloud from whence the lightning issues ; and it may be that Artemis possessed the bow and arrow simply because she was sister of Apollo, and, by analogy, if the sun-god possessed these weapons, so must his sister, the moon-goddess. Again, it may be that she possessed them as a goddess of death. It is strange to find a lunar goddess connected with the chase, that *rôle* being nearly always filled by the thunder- or wind-god.[1]

[1] See the illuminating remarks of Professor Rendel Harris upon this goddess in his *Ascent of Olympus*, pp. 56 *sqq.*

AGRICULTURAL DEITIES

We have seen how a compact for their mutual weal arose between men and the gods when an agricultural elementary basis had been arrived at ; but ere the evolution of departmental deities of agriculture, and of the various grains and plants cultivated, these appear to possess separate guardian spirits. In dealing with the great class of corn-spirits Sir James Frazer distinguished between the spirit and the god as follows. He says :

" As distinguished from gods, spirits are restricted in their operations to definite departments of nature. Their names are general, not proper ; their attributes are generic rather than individual. In other words, there is an indefinite number of spirits of each class, and the individuals of a class are all much alike, they have no definitely marked individuality, no accepted traditions are current as to their origin, life, adventures, and character. On the other hand, gods, as distinguished from spirits, are not restricted to definite departments of nature. It is true that there is generally some one department over which they preside as their special province, but they are not rigorously confined to it. They can exert their power for good or evil in many other spheres of life. Again, they bear individual or proper names, such as Ceres, Proserpine, Bacchus, and their individual characters and histories are fixed by current myths and the representations of art."

The corn-spirit, so characteristic of early agricultural life, is still to be found in present-day folklore. The researches of Mannhardt and Sir James Frazer have supplied numerous illustrations of the manner in which a sheaf at harvest-time is connected with certain rites, more or less similar in all countries, associated with the corn-spirit or corn-mother. Thus it was thought in primitive days that a spirit resided in or watched over the growing grain. In time this animistic conception gave way to the idea of a departmental god of agriculture.

Strangely enough the agricultural departmental deity does not represent the same generally uniform characteristics as do other departmental gods, for example, gods of the sun or gods of the sea. A likeness exists between the myths of Demeter in Greece, Osiris in Egypt, and Ishtar in Babylonia, and it is probable that these three myths had a common origin; but there is no likeness between the person or attributes of the three gods alluded to. The establishment of agriculture may be—indeed, often is—part of the earthly accomplishment of a culture-god. Thus Apollo was guardian of the crops and even of the herds, and during the mythical reign of Quetzalcoatl in Mexico the ears of maize were so heavy that one might scarce be carried by a strong man. Agricultural gods too frequently have a connexion with the Underworld, for seed grows to fruition there. Thus among the Greeks, Persephone, the wife of Aides or Hades, was unquestionably symbolic of the corn sleeping in winter and coming to fruition in the warm months.

The Corn-Spirit and its Abode

The mother of Persephone, or Kore, was Demeter—*i.e.,* 'corn-mother.' Persephone was carried off and wed by Hades, king of the dead, was sought for in his dark country by her mother, and was restored, with the proviso that she must spend so many months every year underground with her husband. Many circumstances in the myth of Osiris point to the same corn-spirit origin. The wanderings of Isis in search of her dismembered husband Osiris throughout the length and breadth of Egypt, the passing of the son of the King of Byblos through the magic flame, as well as other incidents, well illustrate the similarity.

Why do Demeter and Isis wander up and down, the one seeking for her daughter, the other for her husband? Persephone and Osiris in one of his many forms—probably his original form—both represent the sown seed of the wheat, lying dormant for so long, but later resurrected and recovered. Who or what then are Demeter and Isis? It is one of the tenets of animism that the animistic spirit must, as spiritualists would say, 'materialize' in some natural object, and the wandering spirit may thus be enticed by the sorcery of the shaman into the fetish object. When the corn is cut down, whither does the corn-spirit betake itself? It must of necessity become a wanderer on the face of the earth until once more the corn sprouts to give it house-room. If our conclusions are correct, the myths of Demeter and Isis are late and elaborated versions of an early animistic belief that the corn-spirit was driven from its shelter until the green shoots attracted it once more. The myth is most surely an animistic one, and perhaps one of the oldest myths in the world. Demeter and Isis are deified corn-spirits seeking the corn (Persephone and Osiris) for the purpose of rematerializing it. Persephone and Osiris represent the corn-seed as well as the corn-spirit, as is obvious from their sojourn underground.

FIRE-GODS

Fire-gods are usually associated with the sun, but later achieve a certain domestic and mechanical significance. Undoubtedly fire with its movement and appearance of life would be regarded in animistic times as informed by spirit. In later times there is a departmental god of fire who is often an artificer in metals. This idea could not, of course, have arisen before the discovery of the uses of metals, so that departmental deities of this type must be of comparatively recent origin.

In India the great god of fire was Agni, who ruled not only over the lightning and other fires of Heaven, but over those of earth as well. He is occasionally confounded with Indra and Varuna, but in the earlier hymns he is the fire which men prize as an indispensable boon. He bears up sacrifices from men to the gods under the dark canopy of the smoke which arises from the sacred fires below. He is occasionally credited with the wisdom of the sun-god himself. He is 'black-backed' and 'many-limbed'; like the serpent, he is laid hold of with difficulty; he is the regulator of sacrifices, and is regarded as the guide of souls in the unseen world.

Among the Greeks, Hephæstus was regarded as the youngest of the gods. He was a lame and ugly dwarf, the son of Zeus and Hera, who was so displeased with his appearance that she wished to cast him out of Olympus. He took her part in a quarrel with Zeus, however, and thereupon the king of Heaven cast him from the heights to the island of Lemnos, where he fell maimed and wounded. He was the great artificer of the gods, an incomparable worker in metal. He raised the shining palaces of Olympus, forged the marvellous armour of Achilles, and made the necklace of Harmonia. Strangely enough, in Norse myth and English legend, Regin, the smith of the *Volsunga Saga*, and Wieland the Smith are stunted, lame, or limping, and forge arms for heroes, as did Hephæstus for Achilles. In his Latin shape of Vulcan Hephæstus is pre-eminently a god of fire, the conception becoming associated with volcanic districts, especially with Mount Etna in Sicily, where, with the Cyclops for his assistants, he laboured in the bowels of the volcano.

Among the Scandinavian peoples, Loki appears to be the god of fire. He also is limping and misshapen, but one does not espy in him the mechanical ability of the Greek god. He sides now with the gods, now with the giants, thus typifying the twofold nature of fire as a friend and an enemy. He was probably grafted on to an older fire-demon.

In ancient Mexico Xiuhtecutli, the fire-god, was known as Huehueteotl, eldest of the gods, not youngest, as in Greece and India. His body was flame-coloured, and his face black and surmounted by a head-dress of green feathers. A yellow serpent sprawling across his back typified the serpentine nature of fire. He was also the god of the domestic hearth, and on rising in the morning all Mexican families offered him an oblation of food and drink.

From the examples given above it will be seen that although in one instance, that of Hephæstus, the possession of the thunderbolt is assumed, most fire-gods are truly departmental in character, and do not appear to have any connexion with the lightning. They arise from a purely animistic conception of fire, and later become personified. Occasionally we find them, as in the case of Agni, and Yibil, the Babylonian fire-god, partially absorbed by, or having the attributes of, the sun-god.

INTRODUCTION TO MYTHOLOGY

WIND-GODS

Although gods of the winds appear in nearly all mythological systems, in many instances they are neither more nor less than representatives of tempest or gentle breeze. In some mythologies, as in that of Egypt, they occupy a subordinate position, whereas in others the wind, usually as the tempest, is one of the attributes of the supreme god of the pantheon. Odin is undoubtedly in one of his aspects a god of storm and in later folklore figures as the 'Wild Huntsman.' In Mexico, too, the great god Tezcatlipoca was also known as Yoalli Ehecatl, or 'Lord of the Night Wind.' In some mythologies, as in those of India and Greece, every aspect of the wind, whether in gale or breeze, is personified and deified. Of course it is easy to see that wind, like fire, with its movement and utterance, either gentle or boisterous, would lend itself to primitive animistic interpretation. It would seem a very living thing indeed to early man, and was identified with the source of life itself.

In the Vedas of the Hindus we find Veyu personified in the gentler movements of the air, answering in this respect to the Latin Favonius or the Greek Pan. The more violent forces of the wind in Hindu myth are represented by the Maruts, who overturn trees and uproot forests, roar like lions, and shake the mountains. The rain is their raiment, and they are swift as Thor. When the tempest rages, the wayfarer may hear the cracking of their whips as they pass overhead. But their onslaught over and their purpose accomplished, they resume the shape of new-born babes. They are the crushers or grinders, the children of Rudra, father of the winds, who is also the deceiver, the master-thief; this last attribute possibly symbolizing the shifting nature of wind.

In Greek myth we have the gentle or intermittent wind in Pan, who breathes melody through his reed pipes. As the lover of Pitys, the nymph of the pine-tree, he aroused the jealousy of Boreas, the rude north wind, who hurled the maiden from a rock, and changed her into the tree which bears her name. Boreas is the son of the night and the dawn, and is usually figured in Greek myth as dwelling in the north. In

132

the *Odyssey* all the winds are placed by Zeus under the charge of Æolus, to whom is entrusted the power of rousing or quelling them at will. The more vigorous wind from the west was known as Zephyros, husband of Podarge, the white-footed wind who drives before her the snow-white vapours.

The fury of the storm occasionally furnishes the conception of a god of war, as in the case of the Greek Ares. Tezcatlipoca in Mexico, too, was called 'the Slayer.'

EARTH-GODS

The earth was personalized by early man, who regarded it as the parent of all things dwelling thereon. A union is often conceived of between the Sky-Father and the Earth-Mother; and myths from centres as far apart as Egypt and New Zealand tell how these primeval parents were separated. No mere fetishism would suffice for the primeval idea of the earth. Early man seems to have regarded it as his mother, just as the late Mr Andrew Lang insisted that the primeval conception of a heavenly father who dwelt in the sky was prior to animistic belief or, at any rate, came before the polytheistic stage. As previously suggested, the primitive All-Father of Mr Lang may have been no other than the primitive sky-god. In a striking passage in his *Introduction to Mythology and Folklore* Sir George Cox says: " It may seem almost a paradox to say that the thought of the earth as a producer and restorer would be more likely to lead men on to the thought of a power transcending nature, or the forces which we see at work in the outward world, than the impressions made on the human mind by the phenomena of the daily or nightly heavens ; but on further thought we can scarcely fail to see that the continuance of life on the earth, the unceasing restlessness, the perpetual change which is going on upon its surface, the sensitiveness of all vegetable and animal substances to the influences which act upon them from without, must inevitably lead men on to something more like a scheme of philosophy than any which could be furnished by mere phrases describing the phenomena of the day or the year."

The Earth-Mother, then, would be practically universal.

We should expect to find her everywhere, and indeed we do. In the Vedic hymns the earth is the bride of Dyaus; in Greece she was known as Gæa. Bacchus or Dionysus is certainly a deity with an earth connexion. In Mexico more than one god was connected with the earth—for example, Tepeyollotl, usually worshipped in a cavern, and a god of earthquakes. The name signifies 'Heart of the Mountain' and evidently has a seismic meaning. In the worship of Centeotl, the maize-god, there was a ceremony called the Nitiçapoloa, or 'Tasting of the Soil,' consisting in raising a little earth on one finger to the mouth and eating it, thus achieving communion with the earth-god. The Spanish conquerors left it on record that the soil was in reality tasted, and not merely placed to the lips. Like the Babylonians, the Aztecs sometimes painted the Earth-Mother as a woman with countless breasts; the Peruvians called her Mama Allpa, 'Mother Earth,' and the Caribs addressed her as Mama Nono, 'the Good Mother from whom all things come.' In the dialect of the Algonquin Indians the word for 'earth' is derived from the same root as those for 'mother' and 'father,' but the Western Algonquin tribes call her Nokomis, 'My grandmother.' The Passes of Brazil believed that the earth was a great creature, that the rivers and streams were its blood-vessels, and that it circled round the sun, turning first one and then the other of its sides toward that luminary in order to keep itself warm—not a bad guess for the early scientist to make! In some parts of Europe we find the small progeny of the dwarfs connected with the cult of earth.

These teeming animistic spirits are not confined to Europe, however. An earth-goddess in German tradition is the benignant Holda, who preserves the life of the winter-bound world under a mantle of snow.

A group of interesting earth-deities were known to Latin Italy. Ops, a goddess of wealth and fertility, the wife of Saturnus, corresponded to the Greek Rhea. The Latin genii were also closely akin to the dryads and hamadryads of the Greeks, who inhabited groves and trees. Pilumnus and Picumnus too were worshipped as rural deities, but they seem to have had a more agricultural than terrestrial significance.

Pomona was the Latin goddess of fruit-trees and their fruits, and Fauna and Faunus were also rural deities. The satyrs in Greece were cognate types.

Before agriculture proper with its especial pantheon was evolved the forces of fertility may have received a considerable amount of adoration and were probably in some measure connected with the spirit of earth. Rites innumerable were carried out to secure the revival of vegetation in spring, most of them having for object the rejuvenation of nature. In some instances trees, and in others human beings, were sacrificed. Such gods, for example, as Adonis, who was worshipped in Western Asia, Osiris, and Attys represented the decay and revival of vegetation. Much of their ritual is still performed by the peasantry of all parts of Europe, and has been collected by the labours of Mannhardt and Sir James Frazer. It may be interesting to give here an account of such an observance which came beneath the writer's own notice.

THE BURRY MAN

At South Queensferry, near Edinburgh, a strange annual ceremony took place, the chief actor in which was known locally as 'the Burry Man.' It was supposed to commemorate the passage of Malcolm Canmore and Queen Margaret to and from Edinburgh and Dunfermline, but this is local surmise and nothing more. It can be traced back at least to the period of the last battle of Falkirk, for an old woman of eighty, whose mother was thirteen years of age at the date of that battle (1746), stated that the observance had been unaltered from that time till her own old age. It took place on the day preceding the annual fair, usually about the second week in August, and was long upheld by the boys of Queensferry. On the day preceding the fair the Burry Man, always a stout fellow or a robust lad, was dressed in loosely fitting flannels, and his face, arms, and legs thickly covered with burrs. He carried two staves at arm's-length, and these, as well as his hands, were beautifully adorned with flowers. Thus accoutred, he was led from door to door by two attendants, who assisted him in upholding his arms by grasping the staves. As each successive door was reached a shout was raised and the inhabitants came out to bestow greetings and money on the Burry Man, the amount collected being equally divided and spent at the fair by the youths who kept up the custom. On some occasions two persons were thus selected and led in procession from door to door—the one being styled the 'King' and the other the 'Queen,' it is thought in allusion to the passage of the royal couple through the borough. It used to be a popular belief that when this quaint custom was abandoned misfortune would befall the town.

Now what did the Burry Man represent? The custom was certainly a relic of a most ancient festival. The Burry Man of South Queensferry was as elsewhere the representation in human form of a tree- or plant-spirit, for these often are represented in anthropomorphic or man-like shape in folk festival. In Bohemia on the fourth Sunday in Lent the girls of the villages go into a wood, cut down a young tree, fasten to it a puppet dressed in white clothes to look like a woman, and with this figure go from house to house collecting gratuities and singing that they bring summer into the village, summer being represented as the spirit of vegetation, returning or reviving. At Thann in Alsace a girl called the 'Little May Rose,' dressed in white, carries a small may-tree covered with garlands and ribbons, and she and her companions collect gifts from door to door, singing as they go. In Lithuania the lads of the village choose the prettiest girl, swathe her in birch branches, and dress her as the May. In Brie, in the Ile de France, a lad is wrapped in leaves and is called 'Father May.' In the Frankenwald mountains, in Northern Bavaria, on the 2nd of May a man is enveloped in straw from head to foot to personify a sheaf, and in this guise he dances round a tree erected before the local tavern, after which he is led in procession through the streets, which are adorned with sprigs of birch. In Thuringia as soon as the trees begin to grow green in spring the children choose one of their playmates, around whom they twine leaves till only his shoes peep out from the greenery. Two of them lead him about so that he may not stumble or fall, and they address him as the 'Little Leaf Man.' In Carinthia on St George's Day a young fellow called 'Green George' is clad from head to foot in green birch branches. In England, too, a good example of these leaf-clad mummers is 'Jack-in-the-Green,' who walks enshrouded in a framework of wicker covered with holly and ivy and surmounted by flowers and ribbons. Many other examples could be given.

The Burry Man, like these, is a representation of the spirit of vegetation, the festival of which has survived in South Queensferry from early times, just as it has elsewhere.

CHAPTER V
THE VARIOUS CLASSES OF MYTH

MYTHS can to a large extent be classified, and most important myths may be grouped under one of the following heads:

Creation myths (creation of the earth and man).
Myths of the origin of man.
Flood myths.
Myths of a place of reward.
Myths of a place of punishment.
Sun myths.
Moon myths.
Hero myths.
Beast myths.
Myths to account for customs or rites.
Myths of journeys or adventures through the Underworld or place of the dead.
Myths regarding the birth of gods.
Fire myths.
Star myths.
Myths of death.
Food of the dead formula.
Myths regarding taboo.
'Dismemberment' myths (in which a god is dismembered).
Dualistic myths (the good god fighting the bad).
Myths of the origin of the arts of life.
Soul myths.

The first five classes are treated in this volume, in separate chapters or otherwise, according to their importance. Sun myths have already been dealt with individually, as have

THE VARIOUS CLASSES OF MYTH

culture-hero or hero myths,[1] moon myths, beast myths, ritual myths, and birth of gods myths, which leaves for discussion in this chapter fire myths, star myths, myths of death, myths regarding taboo, 'dismemberment' myths, and dualistic myths.

FIRE MYTHS

Fire myths are of two descriptions: those which relate to the destruction of the world by fire and those which tell how fire was stolen from heaven by a demigod, hero, or supernatural bird or other animal. Of the first class it is surprising what a large proportion come from the American continent. In the Old World we have the Jewish idea of a universal conflagration of the 'last day' (not unknown to the childhood of the present generation), the Norse belief that fire should end the heavens and the earth, and (according to Seneca) the Roman idea that some such fate would ultimately overtake the world of men and things; but it is to America that we must go for really striking and picturesque myths of the destruction of the earth by fire in whole or part. Thus the Arawaks of Guiana tell of a dreadful scourging by fire sent upon them by the Great Spirit Aimon Kondi, from which the survivors escaped by taking refuge in underground caverns. Monan, the creator of the Brazilian Indians, vexed with mankind, resolved to destroy the world by fire, and would have succeeded had not Irin Magé, a crafty wizard, extinguished the flames by a heavy rain-storm. The Aztecs at the end of each cycle of fifty-two years dwelt in dread lest the period for the destruction of the earth by fire had at last arrived, and the Peruvians believed that following an eclipse the world would be wrapped in devouring flames. In North America the Algonquin Indians believe that at the last day Michabo will stamp his foot upon the earth, and lo! flames will spring up and devour it. A similar belief was held by the Pueblo Indians and the ancient Maya of Central America.

[1] See *Popul Vuh*, chap. x.

FIRE-STEALING MYTHS

Another class of fire myth is that in which a supernatural being, usually a bird, steals fire from Heaven and brings it to earth for the benefit of mankind. The best-known example of this type of myth is that which recounts how Prometheus brought fire from Olympus in a hollow cane or tube. As has been shown elsewhere in this volume, the myth is almost universal, and the reader is referred to the comparative table at the end of this chapter.

STAR MYTHS

The numerous star myths, the general character of which is of fairly uniform type throughout the world, deal less with single stars than with groups of stars. Where Heaven is the original theatre of creation and the ancestor-land to which the spirits of the forefathers return, as stars, the constellations are, so to speak, the illustration of the cosmogonic legend, the images of objects, animals, persons, which appear therein. Other constellations are formed by their readily perceived similarity to objects and persons, and a myth is invented in explanation. These things are brought into connexion with one another and woven into a narrative, in which one idea gives rise to others. The conception and meaning of such pictures is naturally very varied among individual races, but on the other hand very similar where the characteristic forms and groupings of the constellations must suggest the same or related ideas to independent observers. The constellations which belong to this class are, for example, Orion, the Cross, the Pleiades, the Great Bear, and the Milky Way. Ideas of the Pleiades as heaps of grain, swarms of small animals, birds, bees, kids, or groups of people playing, are universal. But nowhere is the star myth so original or striking as in South America, and as the constellation legends of that sub-continent are but little known, we shall furnish the reader with some account of them in preference to the more hackneyed star tales of Europe and Asia. The Pleiades are thus wheat among the Bakairi, dwarf-parrots among the Moxos and Karayas, bee-

THE VARIOUS CLASSES OF MYTH

swarms among the Tupi, and other tribes. Only among the Makusi in the south is a parallel to be found to the widely spread North American myth which supposes the Pleiades to be children carried off to Heaven while playing in a dance. The Southern Cross is very variously treated. The idea of its being the tracks of an emu seems to be limited to South America, but is very widespread there, for example, among the Bororos and Karayas, inhabitants of the steppe districts. As the four outstanding stars of the Cross lie in the Milky Way, one may identify the four-eyed jaguar which in the Yurakare myth escapes the vengeance of the hero Tin, and, calling upon the moon, is raised to Heaven. The Milky Way, as the most prominent appearance in the darkened heavens at night, receives universal attention, but has given rise to the most diverse traditions. Like the Bushmen and other Africans, the Bororos and Karayas believe that the Milky Way is an ash-track. This, as well as the guanaco track of the Patagonians, resembles the 'Path of the Gods' of the Romans, the bird-track of the Esthonians, and the 'Jacob's ladder' of the medieval church, while the Milky Way seems to be considered as a path of souls by some of the Bolivian nations. Its conception as a stream or lake has not been definitely traced in South America. On the other hand, it appears that its peculiar branching formation caused it to be likened to a tree, and this belief finds expression in the Arawak legend of the world-tree of Akawiro, which bore not only all known fruits and plants, but also all organic beings. Among the central Caribs of the Bakairi it is a hollow tree-stem, such as is used among them as a drum, its roots spreading southward and apart from each other. In its neighbourhood the first acts of the mythical twin-heroes Keri and Kame were performed, and among the Caribs even to this day are to be seen living animals which originally issued from its trunk.

The distinctly circumscribed, sharply defined shape of Orion is compared by the Indian with familiar objects of a rhomboidal form, or similar shaped animals. The Bakairi see in this constellation a dried stack of manioc, the Karayas a beetle, the Ipurinas a turtle, and so on. In myths he appears first in connexion with the neighbouring star-groups of the Pleiades and Hyades (Aldebaran). He then becomes among the Indians a mighty hunter who follows a female, our Pleiades, as Orion in the Greek legends pursues the daughters of Pleion, with whom he had fallen in love, until they are changed by Zeus into a swarm of doves. So in the legend of the Caribs of Guiana the hunter Seriko goes after his faithless wife Wailya, whom the Tapir (Hyades group) had taken away from him.

The wifely relationship of the Pleiades with the Indian Orion is also met with under the sign of Seuci (Tupi), Ceiguce (Amazonia), though it cannot be said that the idea can solely be ascribed to the Tupi. The myth tells how a girl of the kindred Uaupe race (Tariana or Temiana) flees her village in order to escape from the local marriage customs and enters the house of a Yacami chief who takes her to wife. She brings forth two eggs, from which a boy and girl are hatched, both ornamented with stars. The girl, decked with seven stars, is Seuci; the boy, Pinon, is girdled with a star-serpent, and perhaps Orion's belt. The children return home with their mother, where the boy secures recognition by the performance of prodigies, such as the slinging of giant stones.

Myths of Death and Taboo

Myths of death are obviously ætiological—that is, manufactured *ad hoc*, to account for death, usually regarded by primitive peoples as an unnatural event, due to magic or the breaking of a taboo or the neglect of some ritual act. Thus death was let loose upon the world by the breaking of the taboo or prohibition which had been placed upon the opening of Pandora's box. The apple myth of Adam and Eve bears similar evidences of the idea of taboo. An Australian myth recounts how a woman approaches a forbidden tree and thus meets her doom. Several myths relate how death came into the world through the agency of Night—obviously a connexion of mortality with the phenomenon of sleep. Thus a Polynesian myth tells how Mani tried to pass through Night, but a little bird sang and awakened the night-monster, who ate Mani up. In Southern India it is believed that "the death-snake bites while God sleeps." A Central African story tells that when sleep was unknown in the world a woman offered to teach a man how to sleep. She held her victim's nostrils so hard that he could not breathe, but died.

Taboo myths of importance are not so numerous as might be supposed. Perhaps the chief is the tale of Cupid and Psyche. In its later form the bride was forbidden to look upon her husband, but her curiosity overcame her fear and she beheld his face, with dire results. This myth is, of course, a legacy from an age when for various reasons it was taboo for a woman to see her husband for some time after her marriage, just as it is to-day among certain African peoples, the ' reasons ' being to neutralize the dangers supposed to be attendant upon the matrimonial state. Akin to this is the name-taboo, found in the story of Lohengrin, whose bride is not permitted to ask the name and rank of her lord and master, the reason being that the real name, like the soul, is part of one's personality and that it is dangerous for any other person to know it, a pseudo-name being commonly employed among many savage races. Thus, if the names of certain evilly disposed supernatural beings are known and pronounced their power disappears, as in the well-known stories of Tom-tit-tot and Rumplestiltskin.

THE DISMEMBERMENT MYTH

It has been thought that such dismemberment myths as those of Osiris, Dionysus, and Demeter, the Algonquin Lox, and the Polynesian Tangoroa have their origin in a primitive custom, the dismemberment of a human victim, who was buried in the corn-fields and supposed to renew his life in the harvest following his burial. It is considered that such a practice gave birth to the myth of Osiris in Egypt and became symbolic of resurrection. The practice is probably connected in some manner with the almost universal savage custom of preserving the bones of the dead for the owner, who at some future period will desire to claim them.

DUALISM

Dualism is the belief in opposing good and evil deities, and is found in connexion (1) with such peoples as have advanced far on the path of theological thought and progress, (2) with races whose original beliefs have been sophisticated by those of more civilized peoples. A good example of the first is the widely known Persian myth of Ormuzd and Ahriman. The second class is well illustrated by the myth of Joskeha and Tawiscara, already alluded to in dealing with sophisticated myths.

COMPARATIVE TABLES OF MYTHS

The following tables have been compiled for the purpose of bringing together the most important types of myth and indicating their geographical incidence. It is not pretended that these are in any way exhaustive, but much care has been taken in their compilation and it is hoped that they will assist the student of myth as a ready reference to parallels.

BIRTH OF GODS MYTHS

Greeks. Zeus, Poseidon, Pluto, Hera, Demeter, and Hestia, children of Cronus. All but Zeus were swallowed by their father when infants and all disgorged by him at one time full grown.

Perseus, son of Zeus and Danaë.

The Dioscuri (Zeus visits their mother Leda as a swan).

Vedas. Agni, both son and father of the gods—son of Heaven and earth—begotten by the sky, the clouds, and the dawn—born among men, in Heaven and in the waters.

Algonquins. Manibozho, born of a virgin.

Hurons. Joskeha, born of a virgin.

Mexicans. Quetzalcoatl, born of a virgin; Uitzilopochtli (ball of feathers falls from heaven into his mother's breast).

Peruvians. Viracocha, born of a virgin.

Thlinkeets (N.W. America). Yetl's mother by advice of friendly dolphin swallows pebble and sea-water.

Uapès (Brazil). Jurapari (his mother drinks fermented liquor).

BEAST MYTHS.
Beasts and birds are credited with divine or semi-divine attributes.

Greeks. Io as a cow chased into Egypt by gad-fly sent by Hera.

Amphitryon chases the Cadmean fox with the Athenian dog.

Bellerophon slays the Chimæra with the help of Pegasus.

The Centaurs.

Caribs (Antilles). The ibis.

Chinooks (Colombia River). Blue Jay.

Aschochimi Indians (California). The coyote.

Thlinkeet Indians. Yetl the raven.

Australians. Pund-jel the eagle-hawk.

Ahts Indians (Vancouver Island). Tootah, the thunder-bird, universal mother.

Banks Islanders. Marawa the spider.

Tinneh or Déné Indians (Hare-skins). Miraculous dog is creator.

DUALISTIC MYTHS (the good god combating the bad god). This idea is very general, being found practically all over the world. The creator of all good things is constantly thwarted by the evil spirit or principle, who, for every good and beautiful thing that the beneficent god makes, produces a corresponding evil.

Egyptians. Osiris and Set or Apep.

Ra (light and goodness) and Apep (darkness and evil).

Babylonians. Merodach and Tiawath.

Persians. Ormuzd and Ahriman.

Greeks. Zeus and Typhon.

Apollo and Python.

Perseus and the Gorgon.

Teutons (Scandinavia). Thor and Loki.

Sigurd and Fafnir.

Hindus. Indra and Ahi or Vritra.

Hottentots. Gaunab (bad) and Tsui-Goab (good).

Algonquin Indians. Michabo or Manibozho and the prince of serpents.

Great Manitou, whose heart is the sun, made men. His wife, the moon, brought disease and death to the race.

Glooskap and Malsum.

Huron Indians. Joskeha and Tawiscara.

Incas (Peru). Piguerão (day) and Apocatequil (night).

145

Iroquois Indians. Enigorio and Enigohatgea (Good Mind and Bad Mind).

Thlinkeet Indians. Yetl and Khanukh.

Tupi-Guarani (Brazil). Aricoute (darkness) and Tamandare (light).

Australians. Pund-jel, the eagle-hawk (good) and the Crow (bad).

Pentecost Islanders. Tagar (good) and Suque (bad).

Banks Islanders. Qat and Tangaro Lologong (the Fool).

DISMEMBERMENT MYTHS. In which a god or demigod is torn to pieces and the parts widely scattered and afterward collected.

Egyptians. Osiris and Isis.

Greeks. Orpheus and Eurydice.
Dionysus and Demeter.
Medea and Pelias.

Finns (*Kalevala* epic). Lemminkainen and his mother.

Rumanians. Frounse Werdye and Holy Mother Sunday.

Russians. Morevna and Koshchei.

Bushmen. Moon cut down by sun; piece left grows.

Antis Indians (Brazil). See Spence, *Dictionary of Non-Classical Mythology*, p. 43.

Algonquins. The demon Lox.

Caribs. Story of their ancestor.

Dindje. Crow killed by the Navigator.

Pawnee Indians. Pa-hu-ka-tawa.

Zuñi Indians. Woman beloved by the sun becomes the mother of twins.

Madagascar. Ibonia, joiner together and life-giver.

Polynesians. Tangaroa and Mani.

CREATION MYTHS. In these there is nearly always a vast world of waters, over which broods the creative agency, who by a spoken word, force of thought (will-power), or by sheer physical labour creates the earth, or, more often, raises it from the midst of the watery abyss.

Babylonians. Bel or Merodach forms Heaven and earth from the two halves of the body of Tiawath.

Persians. Ormuzd (Ahura Mazda), father and creator.

Greeks. Uranus (Heaven-Father) and Gæa (Earth-Mother) beget all things.

THE VARIOUS CLASSES OF MYTH

Teutons (Scandinavia). Ginnungagap, the gulf existent. World made from body of the giant Ymir.

Finns (*Kalevala* epic). Eagle hatches the land.

Hindus. Brahma, in his avatar as the boar, raised the earth on his tusks from out the waters and then began his work of creating.

Japanese. Izanagi and Izanami (creative pair).

Bushmen. Cagn (the praying mantis) created the world.

Zulus. Unkulunkulu (the great ancestor-creator).

Ahts Indians (Vancouver Island). Quawteaht was the 'framer of all things.'

Algonquin Indians. Michabo or Manibozho, the Great Hare, creates all things.

Arawaks (Guiana). Aluberi (from Alin 'He who makes').

Athapascan Indians. Yetl, the omnipotent raven, descended to the ocean from Heaven, and the earth rose.

Incas (Peru). Ataguju is creator of all things.

Iroquois Indians. Divine woman falls on turtle (earth).

Mexicans. Tonacatecutli breathes and divides the waters of the heavens and earth.

Navaho Indians. Ahsonnatli 'the Turquoise Hermaphrodite' creates Heaven and earth.

Oregon Indians. Coyote is creator.

Peruvians. Mama-cocha (the whale), 'Mother Sea,' was the mother of mankind.

Pawnees. Ti-ra-wa or A-ti-us (Atius Tirawa) is creator.

Papagos Indians (Gulf of California). Coyote or prairie-wolf acts as creator.

Kiche Indians. Nothing but the sea and sky, stillness and darkness. Nothing but the Maker and Moulder, the Hurler, the Bird-serpent. Under sea, covered with green feathers, slept the mothers and the fathers. Hurakan passes over the abyss, calls " Earth," and land appears.

Tacullies (British Columbia). Say earth is mud spat out of mouth of a pre-existing musk-rat.

Tinneh or Déné Indians. The dog is creator.

Tzentals (Chiapas). Alaghom or Iztat Ix, she who brings forth Mind—the mother of Wisdom—creatrix of the mental or immaterial part of nature.

Zuñi Indians (New Mexico). Awonawilona creates the world.

(See chapter on cosmogony.)

INTRODUCTION TO MYTHOLOGY

MYTHS OF THE ORIGIN OF MAN. These are closely allied to the creation myths. Man is usually made out of clay or the 'dust of the earth' by a supernatural being, who sometimes moistens the clay with his or her own blood or sweat, and imparts to it 'the breath of life.' There is sometimes a prior creation of wooden men, who are found wanting.

Greeks. Prometheus makes man and woman, Deucalion and Pyrrha.

Hindus. Brahma or Prajapati makes man.

American Indians (generally). Man is evolved from coyotes, beavers, apes, or issued from caves.

Aztecs. After the destruction of the world Xolotl descends to Mictlan and brings a bone of the perished race. The gods sprinkle this with blood and from it emerge the progenitors of the present race.

Hurons. Joskeha makes men.

Karaya Indians (Brazil). Kaboi led their ancestors from the Underworld.

Peruvians. Apocatequil digs up men from the Underworld with a golden spade.

Kiches (Central America). The gods in council create man. At first they make wooden men, the remainder of whom turn into monkeys. They then create the present race from yellow and white maize.

Zuñi Indians. Janauluha leads men from the Underworld to the world of day.

Bushmen. Men came out of a cave.

Zulus. Men came out of beds of reeds.

Australians. Pund-jel makes two men from clay, one with straight and one with curly hair (bark). He dances round them and breathes life into them.

Australians (Dyiere). Men came out of wattle-gum tree.

Maoris (New Zealand). Tiki makes man of clay.

Polynesians (Mangaians). The woman of the abyss makes man by tearing from her right side a piece of flesh, which becomes Vatea, father of gods and men.

Melanesians. Qat makes man.

THE VARIOUS CLASSES OF MYTH

MYTHS OF THE ORIGIN OF HEROES

Babylonians. Story of Sargon.

Hebrews. Story of Moses.

Greeks. Perseus, son of Danaë. His father Zeus descended in a shower of golden rain.

Heracles, son of Zeus, who deceives the mother of Heracles by pretending to be Amphitryon, her absent husband.

Romans. Story of Romulus.

Celts. Sagas and romances of Arthur, Merlin, and Beowulf.

Indians. Saga of Rama, in *Ramayana*.

Mexicans. Uitzilopochtli, myth of his birth.

Kiches. Hun-Apu and Xbalanque in the *Popol Vuh*.

Peruvians. Ataguju, the creator, begets Guamansuri, who seduces a woman, who gives birth to two eggs. From these emerged Apocatequil and Piguerão. Apocatequil was prince of evil and the most respected hero of the Peruvians.

(See also Culture Myths for other examples.)

MYTHS OF FIRE-STEALING. In which a supernatural being—usually a bird—steals fire from Heaven and brings it to earth for the benefit of mankind.

Greeks. Prometheus.

Vedas. Matarisvan.

Bretons. Golden-crested wren.

Normandy Peasantry. The wren.

Ahts Indians (Vancouver Island). Quawteaht.

Athapascan Indians (N.W. America). Yetl the raven.

Cahrocs and Navaho Indians. The coyote.

Murri Tribe (Gippsland, Australia). Man who became a bird.

Thlinkeets (N.W. America). Yetl the raven.

New Zealanders. Mani.

Andaman Islanders. A bird.

CULTURE MYTHS. MYTHS OF THE ORIGIN OF THE ARTS OF LIFE. A god or culture-hero teaches man the useful arts. The outstanding figures in such myths are:

Egyptians. Osiris.

Babylonians. Oannes.

Greeks. Prometheus, Bacchus, Cadmus.
Celts (Irish). Nuada of the Silver Hand.
Teutons (Scandinavia). Wieland the Smith.
Japanese. Okikurimi.
Bushmen (South Africa). Cagn.
Zulus. Unkulunkulu.
Algonquins. Michabo or Manibozho.
Antis Indians (Brazil). Son of Ulé.
Arawaks. Kamu.
Carayas. Kaboi.
Caribs. Tamu (grandfather).
Cherokees. Wasi.
Chiapas. Votan.
Hurons. Joskeha.
Maya (Yucatan). Itzamná, Kukulcan.
Mexicans. Quetzalcoatl.
Orinoco Tribes. Amalivaca.
Paraguayans. Zumé.
Peruvians. Manco Ccapac ; Viracocha arises from the depths of Lake Titicaca on a civilizing mission.
Toltecs. Hueymactzin.
Australians. Pund-jel.
Melanesians. Qat.

TABOO MYTHS. Myths which relate the existence of, origin of, and necessity for certain taboos or forbidden things.

Hebrews. Adam, Eve, and the eating of the apple.
Greeks. The myth of Cupid and Psyche.
Actæon turned into a stag for observing Artemis when bathing.
Teutons (Scandinavia). Lohengrin and Elsa (name taboo).
Ningphos (Bengal). Think they became mortal by bathing in tabooed water.
Australians. Death introduced by woman going to tabooed tree.

MYTHS OF DEATH. To account for death, regarded by some savage races as unnatural. Usually some custom or taboo is supposed to have been broken, or some ritual neglected or mismanaged, and death has followed. The reasons given by the different races are as follows :

Greeks. Death comes from lifting cover off Pandora's box.

Hindus. Yama is pioneer to the Otherworld.

Southern India. Death (snake) bites men while God sleeps. God makes dog drive away snake ; thus dogs howl at approach of death.

Ningphos (Bengal). Think they became mortal through bathing in tabooed water.

Bushmen. The mother of the little hare is dead. The moon strikes the hare on its lip, splitting it in two, and tells it that its mother is really dead and will not live again as the moon does.

Hottentots. The moon sends the hare to men to tell them that they will live again as he (the moon) does, but the hare forgets the message and tells men that they will surely die, for which mistake the moon burns a hole in his lip.

Namaquas. The hare and the moon's mother.

Central Africans. Sleep unknown ; woman offers to teach man how to sleep ; holds his nostrils ; man never wakes ; dying made easy.

Hurons. Atænsic (the moon) destroys the living.

Australians. Woman goes near a forbidden tree.

New Zealand. Mani was not properly baptized.

Fiji Islanders. The moon desired that men should die and live again like herself, but the rat opposed this, and so men die as rats do.

Polynesians. Mani tries to pass through Night, a little bird sings, night awakes, snaps up Mani, and " so men die."

Banks Islanders. Qat, Mate, Panoi, and Tangaro the Fool. Tangaro the Fool is set to watch the path taken by Death, that men may avoid it, but makes the mistake of pointing to men the path to Hades as that of the path of the upper world. So men have, perforce, to follow this road to Panoi and the dead.

Pentecost Islanders. Tagar makes man die for five days only and live again, but Suque causes them to die for ever.

Solomon Islanders. Koevari resumes cast-off skin.

SOUL MYTHS. (1) In which the idea is found that a person's life, heart, or soul may be separated from him as a life-token or life-index, and that so long as this is kept safe or remains concealed, its owner is immortal. (2) Other myths dealing with the passage of the soul to the Otherworld.

Egyptians. Story of the two brothers.
Hebrews. Samson and Delilah.
Greeks. Meleager and the firebrand.
Misus, King of Megara, and his purple hair.
Souls ferried across the Styx by Charon.
Romans. Silvia and the son of Mars.
Yorkshiremen. 'Brig o' Dread, nae braider than a thread.'
Mohammedans. Reach Paradise across bridge composed of a single hair.
Cingalese. Story of Thossakin, King of Ceylon, who kept his soul in a box when he went to war with Rama.
Ainu (Japan). The 'inao.'
Tinneh or Déné Indians. Etwa-eke and his stone hatchet.
Malays. Tree-trunk across boiling lake to 'Island of Fruits.'
Eskimos. Kujanguak and his life-lock (hair).
Universal. Belief in birth-trees.

FIRE MYTHS. In which the world is destroyed by fire.

Romans. Seneca (see *Natur. Questiones*, iii, cap. 27).
Hebrews. Bible belief.
Teutons (Scandinavia). The "Völuspá": "The sun shall grow dark, the land sink in the waters, the bright stars be quenched, and high flames climb Heaven itself."
Algonquins. Michabo will stamp his foot, flames will devour the earth and only a chosen few (probably one pair) be left to repeople the new earth.
Arawaks (Guiana and N. Brazil). Aimon Kondi.
Aztecs. Extinguished every fire on last night of each cycle of fifty-two years. Then priests made new fire by friction. If this failed the end of the world had come.
Maya. World to be destroyed by ravening fire and the gods with it.
Peruvians. Amantas taught that some day an eclipse would veil the sun for ever, and earth, moon, and stars be wrapped in devouring flame.
Tupi-Guarani (Brazil). Monan, Irin Magé.

THE VARIOUS CLASSES OF MYTH

FLOOD MYTHS. A great deluge in which Heaven or the earth or both Heaven and earth are submerged in water and all living things drowned with the exception of one individual or family favoured by the god or gods.

Egyptians. Tem, Temu, Atem, Atmu.

Babylonians. Ut-Napishtim, the Babylonian Noah.

Hebrews. Noah.

Persians. Yima.

Greeks. Deucalion and Pyrrha.

Teutons (Scandinavia). Bergelmir and Ymir.

Hindus. Manu, son of the sun-god Vivasvat.

Ahts Indians (Vancouver Island). Wispohahp.

Algonquin Indians. Michabo or Manibozho.

Antis Indians (Brazil). Yurukares.

Arawaks. Sigu, Marerewana.

Aschochimi Indians (California). Coyote.

Caribs (Antilles). The ibis.

Hare Indians. Kunyan 'the intelligent.'

Mexicans. Atonatiuh (the Water-Sun) descends upon the earth.

Muyscas (Bogota). Chia or Chin, the moon, floods earth out of spite.

Peruvians. Re-creation after deluge at Tiahuanaco.

Tupi-Guarani (Brazil). Monan, Irin Magé.

MYTHS OF A PLACE OF REWARD (the celestial garden of God).

Country or Race	*Place of Reward*
Egyptians	Aalu
Persians	Alburz
Greeks	The Elysian Fields
Romans	The Fortunate Isles
Celts	The Otherworld beyond or beneath the sea. Tir-nan-og, Avalon, etc.
Teutons (Scandinavia)	Valhalla
Vedas	Agni (or Pushan) conducts the souls to the abodes of bliss
Buddhists	Nirvana
American Indians (generally)	Happy hunting grounds

Country or Race	Place of Reward
Aztecs	Tlalocan 'the east,' 'the terrestrial Paradise.' Tamoanchan, in the west
Caribs	Braves feast in happy islands served by Arawak slaves
Tonga Islanders	Island Paradise of Bolotu

MYTHS OF A PLACE OF PUNISHMENT

Country or Race	Name of Place of Punishment	Name of presiding Deity or Deities
Egyptians	Amenti	Osiris
Babylonians	Sheol or Aralu	Allatu or Nergal
Greeks	Tartarus, Hades	Pluto and Persephone
Celts	Annwn	
Teutons (Scandinavia)	Hel	Hel
Ladaks (Tibet border)	'Bad' men become marmots	
Japanese	Land of Yomi	Eruma-o
Caribs	'Bad' men (i.e., cowards) become slaves to Arawaks in barren land beyond the mountains	
Gallinomero, Californian Indians	'Bad' men become coyotes	
Guatemalans (Kiches)	Xibalba	Hun - Came and Vukub-Came
Mexicans	Mictlan	Mictlantecutli and Mictecaciuatl
Peruvians		Çupay

MYTHS OF JOURNEYS OR ADVENTURES THROUGH THE UNDERWORLD OR PLACE OF THE DEAD

Egyptians. Osiris.

Babylonians. Descent of Ishtar through the Underworld.

Greeks. Orpheus and Eurydice.

Persephone and Pluto.

Psyche.

The punishment of the Danaides.

Alcestis is allowed to return from the Underworld.

Bacchus brings his mother Semele from the Underworld to Olympus.

Medieval Britain. The Harrying of Hell.

Japanese. Izanagi descends into Hades in search of his wife Izanami.

Chinooks (N.W. America). Blue Jay in the Supernatural Country.

Kiches of Guatemala. Adventures of Hun-Apu and Xbalaqnue in the *Popol Vuh.*

FOOD OF THE DEAD FORMULA. An individual 'dies' or is kidnapped, proceeds to the Otherworld, and, having partaken of the food there, is unable to return to earth.

Babylonians. Adapa loses his chance of becoming immortal by refusing the food and drink of life offered him by Anu, as he feared it was the food of the dead of which he had been warned by his father Ea.

Greeks. Persephone.

Finns. In the *Kalevala.*

Chinooks (North American Indians, N.W. coast). Found in shamanistic practice.

SUN MYTHS. The principal figures in sun myths are the following :

Egyptians. Ra and Horus.

Accadians. Amar-utuki or Amar-uduk.

Babylonians. Merodach and Shamash.

Greeks. Apollo (Helios) and Phaethon.

Celts. Lug.

Hindus. Agni.

Aztecs. Piltzintecutli.

MOON MYTHS. These are closely associated with flood myths. In many of the Indian myths deluges are said to have been caused by the moon falling on the earth. She is nearly always held to be the goddess of water, dampness, dews, rain, and fogs. Moon and water are both mythical mothers of the human race.

Egyptians. Isis. All maladies were traced to her anger.

Babylonians. Sin, the moon-god.

Greeks. Selene.

Romans. Diana or Luna.

Algonquins. Moon, night, death, cold, sleep, and water (same word).

Aztecs. Constantly confounded Citatli and Atl (moon and water). Painted moon two colours—beneficent dispenser of harvests and offspring, goddess of night, dampness, cold, ague, miasma, and sleep; the twin of Death. Also known as Metztli, Yohualticitl, or Teciztecatl.

Brazilian Indians. Mothers shield infants from rays which are said to cause sickness.

Hidatsa. Midi is both moon and water.

Hurons. Atænsic is the moon (also water).

Muyscas. Chia the moon floods earth out of spite.

Peruvians. Mama Quilla.

Bushmen. Sun cuts moon down by degrees, but leaves a piece from which a new complete moon grows, and so on.

STAR MYTHS. In both primitive and later myths the stars are metamorphosed men, women, or beasts; in some cases ancestors, in others gods. The belief that the good at death become stars is very widely spread.

Egyptians. Plutarch was shown Isis and Osiris in the sky.

Babylonians. Many gods are represented by stars. Babylonian astrology favoured the evolution of gods into planets.

Greeks. The Pleiades are young girls.
Castor and Pollux are young men.

Hindus. Prajapati and his daughter become constellations.

Bushmen. Metamorphosed men.

American (Chinook Indians, N.W. Coast). Aqas Xenas Xena.

Indians (North American). Ursa Major is a bear.

Mexicans. Quetzalcoatl becomes a planet—our Venus.

Peruvians. Beasts, anthropomorphic gods, and stars are confounded together.

Eskimos. Regard stars as ancestors.

Australians. The Pleiades are young girls.
Castor and Pollux are young men.

South American star myths have not been added to this list as full reference has been made to them in the text.

THE VARIOUS CLASSES OF MYTH

MYTHS TO ACCOUNT FOR CUSTOMS OR RITES (ætiological myths), such as the general belief that water is the mother of all things. This accounts for sacred fountains, lakes, and rivers, baptism, etc. A few examples only can be given.

Greeks. Myth of Dionysus and Pentheus, to explain festival of the former. See Euripides, *The Bacchæ*.

A-Kikuyus (Bantu tribe, E. Africa). To explain sacrifices to Ngai (rain-god).

Todas (Southern India). To explain why the sacred dairyman sacrifices calf to Notirzi.

Blackfeet Indians. To explain sun-dance.

Pawnee Indians. To explain skull-dance, buffalo-dance, beardance (dramatized myths).

Wiradthuri tribes (Australia). Dhuramoolun and the bullroarer.

Almost universal. Belief in ghosts accounts for funeral rites to prevent ghosts' return.

CHAPTER VI
THE MAKING OF THE WORLD AND OF MAN (COSMOGONY)

THE efforts of man to account for his existence and that of the world in which he lives—in a word, for the origin of Heaven and earth and all that is in them — are among the most deeply interesting manifestations of human mental activity and progress. To his speculations the science of comparative mythology has given the name cosmogony (Greek *cosmos*, 'world,' and *gignesthai*, 'to be born'), of which the best literal translation is 'worldbirth.'

Before speculating upon the reason for the similarity between cosmogonic myths in all parts of the globe, or how far they have been coloured one by another or sophisticated by modern culture, we shall find it profitable to study the chief creation tales themselves, so that when we come to discuss their likeness or unlikeness we shall be well furnished with examples in support of the views we adopt. This course is wise in the study of tradition ; for unless the student is well furnished and abundantly fortified with 'instances,' he will never thoroughly apprehend the greater issues of traditional science, never fully grasp its spirit.

Some one has said that quotations are "ready armour, offensive and defensive," and the simile might well be employed of 'instances' in folklore and mythology, where the ability to cite copious parallels is of the highest assistance in argument.

With this in view, then, we shall look at the most important of those tales which relate to the creation of the world and man before analysing them.

158

THE WORLD AND MAN

INDIAN CREATION STORIES

India furnishes manifold ideas concerning the origin of the universe and man. At the first, says the *Rig-Veda*, there was neither non-entity nor entity, and all was water wrapped in gloom. "Then desire (Karma) arose in it, which was the primal germ of mind . . . the bond between entity and non-entity." The following hymn from the *Rig-Veda*,[1] the vigorous translation of which is by the late Dr Muir, gives some account of the process:

> There was neither aught nor naught, nor air, nor sky beyond.
> What covered all? Where rested all? In watery gulf profound?
> Nor death was then, nor deathlessness, nor change of night and day.
> The One breathed calmly, self-sustained; naught else beyond it lay.
>
> Gloom, hid in gloom, existed first—one sea, eluding view.
> That One, a void in chaos wrapt, by inward fervour grew.
> Within it first arose desire, the primal germ of mind,
> Which nothing with existence links, as sages searching find.
>
> The kindling ray that shot across the dark and drear abyss—
> Was it beneath? or high aloft? What bard can answer this?
> There fecundating powers were found, and mighty forces strove—
> A self-supporting mass beneath, and energy above.
>
> Who knows, who ever told, from whence this vast creation rose?
> No gods had then been born—who then can e'er the truth disclose?
> Whence sprang this world, and whether framed by hand divine or no—
> Its lord in heaven alone can tell, if even he can show.

This hymn is among the earliest speculations of the Hindus regarding cosmogonic phenomena, and its pious conclusion did not satisfy the cravings of future still more inquisitive generations. In the *Purusha Sakta* of the *Rig-Veda*, admittedly of considerably later origin than the above composition, the following creation myth is found:

"Purusha has a thousand heads, a thousand eyes, a thousand feet. On every side enveloping the earth, he overpassed (it) by a space of ten fingers. Purusha himself is this whole (universe), whatever has been and whatever shall be. He is

[1] *Original Sanscrit Texts*, London, 1868, vol. v, p. 356.

also lord of immortality, since (or when) by food he expands. All existences are a quarter of him, and three-fourths of him are that which is immortal in the sky. With three-quarters Purusha mounted upward. A quarter of him was again produced here. From him was born Viraj; and from Viraj, Purusha. When the gods performed a sacrifice, with Purusha as the oblation, the spring was its butter, the summer its fuel, and the autumn its (accompanying) offering. From that universal sacrifice sprang the Rich and Saman verses, the metres and the Yajush; from it sprang horses and all animals with two rows of teeth, kine, goats, and sheep. When (the gods) divided Purusha, into how many parts did they cut him up? The Brahman was his mouth, the Rajanya was made his arms, the being (called) Vaisya was his thighs, and the Sudra sprang from his feet. The morn sprang from his soul (manas), the sun from his eye, Indra and Agni from his mouth, and Vaya from his breath. From his navel arose the air, from his head the sky, from his feet the earth, from his ear the (four) quarters; in this manner (the gods) formed the worlds."

Now follows an extract from the *Satapatha Brahmana*, which gives the words used at the creation: "(Uttering) 'bhuh', Prajapati generated this earth. (Uttering) 'bhuvah,' he generated the air; and (uttering) 'svah,' he generated the sky. This universe is co-extensive with these worlds. Saying 'bhuh,' Prajapati generated the Brahman; (saying) 'bhuvah,' he generated the Kshattra; (and saying) 'svah,' he generated the Vis. All this world is as much as the Brahman, Kshattra, and Vis. (Saying) 'bhuh,' Prajapati generated himself; (saying) 'bhuvah,' he generated offspring: (saying) 'svah,' he generated animals. This world is so much as self, offspring, and animals."

The *Taittiriya Brahmana* says, "This entire (universe) has been created by Brahma," and gives an account of the creation of the Asuras, Pitris (or fathers), and gods. "Prajapati desired 'May I propagate.' He practised austerity. His breath became alive. With that breath (asu) he created Asuras. Having created the Asuras, he regarded himself as a father. After that he created the fathers (pitris). That constitutes the fatherhood of the fathers. Having created the fathers, he reflected. After that he created men. That constitutes the manhood of men. He who knows the manhood of men becomes intelligent. To him, when he was creating men, day appeared in the heavens. After that he created the gods."

The *Satapatha Brahmana* relates the creation of men and animals. "Prajapati was formerly this (universe) only. He desired: 'Let me create food, and be propagated.' He formed animals from his breaths, a man from his soul, a horse from his eye, a bull from his breath, a sheep from his ear, a goat from his voice. Since he formed animals from his breaths, therefore men say: 'The breaths are animals.' The soul is the first of breaths. Since he formed a man from his soul, therefore they say: 'Man is the first of the animals and the strongest.' The soul is all the breaths; for all the breaths depend upon the soul. Since he formed man from his soul, therefore they say: 'Man is all the animals'; for all these are man's."

In another passage this Brahmana gives quite a different account. Purusha, as the soul of the universe, was alone. Hence "he did not enjoy happiness. He desired a second. He caused this same self to fall asunder into two parts. Thence arose a husband and wife. From them men were born. She reflected: 'How does he, after having produced me from himself, cohabit with me? Ah! let me disappear!' She became a cow, and the other a bull; from them kine were produced. The one became a mare, the other a stallion; the one a she-ass, the other a male-ass. From them the class of animals with undivided hoofs was produced. The one became a she-goat, the other a he-goat; the one an ewe, the other a ram. From them goats and sheep were produced. In this manner pairs of all creatures whatsoever, down to ants, were created."

The Puranas are very minute and specific as regards the facts of creation. Indeed the first book of the *Vishnu Purana* is largely taken up with accounts of the cosmogonic process. According to this venerable script Brahma first existed in the form of Purusha (spirit) and Kalu (time). "Next proceeded two other forms, the discreet and indiscreet; and Kala (time) was the last. These four—Pradhana (primary or crude matter), Purusha (spirit), Vyakta (visible substance), and Kala (time)—in their due proportions, are the causes of the production of the phenomena of creation, preservation, and destruction. The supreme Brahma, the supreme soul, the substance of the world, the lord of all creatures, the universal soul, the supreme ruler Hari (Vishnu), of his own will having entered into matter and spirit, agitated the mutable and immutable principles, the season of creation having arrived, in the same manner as fragrance affects the mind from its proximity merely, and not from any immediate operation upon mind itself; so the supreme influenced the elements of creation."

After giving an account of the creation, or rather the evolution of the elements, the *Vishnu Purana* goes on to say: "Then (the elements) ether, air, light, water, and earth, severally united with the properties of sound, and the rest existed as distinguishable according to their qualities as soothing, terrific, or stupefying; but possessing various energies, and being unconnected, they could not without combination create living beings, not having blended with each other. Having combined, therefore, with one another, they assumed, through their mutual association, the character of one mass of entire unity; and from the direction of spirit, with the acquiescence of the indiscrete principle, intellect, and the rest, to the gross elements inclusive, formed an egg, which gradually expanded like a bubble of water. This vast egg, compounded of the elements, and resting on the waters, was the excellent natural abode of Vishnu in the form of Brahma; and there Vishnu, the lord of the universe, whose essence is inscrutable, assumed a perceptible form, and even he himself abided in it in the character of Brahma. Its womb, vast as the mountain Meru, was composed of the mountains; and the mighty oceans were the waters that filled its cavity. In that egg were the continents and seas and mountains, the planets and divisions of the universe, the gods, the demons, and mankind.

"Affecting then the quality of activity, Hari the lord of all, himself becoming Brahma, engaged in the creation of the universe. Vishnu, with the quality of goodness and of immeasurable power, preserves created things through successive ages, until the close of the period termed a Kalpa; when the same mighty deity, invested with the quality of darkness, assumes the awful form of Rudra, and swallows up the universe. Having thus devoured all things, and converted the world into one vast ocean, the supreme reposes upon his mighty serpent couch amidst the deep: he awakes after a season, and again, as Brahma, becomes the author of creation."

EGYPTIAN CREATION MYTHS

Turning to ancient Egypt, that dark ocean of myth and mystery, we find in papyrus 10,188, housed in the British Museum, an account of the origin of things written for a priest of Panopolis, called Nes-Amsu, about the year 312 B.C. This papyrus contains many things, chiefly of magical import, but its interest for us is that it introduces two varying accounts of the Egyptian idea of the creation, both of which are a little vague and obscure. In the first, the god Neb-er-tcher, a form of Ra the sun-god, tells how, through his godlike might, all things came into being. Taking upon himself the shape of Khepera, the deity symbolizing creation, he made himself and other "new things," in fact, a whole world, "out of his mouth." The place where he performed this feat was the watery abyss of Nu, from which certain considerations lead us to suppose he took his *materials*. Says Khepera:

"I found no place there (in Nu) whereon I could stand. I worked a charm upon my own heart. I laid a foundation in Maa. I made every form. I was one by myself, I had not emitted from myself the god Shu, I had not spit out from myself the goddess Tefnut. There was no other being who worked with me."

Thus Khepera alone was creator; nor did he have any solid surface to stand upon during the performance of his creative act. To remove the difficulty he worked a charm upon, or made a foundation in, his own heart—that is, by some magical act he found a foothold in the abyss while he produced all things. "There came into being multitudes of things from the things of what was produced"—that is, the objects which had emanated from Khepera continued the work of creation of their own accord. Khepera then produced the god and goddess Shu and Tefnut. Men and women then appeared from his tears. The sun was manufactured from an eye of the god, as was the moon. Plants and creeping things began to grow and move on the surface of the earth, so that they cannot have been included in the original 'things' created by the god. Finally Shu and Tefnut produced the pantheon of the elder gods, and these deities multiplied offspring in the earth.

OSIRIS AS CREATOR

The second version of the creation myth which the papyrus contains makes Osiris take the place of Khepera, or Neb-er-tcher. He is described as the *pautet pautti*, or the very essence of primeval matter, and the source of all created things. Osiris utters his own name as a word of power, and "forthwith came into being under the form of things which were created." Like Neb-er-tcher, he took the form of Khepera as proper to the act of creation. "I came into being," he says, "from primeval matter, and I appeared under the form of multitudes of things from the beginning. Nothing existed at that time, and it was I who made whatsoever was made. I was alone, and there was no other being who worked with me in that place. I made all the forms under which I appeared by means of the god-soul which I raised up out of Nu, out of a state of inertness." Thus we here have the 'god-soul' existent in a quiescent condition in the watery abyss of Nu, awaiting the magic call of Osiris. The next point in which the second account differs from the first is the making of man, made, it states, after the reptiles and creeping things.

Thus in these Egyptian creation myths we have a primeval watery mass peopled by a self-begotten and self-existent god who, uttering his own name as a spell, straightway came into existence, then awakened the slumbering soul of the abyss into activity, and by the utterance of magic words created a place or foundation upon which he could stand. Having done this, he proceeded to the creation of other gods, the light, human beings, vegetation, and creeping things. Of birds, beasts, and stars we find nothing in the myth, which is one of the earliest

THE WORLD AND MAN

Egyptian conceptions of the creation of the world and of mankind.[1]

But as new races entered Egypt as immigrants or conquerors, other myths descriptive of the creation process arose and flourished side by side. There was, for example, that of Ptah, a potter, pictured in the ancient drawings as shaping the world-egg, the 'cosmic egg,' upon his wheel. He is said, in connexion with Khnemu, to have carried out the active work of creation at the command of Thoth. Khnemu was also regarded as the personification of creative force, who formed the cosmic egg from the Nile mud and shaped man on his potter's wheel; and there were others, all more or less akin.

EGYPTIAN IDEAS REGARDING THE SKY

The earlier Egyptians regarded the sky as a flat metal plate or slab, each end of which rested upon a mountain, the mountain of sunrise, Bakhau, and the mountain of sunset, Manu. In the late Pyramid texts the sky is rectangular, each corner resting upon a pillar. In still later times those four pillars were looked upon as the sceptres of the gods who presided over the four quarters of heaven. At a comparatively late date the idea arose that the sky required support in the centre as well as at its angles, and the god who acted as central prop was called Heh. In another myth the heavens were shaped like a man's head, with the sun and moon for eyes, and hair supporting the sky.

Another Egyptian idea of the sky is that the goddess Nut, who personified the upper regions, formed the vault of the heavens by arching her body over the earth and resting her weight upon her hands and feet. Sometimes the god Shu stands beneath, as if to support her. Over her body are scattered the stars. She was alluded to as 'the Lady of Heaven,' and is uniformly painted blue in imitation of the sky she represented.

THE BABYLONIAN ACCOUNTS OF CREATION

The principal version of the Babylonian account of creation is preserved in the 'Seven Tablets of Creation' now in the

[1] See Budge, *The Gods of Egypt* (1904).

British Museum, and originally part of the library of Assur-banipal at Nineveh. In this epic we find two primeval deities, Apsu and Tiawath, personifications of the great abyss, and their son, Mummu. The gods are created, Anu, En-lil, and Ea, but their 'ways' are displeasing to Apsu and Tiawath, who rebel. The original male deities speedily succumb to the power of the new gods. Tiawath creates a host of grisly monsters and carries on unrelenting war against the enemy, but in terrific combat with Marduk or Merodach she is anni-hilated. She is cut in twain, and from one half of her body Merodach forms the heavens. He divides the upper waters from the lower, makes dwellings for the gods, creates the sun, moon, and stars, and ordains their courses. At this juncture a portion of the account (Tablet V) is missing, but in the next slab Merodach is said to have been decapitated, and with his own blood and bone to have made man. Berosus, a priest of Merodach, who lived in the third century B.C., wrote a Greek history of Babylonia, which has been lost, but is known in part from quotations by classical writers. In this work he recounted the above myth, with some variation in the names, and the additional statement that half of Tiawath's body formed the earth.[1]

Tiawath, like the Egyptian Nut, personified the primeval abyss; in fact, the name signifies the sea, Apsu, the name of her spouse, meaning the deep. The sea was to the Semitic mind symbolical of chaos and trouble, as witness the Scriptural promise, "and there shall be no more sea." The strange monsters framed by the goddess of the abyss to combat the gods of light are perhaps associated with the teeming gigantic life the Semites believed the sea capable of propagating, one well-known example of which is the 'whale' or 'great fish' of Jonah.

CHINESE WORLD-MAKING

Chinese myth furnishes a fairly clear account of creation. During countless scores of ages "nothing" condensed into

---

[1] See King, *Seven Tablets of Creation* (1902); and *Babylonian Religion and Mythology* (1899).

unity, and the Mighty Atom was formed. In the course of further ages the atom became divided into the male and female principles, and the universe came into being. But a more simple explanation was necessary for the uninitiated, who were told that the two original elements became four, from the co-operation of which sprang a deity called P'an Ku, whose function it was to supply the constituents of the universe. His eyes became the sun and moon, his breath the wind, his hair trees and vegetation, his flesh the earth, his sweat rain, and the worms which sprang from his decomposing body were men. The god Tien or Shang-ti is generally regarded as the First Cause in Chinese myth; but although he may have inspired the creation of the universe, he does not appear to have taken any hand in its actual manufacture.

THE HEBREW CREATION STORY

The Biblical story of creation is a very complete cosmogony, having affinities with that of Babylon. We are told in Genesis i, 6, 7, 14, 15 that God divided the primeval waters into two parts by an intervening 'firmament' or platform, where he placed the heavenly bodies. This division has some likeness to the Babylonian account of the cleaving of the carcass of Tiawath into two parts, one of which kept the upper waters from coming down. The words *te hom*, rendered in the English Bible 'the deep,' closely resemble the name Tiawath, 'the sea.' Here, then, we seem to possess irrefragable philological evidence of early Babylonian influence upon Hebrew belief. Verse 2 of Genesis i also mentions the earth-matter out of which the earth and all its products were to appear. This is called *tohu* and *bohu*, 'devoid of living things,' and so would appear to equate with "the lands" that "altogether were sea" of Babylonian cosmogony. The creation of light which appears in Genesis is not found in the Babylonian account, but the Babylonian creator, Merodach, is a god of light. In brief, the Hebrew account of the successive stages of creation corresponds so closely to that of Babylon that it is obvious one has been influenced by the other—naturally the younger by the elder.

INTRODUCTION TO MYTHOLOGY

JAPANESE ORIGINS

In the beginning, according to Japanese myth, Heaven and earth were not separated and the In and Yo (the male and female principles) not divided. The *Nihongi* states that these male and female principles formed a chaotic mass like an egg which was of obscurely defined limits and contained germs. This egg quickened with life, the clearer part became Heaven, while the more ponderable portion settled down as the terrestrial sphere, like the floating of a fish sporting on the surface of the waters. An object like a reed-shoot appeared between Heaven and earth, and as suddenly became transformed into a god, Kuni-toko-tachi. Other divine beings were born, but those responsible for most of "this sorry scheme of things entire" were Izanagi (Male who invites) and Izanami (Female who invites), concerning whom a very charming and original myth was told.

They stood on the floating bridge of Heaven and peered downward into the abyss below, asking each other what might exist so far below. Puzzled, yet determined to probe the mystery of nothingness beneath them, they thrust a jewel-spear downward, and touched the ocean. Drawing the spear upward, some water dripped from it, coagulated, and became an island, upon which the god and goddess set foot. Desiring each other as husband and wife, although they were brother and sister, they set up a pillar on the island, and by walking round it lost their relationship. Izanagi walked round one way and Izanami the other, exclaiming when they met: "Delightful! I have met with a lovely maiden," and "I have met with a lovely youth." They espoused each other, and Izanami gave birth to islands, seas, rivers, herbs, and trees, and having produced the Great-Eight-Island Country was desirous of bringing forth a living being who would be head of the Universe. In due season Ama-terasu, the sun-goddess, was born, and the moon-god, Tsuki-yumi. After the birth of the fire-god, however, Izanami suffered so greatly that she betook herself to the land of Yomi or Hades and was subsequently disowned by her husband.

THE WORLD AND MAN

IRANIAN COSMOGONY

The Iranian account of creation states that Ormuzd (Ahura Mazda), the creator and good agency, fixed the duration of the world at twelve thousand years. He created the spiritual world during the first thousand of these. Ahriman, the principle of evil, did not know of his existence until he espied the beams of light which emanated from his glorious presence, but when he discovered it he commenced to plot evil. During the next three thousand years Ormuzd created the world, the sun, moon, and stars, plants, animals, and man. But Ahriman instituted a malevolent counter-creation, and for every desirable thing Ormuzd made Ahriman produced something evil, so that he became the creator of all noxious plants and beasts of prey, diseases, and death. For a third three thousand years a bitter strife was waged between the deities, but with the birth of Zarathushtra or Zoroaster, a better day dawned for the forces of good. The first animal created by Ormuzd was an ox, which was assailed by the plagues and diseases of Ahriman and died ; but from its members sprang every description of cereal and plant, and two other oxen. Ormuzd took of his sweat, and uttering words of power produced the man Gayomart. He was also slain by Ahriman, but his seed having fertilized in the earth, twins Mashya and Mashyana sprang up, at first in the form of shrubs, and were the progenitors of humanity.

THE CELTIC IDEA OF THE ORIGIN OF MAN

The Celtic idea of creation as exhibited in the Welsh work *Barddas* provided for two primary existences, God and Cythrawl, standing respectively for life and death. Cythrawl has his abode in Annwn, the Abyss of Chaos. In the beginning naught was but God and Annwn. God pronounced his ineffable name, and Manred, the primal substance of the Universe, was formed. Manred was composed of thousands of teeming atoms, in each of which God was present, and each was a part of God. They were arranged in concentric circles representing the totality of being, and the innermost, the first on which life gets a footing on emerging from Annwn, is Abred. This is the stage of struggle and evolution, the contest of life with Cythrawl. The second is Gwynfyd, the Circle of Purity, in which life triumphs, and the last is Ceugant, inhabited by God alone, with whom, presumably, it is merged.

NORSE COSMOGONY

The Scandinavian conception of creation bears, strangely enough, some general resemblance to those of ancient China and India (Purusha variant). In the beginning yawned the great abyss of Ginnungagap and naught beside, save that it was flanked on the north by the dreary realm of Niflheim, a region of cold and mist, and on the south by Muspelheim, a region of fire. Flowing from Niflheim, the rivers called Elivagar froze, and the ice formed upon them was covered with congealed vapour. The hot air from Muspelheim beating upon the ice melted it, and the drops of moisture so formed took life and became a giant called Ymir, the progenitor of a race of gigantic beings. From the cow Audhumla, formed at the same time, Ymir was nourished by four streams of milk. For sustenance she licked the stones covered with brine and moisture; and on the first day she licked there appeared a single hair, on the second day a head, on the third an entire being, beautiful and glorious to look upon, Buri, the grandfather of Odin. Ymir, while asleep, engendered the race of giants from the sweat of his body, but the grandchildren of Buri slew him, and all his progeny were drowned in his blood, except Bergelmir and his wife, who saved themselves in a boat. His body was then cast into Ginnungagap, and from his blood were created the sea and waters, from his flesh the solid earth, from his bones the mountains, from his skull the dome of the sky, from his brain the clouds, and from his eyebrows Midgard, the dwelling of the race of men. Odin, Vili, and Ve are then spoken of (in a myth apparently a variant) as raising the disk of the earth out of the waters. Later Odin and his brothers find a couple of inanimate figures fashioned by the dwarfs out of trees, and endowed them with the breath of life and understanding, calling them Askr and Embla. These were the first human beings.

170

THE WORLD AND MAN

MEXICAN BEGINNINGS

In the Mexico of the Aztecs the sun was held to be the cause of all material force, and the gods the holders of the fluctuating fortunes of man. The sun, like man himself, was considered dependent upon food and drink ; and according to Aztec cosmology several suns had perished through lack of provision, as had older races of men. The original sun had no other nourishment than the water it absorbed from the earth, and was thus nothing but a semi-liquid mass, designated Atonatiuh, the 'Water-Sun.' It was supposed to have absorbed enormous quantities during the course of centuries, and ultimately discharged the whole over the world, causing a complete destruction of animal and vegetable life. The Water-Sun was sometimes identified with Tlaloc, the god of moisture, but this is a comparatively recent addition to the popular account. The general destruction of terrestrial life by elementary physical forces was accompanied in Mexican belief by myths of other great catastrophes wrought by earthquake, wind-storms, or fire, and a tale of the collapse of the vault of heaven itself.[1] These holocausts were traced to some defect in the sun. Other accounts relate that the gods Tezcatlipoca, Quetzalcoatl, and Xiuhtecutli each attempted the *rôle* of the god of day without success. At length it became evident that a special god must be created for the express purpose of fulfilling the functions of the office, so the existing sun was brought into being. However the Mexican myths may vary according to the method by which the creation of the sun was achieved authorities agree on these points of Aztec belief. The luminary was an animal which was originally a man, but, by the action of fire, became transformed, and received the intense vitality necessary for the performance of his functions from the blood of the gods, voluntarily shed for that purpose. The gods met at Teotihuacan in order to make a sun. They kindled a mighty fire, and signified to the worshippers that whosoever should first leap into it should become the new sun personified. One of them sacrificed himself by doing so ; and arose as the sun from the midst of the

[1] Gomara, *Conquista de Mejico*, chap. ccxv (Madrid, 1749).

fire, but was unable to ascend into the sky for lack of strength. In order to give him the necessary motive force the gods resolved to sacrifice themselves in the usual Mexican manner, by having their hearts torn out. This was done by the god Xolotl, who had in this way created man, and now performed the act of sacrifice upon himself. The sun then ascended the sky.[1] According to another tradition, the creation of man was subsequent to that of the sun. Men were only created to be the food of the luminary, and were ordered to fight and slay one another so that the sun might be supplied with food. The Mayas of Yucatan increased the previous number of suns by one. Two solar epochs terminated by devastating plagues known as the 'sudden deaths.' So swift and mortal were the pests engendered by solar failure that vultures dwelt in the houses of the cities, and devoured the bodies of their former owners. The third epoch closed with a hurricane or inundation known as *hun yecil*, 'the inundation of the trees,' as all the forests were swept away.

The Kiches of Guatemala had a very complete creation story, which may be studied in the *Popol Vuh*, their sacred book. To begin with, there only existed the vast waste of primeval waters, in which slept "the Old Ones covered with Green Feathers," the father- and mother-deities, Xpiyacoc and Xmucane. Then came Hurakan the mighty, "he who hurls below," a Kiche variant of the Aztec deity Tezcatlipoca. He commanded light to be and the solid earth, by his spoken word. The gods in council created animals. They carved mannikins out of wood, but these were intractable and disobedient, so the gods resolved to destroy them. They sent a deluge upon the world, and the mannikins were drowned. The posterity of the few who were saved are the monkeys. After the catastrophe the earth-god Vukub-Cakix (Macaw) and his progeny gave more trouble to the gods, but were ultimately destroyed. Hurakan latterly created four perfect men from yellow and white maize, and supplied them with wives, after which the sun was created, and the cosmological scheme was complete.[2]

---

[1] Mendieta, *Hist. Eccl. Ind.*, lib. i, chap. 2 (Mexico, 1870).
[2] See my *The Popol Vuh*, pp. 9–26 (London, 1908).

THE WORLD AND MAN

CREATION IN ANCIENT PERU

The Incan Peruvians held that all things emanated from Pachacamac, the universal spirit, from whom proceeded the spirits of the animals or plants produced by the earth. The earth itself they designated Pachacamama, or 'Earth-Mother.' Thus we have two distinct conceptions welded together—a general spirit of living things coalesced with the originally totally distinct Creator. The idea of a Great Spirit, a former and shaper, though not necessarily a Creator, is almost universal throughout America, but it must sooner or later occur to the barbarian mind that the making of living beings requires something more than matter : they must receive the breath of life. A true Creator the Peruvians found in Pachacamac, an anthropomorphic deity representing the creative mind. The conception of Pachacamac as a ruler and director of the universe belongs to a later period of Incan rule, when a shrine was built to him in the new aspect by Apu-Ccapac-Inca Pachacutic, at the north angle of Cuzco. The Peruvians declared that all things were made by the word of the spirit, by the mere exercise of will, or thought. In the prayers to the Creator, and in other fragments of aboriginal rite which have survived, we read, for example : " Let a man be : let a woman be," and such expressions as " the creative word." Occasionally the sun acts as a species of demiurge. For example, it is he who creates the city of Cuzco, and sends to earth the three eggs of gold, of silver, and of copper, from which issue the Curacos and their wives and the Mitayocs and their wives. Tiahuanaco was the theatre of the new creation of man which followed upon the Deluge. In that district the Creator made man of clay, and separated him into nations, making one for each nation, and painting the dresses that each was to wear, besides giving national songs, languages, seeds suitable to the soil of each, and food. Then he gave life and soul to each one, and ordered that they should pass under the earth. Thence each national type came up in the place to which he ordered it to go. This myth again is obviously an attempt to harmonize two conflicting creation stories, an original one of genesis from caves, and the later one of the creation in Tiahuanaco. We also find local creation myths in some of the Peruvian valleys. For example, Pachacamac, in the coast valley of Irma, was not considered the creator of the sun, but a descendant of it. Of the first human pair created by him the man perished of hunger, but the woman maintained herself upon roots. The sun took pity upon her and gave her a son, whom Pachacamac slew and buried, but from his teeth there grew maize, from his ribs the long white roots of the manioc, and from his flesh pumpkins and esculent plants.

AMERICAN INDIAN CREATION MYTHS

In the preface to his *Creation Myths of Primitive America* Mr Jeremiah Curtin says:

"The creation myths of America form a complete system: they give a detailed and circumstantial account of the origin of this world and of all things and creatures contained in it. In the course of the various narratives which compose this myth system an earlier world is described to us, with an order of existence and a method of conduct on which the life of primitive man in America was patterned.

"That earlier world had two periods of duration—one of complete and perfect harmony; another of violence, collision, and conflict. The result and outcome of the second period was the creation of all that is animated on earth except man. Man, in the American scheme of creation, stands apart and separate; he is quite alone, peculiar, and special. Above all, he belongs to this continent. The white man was unknown to American myth-makers, as were also men of every other race and of every region outside of the Western Hemisphere.

"Described briefly and by an Indian, the American myth system is as follows: 'There was a world before this one in which we are living at present; that was the world of the first people, who were different from us altogether. Those people were very numerous, so numerous that if a count could be made of all the stars in the sky, all the feathers on birds, all the hairs and fur on animals, all the hairs of our own heads, they would not be so numerous as the first people.'

THE WORLD AND MAN

"These people lived very long in peace, in concord, in harmony, in happiness. No man knows, no man can tell, how long they lived in that way. At last the minds of all except a very small number were changed; they fell into conflict—one offended another consciously or unconsciously, one injured another with or without intention, one wanted some special thing, another wanted that very thing also. Conflict set in, and because of this came a time of activity and struggle, to which there was no end or stop till the great majority of the first people—that is, all except a small number—were turned into the various kinds of living creatures that are on earth now or have ever been on earth, except man—that is, all kinds of beasts, birds, reptiles, fish, worms, and insects, as well as trees, plants, grasses, rocks, and some mountains; they were turned into everything that we see on the earth or in the sky.

"The small number of the former people who did not quarrel, those great first people of the old time who remained of one mind and harmonious, 'left the earth, sailed away westward, passed that line where the sky comes down to the earth and touches it, sailed to places beyond; stayed there or withdrew to upper regions and lived in them happily, lived in agreement, live so to-day, and will live in the same way hereafter.'

"The American system, as we see, begins with an unknown, great, indefinite number of uncreated beings—in other words, of self-existent personages or divinities. Those divinities were everything at first; there was nothing except them, nothing aside from them, nothing beyond them. They existed unchanged through untold periods, or rather through a duration which would be periods were there a measure by which to divide it. They lived side by side in perfect concord, in the repose of a primeval chaos of quiescent mind which presents a most remarkable analogy with the attenuated, quiescent, undifferentiated matter which, according to the nebular hypothesis, filled all points of space in the physical universe before the first impulse of motion was given to it.

"At last this long period is ended, there is mental difference among most of the first people, character is evolved and has become evident; rivalries, collisions, and conflicts begin.

"The American creation myths, as far as we know them, form simply a series of accounts of the conflicts, happenings, and various methods by which the first world was changed into the world now existing. This change was effected in various ways. In the myths of certain tribes or nations, it is mainly by struggles between hostile personages. One god of great power and character overcomes a vast number of opponents, and changes each into some beast, bird, plant, or insect; but always the resultant beast or other creature corresponds in some power of mind or in some leading quality of character with the god from whose position it has fallen. In certain single cases opponents are closely matched, they are nearly equal in combat; the struggle between them is long, uncertain, and difficult. At last, when one side is triumphant, the victor says, 'Hereafter you shall be nothing but a——'; and he tells what the vanquished is to be. But at this point the vanquished turns on the victor and sends his retort like a Parthian arrow, 'You shall be nothing but a——'; and he declares what his enemy is to be. The metamorphosis takes place immediately on both sides, and each departs in the form which the enemy seemed to impose, but which really belonged to him. . . .

"With the transformation of the last of the first people or divinities, which was finished only when the Indians or some sign of them appeared in every remote nook and corner in which a remnant of the first people had taken refuge, the present order of things is established completely. There are now in the world individualities of three distinct sets and orders. First, that small number of the first people whose minds had never changed, those gods who withdrew and who live in their original integrity and harmony, who retired to places outside the sky or above it; second, the great majority of the gods, who have become everything in the present world save and except only Indians. This cycle finished, there is a new point of departure, and we meet a second group of myths concerning the existent world as it is now with its happenings— myths containing accounts of conflicts which are ever recurrent, which began before all the first people were metamorphosed, conflicts which are going on at present and which will go on forever; struggles between light and darkness, heat and cold, summer and winter, struggles between winds that blow in opposite directions—in fact, accounts of various phenomena and processes which attract the attention of savage men more than others because savage men are living face to face with them always.

"This second group contains a large number of myths, many of them exceedingly beautiful and, so far as they are known, highly pleasing to cultivated people. Unfortunately few of these myths have been given to the world yet, for the sole and simple reason that comparatively few have been collected from the Indians."

Many and diverse indeed are the tales regarding creation current among the red men of America; but, notwithstanding their variety, they possess a fundamental likeness to each other whether they hail from the pampas of Argentina or the region of the Great Lakes. Among the North American Indian myths we find the animal creator strongly in evidence. Thus among the Algonquin Indians we have the Creator Michabo or Manibozho, the Great Hare, who through philological confusion (the likeness of the words for 'light' and 'rabbit') has changed his original status of sun-god for that of an animal deity. While hunting he observed his dogs disappear in the waters of a mighty lake. He himself entered the waters, which suddenly overflowed and submerged 'the world.' The god dispatched a raven to discover a piece of earth, but it returned. Another was equally unlucky, whereupon Manibozho sent out a musk-rat, which returned with a sufficiency of earth to recreate the terrestrial sphere. Marrying the musk-rat, he peopled the world.

ARAWAKS

The Arawak family, inhabiting the Guianas, Northern Brazil, and part of Columbia, believe that in the beginning the animals were created by Makonaima, the great spirit, whom no man has seen.[1] They had at that time the power of speech, and

[1] W. H. Brett, *Indian Tribes of Guiana*, p. 378 *et seq.* (1868).

Sigu, the son of Makonaima, was placed to rule over them. Makonaima created a marvellous tree, each branch of which produced a different kind of fruit. The agouti discovered it first, and, coming daily to the tree, ate his fill without apprising the other animals. Sigu, suspecting him, ordered the woodpecker to keep him in sight, but the bird failed to detect him, and he was ultimately convicted by the rat. The tree was now open to all, and the animals were about to consume the fruits *in toto* when Sigu determined to cut down the tree and extend it over the whole earth by planting every seed and slip which it would furnish. To this end he employed the birds and beasts, all of which assisted willingly, except Iwarrika, the monkey, who thwarted the labours of the others. The stump of the tree was discovered to be full of water containing the fry of every description of fresh-water fish. The water beginning to flow, Sigu covered the tree-stump with a closely woven basket, but the monkey removed this and precipitated a terrible flood. Sigu then led the animals to an eminence where some high cocorite palms grew, and these he made the birds and climbing animals ascend. Those which could not climb and were not amphibious he placed in a cave, and closed and sealed it with wax. He then ascended the cocorite palm himself. During the terrible period of darkness and storm which followed Sigu dropped the seeds of the cocorite into the water beneath to judge by the sound of its depth. When at length he heard them strike the soft earth he knew that the period of flood had passed. The Macusis believe that the only person who survived the deluge repeopled the earth by converting stones into human beings, as did Deucalion and Pyrrha. The Tamanacs say that one man and one woman were saved by taking refuge on the lofty mountains of Tamanucu, and that they threw over their heads the fruits of the Mauritius palm, from the kernels of which sprang men and women. The Warrau tribe of the Arawaks possessed the following legend of their own origin and that of the Caribs. The Warraus originally dwelt in a pleasant region above the sky, where there were neither wicked men nor noxious animals. Okonorote, a young hunter, having wandered far in pursuit of a beautiful bird, espied it and

THE WORLD AND MAN

discharged an arrow which missed its mark and disappeared. While searching for his arrow he found a hole through which it had fallen, and on looking through it descried the lower world. He made a rope by which he descended with his tribe, a corpulent woman, as in several of the North American myths, remaining fixed in the aperture, and filling it up. In answer to the people's cries for water the Great Spirit created the Essiquibo river. Later, Korobona, a Warrau maiden, produced the first Carib—a terrible warrior, who slew many Warraus. The Paressi tribe of the Arawaks believed that the neglect of certain customs was the origin of misfortune in the world. They also related that Maiso, a stone woman, produced all living beings and all rivers. Even the domestic animals and iron tools of the whites were borne by this original mother.

The Arawaks of Guiana had a myth that Aimon Kondi, the Great Spirit, scourged the world with fire, from which the survivors sought refuge in underground caverns. A great flood followed, and Marerewana and his followers saved themselves in a canoe. Still another Arawak myth relates that the Creator, having completed the cosmic scheme, seated himself in a great silk-cotton tree by a river side and cut off pieces of its bark, which he cast all around. Those which reached the water became fish, those which touched the air birds, those which alighted upon the earth animals and men.

The Athapascan Indians of North-west America believe the creator of the world to be Yetl, the bird from whose wings came thunder. The plane of earth arose from the waters as Yetl brooded thereon. The Athapascans trace their descent from Yetl, who, they believe, saved their ancestors from the flood and, like Prometheus, brought them fire from Heaven.

IROQUOIS INDIANS

The Iroquois tribes believe that their female ancestress fell from Heaven into the waste of primeval waters; but the dry land bubbled up under her feet and quickly grew to the size of a continent. Several of these tribes, however, are of opinion that some amphibious animals, such as the otter, beaver, and musk-rat, noticed her fall, and hastened to break it by shovelling up earth from the mud beneath the waters. Indeed, the Indians of this family were wont to point to the mountain so raised near the falls of the Oswego river.

CALIFORNIAN INDIANS

Although there are no less than twenty-one different linguistic divisions in California, the similarity of their myths is remarkable. The Maidu have a most intricate creation myth of Kodoyanpe, the Creator, and the Coyote, who discovered the world and rendered it habitable for men. The first human beings were small wooden images like those in the *Popol Vuh*, but these mannikins were no more tractable than were those of Guatemala, and were at last changed into animals. Kodoyanpe, the Beneficent, perceived that Coyote was bent upon evil courses, and conceived the idea of his destruction. In this he was aided by a being called the Conqueror, destroyer of many monsters and evil things which would have menaced the life of man still unborn; but at length Kodoyanpe was defeated by Coyote and fled eastward, as did Quetzalcoatl in Mexican myth. The Indians then sprang from the places where the mannikins of the first creation had been buried. Other versions of the myth tell of a primeval waste of waters upon which Kodoyanpe and Coyote dropped in a canoe. "Let this surf become sand!" cried Coyote, and it became sand.

The Achomawi, neighbours to the Maidu, state that the Creator originally emerged from a small cloud, and that Coyote sprang from a fog. The Aschochimi of California had a flood myth of the total destruction of humanity; but by planting the feathers of divers birds the Coyote grew a new crop of men of various tribes.

Mr W. Barbrook Grubb in his recent book on the Lengua Indians of South America describes their creation myth as follows:

"Their whole mythology is founded upon their idea of the Creation, of which we know only the bare outlines. The Creator of all things, spiritual and material, is symbolized by a beetle. It seems that the Indian idea is that the material universe was first made. The Creator, in the guise of the beetle, then sent forth from its hole in the earth a race of powerful beings—according to many in an embodied state—who for a time appear to have ruled the universe.

"Afterwards the beetle formed man and woman from the clay which it threw up from its hole. These were sent forth on the earth, joined together like the Siamese twins. They met with persecution from their powerful predecessors, and accordingly appealed to the creating beetle to free them from their disadvantageous formation. He therefore separated them, and gave them power to propagate their species, so that they might become numerous enough to withstand their enemies. It then appears that some time after this, or at this time, the powerful beings first created became disembodied, as they never appear again in the tradition of the Indians in material form. The beetle then ceased to take any active part or interest in the governance of the world, but committed its fortunes to these two races, which have been antagonistic ever since.

"It is rather remarkable, when we consider that they have no written records, and no system of carefully transmitted tradition, that they should retain a belief in an original Creator, in the immortality of the soul, and in the existence of these powerful and numerous evil personifications which they call *kilyikhama*.

"That the Indian should regard the beetle as the symbol of creative power is, perhaps, the most remarkable feature in their mythology, for it closely resembles the Egyptian Scarabæus and the ideas associated with it."

UNDERWORLD ORIGINS

Some American myths recount the manner in which mankind originally emerged from the earth. Thus the Caddoan family (Pawnees, Wichitu, etc.) believed that they came from the Underworld. Atius Tirawa, their creative agency, was omnipotent and invincible, dwelt in the upper air, and guided the constellations. A similar myth is that of the

Mandan Sioux, who suppose that the progenitors of their 'nation' lived in a subterranean village near a vast lake. A grape-vine penetrated the earth, and clambering up this several of them gained the upper world.

CARIB CREATION MYTH

The ancient Caribs of the Antilles, now extinct, regarded the earth, which they designated Mama Nono, as "the good mother, from which all things come." They believed that their original founder created the race by sowing the soil with stones, or with the fruit of the Mauritius palm, which sprouted forth into men and women (Müller, *Amerikanische Urreligionen*). The Bakairi Caribs possess a belief akin to that of the Zuñi Indians of New Mexico regarding the coming together of the Sky-Father and the Earth-Mother, originally in opposition to one another, communicating, then touching, and at last moving away from one another until they exchanged places. In the legends of the Bakairi, the mystical twin heroes Keri and Kame brought the first animals from the hollow trunk of a tree, which they connect with the Milky Way. The Caribs possess the same myth as the Arawaks regarding the efforts of the primitive culture-hero to gauge the depths of the volume of water which enshrouded the earth. Another Carib deluge myth related that excessive rains brought about a great flood, and that humanity was saved by the ibis, which had scooped up so much earth with its beak that hills could be formed from the heap. The Bakairi believe that the sun and moon were in the beginning aimlessly carried about by two birds, until at last Keri and Kame seized them by cunning, and made them proceed in a regular course. They aver that the luminaries are concealed by certain animals—lizards, birds, and spiders—which swallow the sun at night and the moon by day, disgorging them in the morning and evening respectively. Others believe that the moon is obscured at night by a shaman taking the form of a bird, and covering its disk with his wings. The Pleiades the Bakairi believe to be parakeets. In Orion they see a dried stick of manioc.

THE WORLD AND MAN

TUPI-GUARANI CREATION MYTH

A twofold destruction befell the original Tupi-Guarani people of Brazil. According to the myth, Monan the Creator, vexed with mankind, attempted to destroy the world by fire; but one Irin Magé, a magician of might, extinguished the conflagration by a heavy rain-storm. This in turn caused the rivers and lakes to overflow. When the flood subsided, a quarrel between the hero-brothers Tamandare and Aricoute precipitated another deluge, for the former stamped his foot so deeply into the ground that a flood of water issued therefrom, and the two brothers and their families were forced to take refuge in trees. The Mundruku tribe possesses a myth that a god Raini formed the world by placing it in the shape of a flat stone upon the head of another demiurge. Some other Tupi tribes believe in an interchange of Heaven and earth, as do the Zuñi Indians, while the Mundruku hero, Karu, creates mountains by blowing feathers about. The River Chaco Indians, cognate to the Guarani, believe that the universe was created by a gigantic beetle. After having made the plains, mountains, and forests, it scraped a hole in the ground and entered the earth. From this hole numerous living beings issued and covered the face of the earth. These beings after death became evil spirits, and constantly torment mankind. From the particles of soil thrown up by its excoriations the beetle constructed a man and woman, the progenitors of all human kind. Subsequently other evil spirits came from the hole, and attempted to overthrow the man and woman. The beetle gave power to the human beings to resist, but then withdrew, taking no further interest in their fate. An early traveller, Hans Staden, writing in 1550 of the Tupi-Guarani tribes, states their belief in the destruction of their ancestors by a powerful supernatural being, Maire, in an inundation from which but a few were saved by climbing trees and hiding in caves. The same authority gives the names of three brothers, Krimen, Hermitten, and Coem, from whom these tribes claimed descent. The southern tribes speak of four brothers, two of them called Tupi and Guarani respectively, and parents of the racial divisions designated after them. Among the northern Tupi proper a very definite cosmogony is discovered. Toru-shom-pek, the sun, is their principle of good, and Toru-guenket, the moon, the power of evil. The latter is supposed to fall periodically and destroy the earth, and from her emanate all baneful influences, such as thunderstorms and floods. Tupi cosmology rests primarily upon the idea that all created things possess a maker or 'mother' who is solely responsible for the scheme of creation, no male influence being traceable. There are three other superior deities, who made the various natural families and are generally known among the Tupi tribes as Guaracy, the sun, creator of all animals, Jacy, the moon, creator of plant-life, and Peruda or Ruda, the god of generation, who promotes the reproduction of human beings. Each of these has a number of demiurges under him, served by numerous spirits who protect every individual animal, plant, and person. But Tupi cosmology varies with locality, and this accounts for the conflicting notices of its several investigators. Like the Arawaks, the Tupi believe in Tupan, who alone of his four brothers survived the deluge, but he does not appear as a creative agency. The conception of natural phenomena among the Tupi-Guarani tribes is no less curious than their theories of creation. They believe the Pleiades to be a swarm of celestial bees. The Bororos Indians and other tribes believe the Southern Cross to be the track of an emu, and the Milky Way an ash-track.

A Tupi-Guarani Legend

During their voyage of exploration along the Rio Maraca, a tributary on the right bank of the Amazon, the mightiest river of the world, the leaders of the Croatian Scientific Mission in South America heard from native lips an interesting creation legend concerning the brothers Tupi and Guarani, the first forefathers of the tribes speaking the sister tongues called after them. This legend freely translated, runs as follows :

Tupi was once proceeding on a great journey to Pará, with his bow and arrow in his hands, and his inseparable companion, the wise parrot Maitá, on his shoulders. His younger brother Guarani followed in his track with the evil purpose of stealing

Maitá, because Fortune (Toryba) had decreed that the possessor of this bird should have his daughter, the beautiful maiden Maricá ('fine leaf'), as his wife.

Maitá, endowed with all magic wisdom, was a unique bird. He spoke with his companion, knew exactly the spots in the primeval forest where game and fruits were to be found, and likewise kept watch and gave warning of the approach and the number of enemies. Tupi, although aware of the evil intentions of his younger brother, went cheerily and carelessly on his way, the magic bird shielding him against all surprise. The steps of the two brothers were to bring them to the banks of the Pará. Guarani, fitly known as 'the patient one,' did not fret. Maricá, the amiable daughter of Toryba, had long been in love with the younger of the brothers; their hearts had long been united in the primeval forest, where the world had often been forgotten in sweet kisses and embraces.

"Wait three days for me!" said the maiden. "I will bring you Maitá or be the prisoner of Tupi."

In the meantime Tupi reached the banks of the Pará and lay fast asleep under the shade of a great banana-tree (Pacobahyba).

"Awake, comrade!" cried Maitá. "The enemy is yet far distant, but the treacherous Maricá is in sight."

Hastily the warrior sprang up, and became aware of a mocking titter from the neighbouring bushes.

"Do not fear to come nearer, Maricá, my love. I will marry you, and you shall become the mother of my children."

"Thou liest, Tupi!" answered the girl. "Give me thy bird and I will believe it!"

The eyes of the charming wood-nymph flashed alluringly upon the youth; he could not resist their magic and ordered the parrot to fly to the shoulder of his new companion; but the wise bird had no intention of furthering the false designs of the maiden, and did not move from the spot.

Tupi angrily repeated his order and made as if to strike the inattentive bird. Then Maitá flew to the very top of a slender palm, while the fleet-footed maiden endeavoured to disappear into the depths of the forest.

INTRODUCTION TO MYTHOLOGY

Tupi was by no means willing to lose the beauty, and set out after her with swinging strides, but in vain. Laughing heartily, the active little maid clambered up a thousand-year-old giant tree and would not be caught.

As if grown out of the earth Guarani suddenly appeared between them. The game of hide-and-seek came to an end, the rivals measured each other with glances of hatred, fell upon and grappled with one another. Like a squirrel the lovely Maricá climbed up a palm and seated herself beside the fugitive magic bird Maitá. Both desired to witness this unworthy fight between the twin brothers.

The day-star set, the moon arose, but the brothers did not move from the spot. They gripped each other fast, bloody sweat dripped from their brows, and their fiercely sparkling eyes declared that one of them must have no place on earth. The parrot screeched, and Maricá wept, for Guarani's strength seemed to be leaving him.

"Be gracious, mighty Tupan!" pleaded the daughter of Fate to the father of mankind. Tupan, the almighty, heard the maiden's prayer and ordered the bride of the Wind to separate the brothers. Forthwith the Flood (Pororoca) rose in storm amidst peals of thunder; uncanny crashings and rumblings broke the stillness of the primeval forest, the earth shook, and all the elements seemed to have broken loose. Trees and palms were overthrown, and fell into the foam-covered waves of the giant river. The parrot was lost in the skies, while Maricá was carried off by the wind and came to herself in her mother's hut. The terrified wrestlers ceased their struggle and looked in surprise at each other.

In the hope of catching Maricá, Tupi sprang upon a floating tree-trunk and entrusted his fate to the will of the waters, finally anchoring his ship of life to the opposite bank. There he settled down and became the ancestor of numerous Indian peoples, the Pitiguaras, Tupinambas, Tabajaras, Cahetes, Tupiniquias, and many others.

Guarani returned southward and founded the Guayanas, Carijos, Tapes, and many other generations of warlike Indian races.

THE WORLD AND MAN

THE RELATIONSHIP OF COSMOGONIES

We have now summarized the chief creation myths, and the question arises, How far have these influenced each other? The further question, Can they be traced to a common original account or accounts? we do not put, as it appears to us quite as futile as those 'researches' into the 'original language' of mankind.

Although not in any way denying the circulation of myth and its dissemination, we do not think that the theory of complete and wholesale borrowing from advanced races by savage peoples is confirmed by actual research. There are, it is admitted, well-authenticated examples of the colouring of savage myth by civilized cosmogonies; but these examples are easily distinguished by the practised student of myth, as they lack the fundamentals of barbarian myth—simplicity, 'savagery,' in short, that aboriginal artlessness and primitiveness which mark all early and unsophisticated religious thought. Unlike primitive myths, they possess the idea of the creation of something from nothing (that is, they do not describe re-creation instead of creation). Of creation myths exhibiting cultured influence there are very few, and when one creation tale resembles another a great deal of proof should be forthcoming before it is inferred that one has sophisticated the other or that both proceed from a common story.[1]

How absurd it is to credit all or most barbarian theology with an alien origin is seen from the *Popol Vuh*, already quoted, an aboriginal composition of the Kiche Indians of Guatemala. This work was written by a Christianized native of Guatemala some time in the seventeenth century, and was copied (in the Kiche language, in which it was originally written) by a Dominican friar, Francisco Ximenez, who added a Spanish translation and *scholia*. The Abbé Brasseur de Bourbourg, a profound student of American archæology and languages,[2] deplored, in a letter to the Duc de Valmy,[3] the supposed loss of

---

[1] This question has been dealt with at greater length elsewhere (see p. 158).

[2] His euhemeristic interpretations of the Mexican myths are as worthless as the materials he unearthed are priceless.

[3] Mexico, October 15, 1850.

the *Popol Vuh*, which he was aware had been made use of early in the nineteenth century by a certain Don Felix Cabrera. Dr C. Scherzer, an Austrian scholar, thus made aware of its value, paid a visit to the republic of Guatemala in 1854 or 1855, and was successful in tracing the missing manuscript in the library of the University of San Carlos in the city of Guatemala. It was afterward ascertained that its scholiast, Ximenez, had deposited it in the library of his convent at Chichicastenango, whence it passed to the San Carlos library in 1830. Scherzer made a copy of the Spanish translation of the manuscript, which he published at Vienna in 1856 under the title of *Las Historias del origen de los Indios de Guatemala, par el R. P. F. Francisco Ximenez*. The Abbé Brasseur also took a copy of the original, which he published at Paris in 1861, with the title *Vuh Popol: Le livre sacré des Quiches, et les mythes de l'antiquité américaine*. In this work the Kiche original and the Abbé's French translation are set forth side by side. Unfortunately both the Spanish and the French translations leave much to be desired in accuracy, and the notes which accompany them are misleading. The name '*Popol Vuh*' signifies 'Record of the Community,' and its literal translation is 'Book of the Mat,' from the Kiche words *pop* or *popol*, a mat or rug of woven leaves on which the entire family sat, and *vuh* or *uuh*, paper or book, from *uoch*, to write. The *Popol Vuh* is an example of a world-wide *genre*—a type of annals of which the first portion is pure mythology, shading off into pure history, evolving from the hero-myths of saga to the recital of the deeds of authentic personages. It may, in fact, be classed with the *Heimskringla* of Snorri, the Danish History of Saxo Grammaticus, the Chinese History in the Five Books, the Japanese *Nihongi*, and its fourth book somewhat resembles the Pictish Chronicle. The cosmogony of the *Popol Vuh* exhibits no signs of Christian influence, and even if it did, it would be quite erroneous to infer that such influence was direct—that is, that the original compiler deliberately infused into the narrative what he knew of Hebrew cosmogony. The resemblance between the first few chapters of the *Popol Vuh* and the creation myth in Genesis is slight and fortuitous. There are

188

THE WORLD AND MAN

no precise points of contact, and the supposed resemblance has been drawn by writers only superficially acquainted with Kiche myth and wholly ignorant of its spirit and the processes which developed it. It is by no means difficult to prove the genuine American character of the *Popol Vuh*. A perusal should suffice. Macpherson, in his preface to the first edition of the poems of Ossian, says an "ingenious gentleman" before reading those poems imagined that out of modesty he had ascribed them to an ancient writer, but after reading them said they abounded too much in ideas only belonging to an early state of society to be the work of a modern poet. We need not trouble about the authorship of the poems of Ossian ; but the ingenious gentleman could have said the same thing with justice of the *Popol Vuh*. To anyone who has given it a careful examination it must be abundantly evident that it has passed through several stages of development ; that it is of aboriginal origin ; and that it has not been influenced by European thought in any manner whatsoever. The fact that it was composed in the Kiche tongue is almost sufficient proof of its genuine American character. The scholarship of the nineteenth century was unequal to the adequate translation of the *Popol Vuh* ; the twentieth century has as yet shown no signs of being able to accomplish the task ; and if modern scholarship is unable to translate the work, the eighteenth century was unable to create it. No European of that time was sufficiently versed in Kiche theology and history to compose in faultless Kiche such a work as the *Popol Vuh*, breathing as it does in every line an intimate and natural acquaintance with the antiquities of Guatemala.

From these considerations it will be clear that the Hebrew cosmogony has neither coloured nor veneered the account of creation in the *Popol Vuh*, nor have its transcribers destroyed the veritable aboriginal thought which lies beneath. The account of the making of man, for example, is totally different in Genesis and in the Kiche production. "Giants in those days" appear in both, but in the first they are merely alluded to, whereas in the second a very full account is provided of their destruction. The star and sun myths of the two accounts have no resemblance, and the sole likeness is in the opening scene,[1] where the vast abyss in which the original deity or deities sleep is pictured. Its resemblance to other American cosmogonies has been amply proved ; and to credit the whole, as has been done, to Christian influence *alone* is characteristic of the period in which the criticism was promulgated—a period of superficial learning and cheap generalization like that of certain present-day critics and ultra-popular writers on mythology and folklore, and improperly equipped persons at all times.[2]

We do not desire, as we have already said, to deny the existence of borrowed or sophisticated cosmogonies, but these are of late origin, easily perceived, and as a rule merely veil a primitive or much earlier original. The following instance, alluded to by the late Professor Brinton, well serves to illustrate the point in question. He says:

"Very soon after coming in contact with the whites, the Indians caught the notion of a bad and good spirit, pitted one against the other in eternal warfare, and engrafted it on their ancient traditions. Writers anxious to discover Jewish or Christian analogies forcibly construed myths to suit their pet theories, and for indolent observers it was convenient to catalogue their gods in antithetical classes. In Mexican and Peruvian mythology this is so plainly false that historians no longer insist upon it, but as a popular error it still holds its ground with reference to the more barbarous and less known

---

[1] This has, in fact, quite as strong a resemblance to the cosmological account in the *Satapatha Brahmana* in some details.

[2] A disquieting circumstance attending such ignorant criticism is that those who criticize appear in many instances to be quite unable to apprehend the substantial difficulties in the way of barbarian borrowings. Thus a reviewer in a weekly journal of standing actually inferred that certain North American Indian myths presented by the author had been sophisticated by Greek and classical tales. However well the theory of borrowing may explain things, and although borrowing does at times occur, the difficulties in this especial instance are overwhelming. They were quite unappreciated, however, by the reviewer, whose experience of myth was, of course, obviously limited. Students of myth would do well to bear the point of virtual impossibility in mind, as it is of constant occurrence, and one regarding which no fixed or definite rules or laws can possibly obtain.

THE WORLD AND MAN

tribes. Perhaps no myth has been so often quoted in its confirmation as that of the ancient Iroquois, which narrates the conflict between the first two brothers of our race. It is of undoubted native origin and venerable antiquity. The version given by the Tuscarora chief Cusic in 1825 relates that in the beginning of things there were two brothers, Enigorio and Enigohatgea, names literally meaning the Good Mind and the Bad Mind. (Or more exactly, the Beautiful Spirit, the Ugly Spirit. In Onondaga the radicals are *onigonra*, spirit; *hio*, beautiful; *ahetken*, ugly.) The former went about the world furnishing it with gentle streams, fertile plains, and plenteous fruits, while the latter maliciously followed him, creating rapids, thorns, and deserts. At length the Good Mind turned upon his brother in anger, and crushed him into the earth. He sank out of sight in its depths, but not to perish, for in the dark realms of the Underworld he still lives, receiving the souls of the dead, and being the author of all evil. Now when we compare this with the version of the same legend given by Father Brebeuf, missionary to the Hurons in 1636, we find its whole complexion altered; the moral dualism vanishes; the names Good Mind and Bad Mind do not appear; it is the struggle of Ioskeha, the White one, with his brother Tawiscara, the Dark one, and we at once perceive that Christian influence in the course of two centuries had given the tale a meaning foreign to its original intent." [1]

No student of myth of any experience would for a moment accept the first-mentioned tale as solely of aboriginal origin. Its ethical trend would make this at least doubtful. It would not be correct to say that an ethical spirit never enters into the religious tales of savages, but it should certainly be regarded with suspicion until it is proved to be aboriginal. It is not surprising to find it in the tales of Egyptians, Hebrews, Peruvians, and people of considerable culture; but to encounter it in the stories of Africans, American Indians, and savages who have been long in contact with Europeans should at once arouse suspicion. Never let us neglect, however, the matter which lies beneath the cultural veneer. The Uapès Indians

[1] *Myths of the New World*, by Professor D. G. Brinton (Philadelphia, 1905).

INTRODUCTION TO MYTHOLOGY

of Brazil include both Jurupari and the Christian hierarchy in their pantheon. We know that the latter are new-comers there; but let us not neglect Jurupari! We know that Roman belief sophisticated Gallic religious practice; but is that to say that it submerged it?

In order to show exactly where the most notable creation myths impinge upon each other and exhibit resemblances, the following tables have been drawn up, which indicate this at a glance. It will be seen that most of those which bear resemblances are situated in regions excessively remote—an argument in favour of those who believe that the religious evolution of man has followed similar lines in all parts of the habitable globe.

CONCLUSIONS

The idea of a primeval abyss is common to Egypt, Babylonia, India, Scandinavia, the Celts, some North American Indians.

The original god (or gods) finds himself in this abyss in the myths of Egypt, Babylonia, India, the Hebrews, the Maya-Kiches.

The original god (or gods) broods over the face of the waters in Hebrew, Polynesian, North American Indian, and Maya-Kiche myth.

The universe is manufactured from the corpse of a primeval being in the myths of Babylonia, China, Scandinavia, Hindus (Purusha).

Life or matter is created by the spoken word of the original god in the myths of Egypt, the Hebrews, the Celts, the Maya-Kiches.

The idea of the cosmic egg appears in the myths of Egypt, India, Japan, Peru.

Man emanates: from the tears of a god (Egypt), from the blood and bones of a god (Babylonia), from clay (the Hebrews and North American Indians), from worms (China), from wooden images or trees (Scandinavia, Maya-Kiches, Iran), from the sweat of a god or giant (Iran and Scandinavia), from the union of a god and an animal (some North American Indians).

The eyes of a god or demiurge become the sun and moon in the cosmogonies of Egypt, China, Scandinavia (?).

192

THE WORLD AND MAN

The piece of earth from which the new world is constructed is fished out of the waters of the deluge by an animal in some North American Indian myths, and perhaps in the original form of the Hebrew myth.

PRINCIPAL CREATION MYTHS SUMMARIZED

EGYPT

(1) A god finding himself in a primeval abyss, where he has been since the beginning of time, utters his name. This act causes him to 'live.'

(2) He next creates, by a magical act, a foundation upon which to stand, probably the earth.

(3) From his mouth he brings objects which reproduce themselves.

(4) He creates two other deities, male and female, who in turn propagate other gods.

(5) Vegetation and creeping things are formed on the earth.

(6) Man is then created from the tears which fall from the original deity.

BABYLONIA

(1) Primeval deities dwell in an abyss.

(2) New gods arrive (?) and quarrel with them.

(3) Two of the primeval deities are slain, but the third, a female, creates monsters and gives battle to the new-comers, and is annihilated.

(4) The new gods create the earth and firmament from her corpse.

(5) Their champion is decapitated, and from his blood and bones springs the race of mankind.

CHINESE

(1) From nothingness an atom is formed.

(2) In the course of ages it splits into a male and female principle which again split in two.

(3) From the co-operation of these four elements springs a being whose body is broken up into the constituents of a universe, and the worms from its decomposing corpse become men.

SCANDINAVIAN

(1) There exists a yawning abyss, bordered on one side by a realm of mist and cold, on the other by a region of fire.

193

(2) A giant is brought into being through the melting of the congealing vapour in the place of cold by a spark of fire from the region of Muspelheim.

(3) This being becomes the progenitor of a race of giants.

(4) He has a cow which, by licking a brine-covered rock, produces the father of the gods.

(5) These gods slay the giant and all his progeny save two, and manufacture the earth from his corpse.

(6) Alternatively the gods lift the earth out of the primeval waters.

(7) The dwarfs fashion two figures out of trees, and the gods give them life and understanding.

CELTS

(1) Two principles, creative and destructive, are alluded to.

(2) The latter dwells in an abyss.

(3) Atomic life originates through the spoken words of the creative principle.

(4) Man passes from the abyss to the earth-circle.

JAPANESE

(1) Male and female elements separate from the original atom.

(2) These form an ovoid body containing germs from which heaven and earth are formed.

(3) A species of reed-shoot appears between them and is transformed into a god.

(4) Divine beings are born, two of whom unite and give birth to islands, seas, rivers, herbs, and trees, and the celestial bodies.

CHAPTER VII
PARADISE AND THE PLACE OF PUNISHMENT

A PLACE of reward and a place of punishment are ineradicably associated with mythology. The idea that the human soul must betake itself to a realm of brightness and bliss, where it will ever bask in the smile of the gods it has adored upon earth, or be tormented by beings—still god-like—in an atmosphere of suffering or torture, appears to be common to most mythological systems of an advanced type. Thus Egyptian, Indian, Babylonian, Hebrew, and Mexican mythology all possess a place of bliss and a region of sorrow. In Greek, Roman, Scandinavian, and Celtic myth, however, we have merely a Hades, an Otherworld, a place of the dead. Would it be true to say that it is only among those peoples in whom the moral standpoint is high that the places of reward and punishment are conceived, instead of the mere place of the dead, the abode of shadows? If so, the Aztec who delighted in human sacrifice was upon a higher ethical level than the cultivated Greek. Again, the myths of races of low civilization sometimes refer to a place of reward, although more often their abode of the dead is merely a shadowy extension of their mortal existence.

Let us examine the outstanding myths of civilized antiquity, then their savage counterparts, ere we decide how far mankind owes its conception of Heaven and Hell to ethical promptings. This is one of the junctures where religious science is not to be distinguished from the science of mythology, for both explain the origin of ideas dealing with the next world, or attempt to place them in their proper sequence of evolution. But it must be borne in mind that the science of myth is not concerned with the purely religious aspect of the abode of the dead, whatever form it takes, but with its 'geography,' scenery, and supernatural inhabitants only. If it asks "How far have the myths of a place of punishment and reward been affected by ethical promptings?" it is merely for the sake of the myths, not for any concern with these promptings.

THE TEUTONIC REALM OF WOE

The Teutonic peoples believed that the dead passed to the realm of Hel (our 'Hell'), daughter of Loki. The word Hel appears to be derived from a root which means 'to conceal' (old Teutonic 'Halja,' the Coverer-up or Hider), and signified both the realm of the dead and the goddess who presided over it. But it is probably a later development of the myth, perhaps sophisticated by Christian influences, that makes Hel a place of punishment. In Hel's later habitation we find "Hunger her table, starvation her knife, delay and slowness her servants, precipice her threshold, care her bed." The realm of this dark goddess, the Proserpine of the North, was not originally associated with the idea of punishment, but was pictured rather as a delectable region. Thither fared Balder when slain, and on his arrival 'Eljudnir,' the high hall of Hel, was bravely decorated, while foaming horns of mead were prepared for his reception. In later days, when the conception of Valhalla, the warriors' Paradise, was popularly accepted, Hel became the residence after death of those who had not perished by the sword, who had died a 'straw' death. The Teutonic defunct, then, were divided in death according to the manner of their dying, as in ancient Mexico, where dead warriors went to the palace of the sun-god and those who died of dropsy or were struck by lightning betook them to the luscious and fertile Paradise of Tlaloc the water-god, while the common herd were swallowed pell-mell by the capacious death-cavern of Mictlantecutli, lord of Mictlan or 'Hades.' The Teutonic goddess Hel (or 'Hela' in its Latinized form) was, according to Meyer and Mogk, more closely related to the demonic class of beings than to the gods proper. This is sometimes the case with the infernal powers, and examples occur where they are scarcely more than mere demons; but most commonly the rulers of the Underworld rank as gods proper. Again, they are often the deities of a subject, conquered, or outcast race. This question will receive further treatment at the end of this chapter.

Hel, as has been said, was the child of Loki and the giantess Angurboda; and a shadowy Teutonic All-Father (a 'god behind the gods,' who recalls Mr Lang's Australian and Andaman original monotheistic figures), fearful of the innate and abounding evil in her, cast her into Niflheim and gave her power over the nine worlds of Helheim, where she housed the dead. Hel was a place of gloom and dreariness, but within it was a grove inhabited by sinless beings destined to repeople the world. It is possible to discern in the myth of Hel as we know it a later sophistication of the original, most probably due, as we have said, to Christian influence. Early Teutonic ideas concerning the dead were by no means well defined. We read of the souls of the departed accompanying the Wild Huntsman (no other than Odin) on his weird nightly chase. Other tales describe them as dwelling with Odin in the hills, or, indeed, beneath them. This last is a very much more widespread Teutonic tradition than is generally credited. Charlemagne sleeps in the Odenberg, Frederick Barbarossa in the Kyffhäuser, and, all unknown to the writer until the day before penning these words, King Arthur was once thought to slumber beneath the lion-like mass of Arthur's Seat on the outskirts of Edinburgh.

VALHALLA, THE WARRIORS' HEAVEN

Valhalla, the hall of Odin, where Teutonic warriors fallen in battle dwelt ever with the god in feast and fray, was the warriors' Paradise, and was built round the trunk of a tree Laeradhr. On its leaves browsed the stag Eikthyrmir and the goat Heidbrun, from whose udders flowed inexhaustible streams of mead to quench the thirst of the heroes. Its portals were five hundred and forty in number, and were capable of admitting eight hundred warriors at a time. Its roof was made of the shields of the mighty dead, its leaves of their spear-shafts, and round the walls glittered their swords and mail, while on the western wall hung a stuffed wolf surmounted by an eagle. At some distance from the hall was the forest Glasir, the trees of which bore golden foliage, encircled by a sacred wall. The champions or 'Einherjar' went forth to combat each other every day, returning to feast on boar and mead.

Now it is obvious that this myth is a comparatively late conception created by a military aristocracy. A similar phenomenon is to be observed, as has been said, in ancient Mexico, where the military caste supplied the altars of the war-god with sacrificial victims, and maintained the food-compact between the people and their deities. As you will remember, if the gods perished for lack of sustenance (human blood) they could not bless the harvests, and the people would also die. The future reward of a valiant Mexican warrior was the continuous company of the sun-god. Now we find that at one time human sacrifice was rendered to Odin. Prisoners of war were sacrificed to him, precisely as they were to the Mexican war-god Uitzilopochtli by *stabbing* (see Chadwick, *Cult of Othin*), and sometimes the 'blood eagle' was carved on their backs. King Domalde of Sweden and a certain King Olaf were sacrificed to Odin in order that he might be induced to put an end to a famine. Thus early Scandinavia resembles Mexico. By such instances does the science of comparative religion triumphantly assert its value. Thus the myth of Valhalla appears to have had the same genesis as the myth of the reception of dead Mexican warriors into the sun-god's train.

THE OLYMPUS OF OLD EGYPT

But scanty information is to be gleaned concerning the abode of the gods of Egypt. In the Pyramid texts of King Pepi I we read that the whole universe was divided into three portions, Heaven, earth, and the Underworld or 'Duat,' each with its own gods. Besides the gods, Heaven contained other classes of beings, the Shesu-Heru or Shemsu-Heru, a name which may, perhaps, be translated 'Followers of Horus.' They were those who attended upon Horus, his satellites, and on occasion his defenders, obviously followers of the sun, the hosts of the sun-god, resembling in nature the 'pages' of the Mexican

PARADISE AND PUNISHMENT

Quetzalcoatl, the Knights of King Arthur of the Round Table (also perhaps the sun[1]), or the dead warriors who caroused with Norse Odin in Valhalla. Indeed, we find them assisting Horus in his war against the powers of darkness exactly as the dead warriors help Odin. These powers are alluded to in the texts of Pepi I as if they were of very considerable importance in the Egyptian heavenly economy. Pepi placates them and they purify him and recite the 'Chapter of those who rise up' on his behalf. Another class of heavenly beings is the Ashemu, whose characteristics are unknown. The Henmemet or Hamemet were either those who have been or were to become human beings. A text of Hatshepset seems to ascribe mortal attributes to them, as it employs the determinative signs which stand for human beings, and a passage in a hymn to Amen-Ra edited by Grépaut shows that the Egyptians believed them to live on grain. Of other beings, the Set, the Afa, and the Utennu, we only know the name. The souls of righteous men also dwelt in Heaven.

The Egyptian Heaven, so far as we can glean, realized the idea of Paracelsus, 'as above, so below'; for it was the macrocosm of the earth's microcosm, the greater world above, which was mirrored in the earth below, one being the complement of the other. The denizens of the Egyptian Olympus were the 'Great,' the 'Little,' and the other companies of gods; the different classes of beings already alluded to; and the souls of men, or their 'shadows,' 'doubles,' 'souls,' 'spirits,' 'powers,' 'hearts,' or 'spiritual bodies.' The denizens of Heaven directed the course of the celestial bodies, overlooked the affairs of mortals, and accompanied the greater gods in their progress through the heavens. Constant prayers and hymns of praise arose to Ra, the king and chief of Heaven. The gods were nourished on celestial food which came from the Eye of Horus—that is, they subsisted upon the beams of light which emanated from the sun. In a text of Pepi I we read of a 'plant of life' which the gods subsisted on, and it apparently grew near the great lake Sekhet-hetep, on the banks of which the gods usually reclined. The just who abode with the gods

[1] See above, p. 122.

199

were apparelled in similar manner to them; but they also wore white linen garments, and were shod with white sandals.

From the Pyramid texts of Unas we glean some further information concerning the celestial sphere. It is called Aaru (perhaps 'the Place of Reeds'), or, in another part of the text, Sekhet-Aaru, and was divided into a number of districts, the names of which may be translated 'the Field of Offerings,' 'the Field of Peace,' and 'the Field of Grasshoppers.' It was watered by extensive lakes, where Ra bathed and the dead purified themselves before beginning their heavenly existence. Originally Aaru was thought to be located in the sky, but there is evidence that it could be entered from certain places in the Delta, called Pe-Tep and Tettu. The vignettes of Sekhet-Aaru in the Theban recension of the *Book of the Dead* indicate that it was placed in the north of Egypt. It seems to have been composed of good agricultural country bearing heavy crops, a pleasant and well-watered land where the justified soul might rest from the labours of earth, secure in an eternity of bucolic delights. This, be it noted, was the Paradise of the cult of Osiris, a worship anciently connected with the land and the tillers thereof. There is little or no ground for its being confounded, as it certainly appears to have been confounded at a later period, with the Heaven of Ra. The myth of the Paradise of Ra, with its choirs of chanting spirits and its different classes of supernatural beings, bears traces of ecclesiastical elaboration, whereas the Paradise of the Osirian cult is the Otherworld of a race purely agricultural—the cult of the peasant as opposed to that of the dweller in towns.

THE DUAT

It was probably only in later times that the 'Duat' was regarded as a place of punishment. Originally it seems to have been merely the place through which the dead sun-god Ra passed, after his setting or death each evening, on his journey to the east, where once again he might rise. The Duat was peopled by the powers of night and darkness, the natural enemies of the sun. At a later period these powers were confounded with the damned—that is, they met with the fate generally accorded to the deities of gloom and chaos at the hands of more distant generations. There was no Hell proper for 'lost souls' in the Egyptian religious economy; but a region existed at the end of the Duat where infernal goddesses presided over pits of fire, slaying, beheading, and dismembering the enemies of Ra, and burning the remains. Once the god had quitted this region, however, the fires went out and his enemies were granted a period of rest until he reappeared on the following night. As these beings appeared in Egyptian pictorial art with human forms, the idea gradually took shape that they represented the souls of the damned. Dr Budge very shrewdly says: "The souls of the damned could have done nothing to hinder the progress of Ra, and the Egyptians never imagined that they did, but it is possible that in late dynastic times certain schools of theological thought in Egypt, being dissatisfied with and unconvinced of the accuracy of the theory of the annihilation of the wicked, assigned to evil souls dwelling-places with the personifications of the powers of nature already mentioned."[1] The description of the Duat is hard to fit to any known mythic locality, but it is usually employed in the texts as a name for a place of the dead—a Hades, not a place of retribution.

ASSYRIA'S 'LAND OF NO RETURN'

The Hades of Assyria is a vast expanse of emptiness and gloom, from which, as we learn from a mythological poem on the descent of Ishtar, "there is no return." Mud and dust feed its population, darkness is their heritage, it is a house with no exit. A keeper guards the entrance and exacts homage to Allatu, the queen, from all who enter the gate. A spell is then cast over the ill-fated new-comer and he is led through seven successive gates and stripped of all earthly possessions. In the end he is bereft even of the power of speech.

Allatu and her chiefs enjoy thrones of gold adorned with precious stones, as though to mark emphatically the difference between themselves and the culprits. Allatu may recompense or condemn, according to the needs of the cases that come

[1] *The Gods of the Egyptians*, vol. i, pp. 264-265.

before her, and has the power, for instance, to strike an offender with disease of the body, or to consign him to prison.

The Assyrian Hades was separated from the land of the living by a river of Death. It had no substance, shape, or atmosphere, but was filled with chilling cold and melancholy gloom. It boasted a department of judgment, like the Hebrew Sheol, which in later years became further developed, and marks a most important variation in the evolution of the idea of a place of punishment. The journey to this hall of judgment was full of dangers and horrors of every description, through which the deceased must pass.

The Babylonian Hades resembles the medieval Hell inasmuch as the disembodied souls wander about in search of escape. Allatu, with her divining rod, ruled her dominion with relentless power ; and being the goddess of death and barrenness, she lived in constant dread of Ea, the god of wisdom, who could alone cancel the spells of the Underworld and cause men to live again.

The idea of personifying the stars and planets, so that besides appearing in the sky they presided on the earth in living bodies, is exemplified in the later Babylonian mythology. This astral system had the outstanding feature that occurrences on earth closely corresponded to the movements in Heaven. The gods and goddesses had seats assigned to them in the heavens while their spirits pervaded the earth. Shamash and Sin, the two greatest deities, represented the sun and moon, and were followed by the other planetary gods. Anu became the greatest of the gods and assumed supreme command of the heavens.

The Babylonians pictured a region in Hades for the reception of righteous souls. Into this region those who after judgment appeared to merit recompense gained admission. Under a peaceful silver sky ancient prophets, crowned in triumph, sat amid pleasant fields. A clear stream rippled past and quenched the thirst of the seers from year's end to year's end. This was the water of life, belonging to Ishtar, and endowing her with the power to return to earth. From this region spirits passed into a firmament above, consisting of the earthly sphere in addition to the heavenly. It had windows from which the rain descended, and a flight of steps leading from the zenith to the earth.

THE HEBREW HELL

The Jewish place of punishment was Gehenna, where corporal as well as spiritual torment was meted out to the wicked. In later Jewish eschatology, it was the place of eternal punishment for the Gentile races, apostate Jews being retained there in a description of purgatory until, their sin atoned for, they could pass to Paradise. Sheol, on the other hand, was perhaps a more purely Hebrew conception than Gehenna, which probably had its origin in the old Accadian Gi-umuna. Sheol is the common abode of just and unjust alike after death, and life there was shadowy and unsubstantial as in the Greek Hades. It is well described in Isaiah xiv, 9–11 :

" Hell from beneath is moved for thee to meet thee at thy coming : it stirreth up the dead for thee, even all the chief ones of the earth ; it hath raised up from their thrones all the kings of the nations.

" All they shall speak and say unto thee, Art thou also become weak as we? art thou become like unto us ?

" Thy pomp is brought down to the grave, and the noise of thy viols : the worm is spread under thee, and the worms cover thee." [1]

[1] The writer does not recall having read this passage until a few weeks ago, yet in a volume of verse published in 1913 he included some stanzas the two last of which offer such a striking resemblance to the Biblical verses just quoted that he ventures to print them here as an example of the manner in which the imagination of men may run on similar lines, although centuries of time separate them ;

THE DEAD

Do ye hearken, ye dead, with your faces so nobly quiet,
Do ye list to the lays that are sung, and the lusts that are said,
Do ye wot of the frenzies, the fears, the desires, and the riot,
    Do ye hearken, ye dead?

" O'er our lips and our hearts are the sods and the cerements spread,
But we hearken the harps and the whispers, the songs that ye sigh at,
All your manifold furies and fears do we list in our bed.

" We would rise, we would rise to partake of your doom and your diet,
But on lips and on eyen the worms and the vampires have fed,
We can kiss, we can smile not—awaiting eternity's fiat.
    We hearken, we dead !"

INTRODUCTION TO MYTHOLOGY

After the captivity, and consequently under Babylonian influences, Sheol became a region principally devoted to punishment, with Gehenna as the place of especial torment and abasement. The Talmud describes this place of woe as follows : "Ordinary transgressors of Israel, whose merits preponderate, though they descend into Hell, do not feel the effects of the flames, and rise at once. Some who sin with their bodies, such as those who put their neighbours to shame publicly and who neglect the phylacteries, etc., are annihilated after twelve months' endurance of hell-fire. Adulterers, though they sin with their bodies, ascend to happiness at the end of the same period. Christians, informers, and those who systematically despise the words of the Rabbis are consigned to eternal punishment. Of course, all may escape punishment altogether by repentance in this life."

No departmental god rules in this dreary realm, Sheol being directly under the eye of Yahweh ; for, according to Job xxvi, 6, Sheol and destruction are naked before Him, and being omnipresent He is also in Sheol. Sheol was silent as the grave, its inhabitants raising not a murmur ; neither in their grief could they work to praise God. It had gates and bars, alluded to in the Song of Solomon as "jealous" and "cruel as the grave."

The Talmud obviously borrows from Persian doctrine ; or it might be more correct to say that both conceptions spring from a common source. In Psalms xxxvi, 8, and xlvi, 4, a river of life is alluded to which makes glad the abode of the Elohim or gods. Says the anonymous author of *Bible Folklore* : "In the discourse of Josephus to the Greeks on Hades we find the opinions of the more liberal Pharisees clearly set forth about the Christian era. He believes in a Hades of temporary punishment, and an Elysium of light called Abraham's bosom. The Messiah Logos (as at Alexandria) is, according to the Jewish historian, to be the judge who will condemn the wicked to a lake of fire already prepared, but as yet not used for torture, and will reward the righteous in the heavenly kingdom. The wicked are to resume their old bodies unchanged, but the righteous will obtain pure and immortal forms fashioned from

204

their old bodies which have been sowed in the ground. The simile of the corn sown as seed, and springing up with a glorified body, is used by Josephus as by St Paul, and it was evidently a widely known parable, which occurs also in the Talmud, for Rabbi Meir is said to have told Cleopatra that as a grain of wheat buried naked springs forth with many clothes so will the righteous also. . . .

"In the future happy age, says Josephus, after the judgment of the wicked, there will be inhabitants of Heaven and of earth, but no more birth, no wild animals, no storms, no darkness or change. Man will be able to walk across the sea, and to ascend into Heaven; he will never grow old or die, but continue to enjoy a material or semi-material existence in his spiritual body. . . .

"In the Mishnah the world to come is mentioned as the heritage of 'all Israel,' but the wicked, the Sadducee, the Epicurean, readers of foreign books, and sorcerers, together with certain historic personages, are excluded. Some of these are to be slain by plague in the world to come, and some are to be scattered. Thus the doctrine of immortality in the Mishnah is confined to the future resurrection of pious Israelites. In Daniel also a partial resurrection only is foretold to follow a judgment day. The Sibyl believes that the righteous will live again on earth, but the wicked will remain in Gehenna. The Book of Enoch is full of the same doctrine. A sealed volume is to be opened in the last day, and the good will be selected and become angels, but Azazel and his hosts will be judged, and cast into a lake of fire. A great fire is also to burn up the present Heaven and earth according to the Sibyl, and a new creation will emerge from the ashes.

"Such, then, was the development of Jewish eschatology as compared with that of Egypt, Assyria, and Persia. At first an 'eternal house' beneath the earth is imagined to hold for ever the shades of good and evil in appropriate habitations. Gradually the expectation of a return to earthly life grows up, and the idea of spiritual and immortal bodies. These are, however, reserved for the elect few, and the wicked are condemned either to a second death or to eternal torment in their former bodies in a Hell of flame, where, according to Isaiah, a fiery worm gnaws upon them."

THE HELLENIC PLACE OF THE DEAD

The Greek place of punishment embraces three abstract regions, Hades, Tartarus, and Elysium. Spirits leaving the earth entered 'the Unseen,' passing, according to their worth, into one of these three abodes.

According to one writer, Oceanus, greatest of rivers, rolled between the place of perfect happiness on its southern banks and the realms of eternal darkness on its western, where fog and gloom encircled a place of everlasting punishment. This stream had no mouth and no source, and did not mingle with the sea which, according to Homer, it enclosed. Earlier than this, Plato described a still more gloomy region. He speaks of the plain of Lethe (situated near the two springs of Lethe and Mnemosyne, which represented oblivion and memory), whose waters give forgetfulness.

In the *Iliad*, again, the place of Oceanus is usurped by the Styx, which wound its course seven times round the world of the dead.

Those who had been taught the divination of the mysteries of infernal life could find guidance as to the future engraved on a gold plate in a tomb in Petelia at the oracle of Trophonius; and this tomb came to be regarded as one of the entrances to Hell.

The supreme sovereign of the infernal regions was Pluto, brother of Zeus and Poseidon, and a willing accomplice in deposing Cronus, their father, and sharing his kingdom. Pluto, spouse of Persephone, whom we have mentioned before, ruled with merciless severity, striking terror to the hearts of his subjects. He possessed a helmet which rendered him invisible, and he was feared by the gods as well as by the dead. He was assisted by a tribunal of judges, the chief being Æacus, son of Zeus and Ægina (appointed to this trust in the Underworld because of his just dealings with men in his kingdom above), Minos, and Rhadamanthus. Elysium and Tartarus were two late offshoots of the region of Hades. In the *Odyssey*, the souls who were

utterly worthless fell into the 'deep bottomless pit' of Tartarus, while those who merited reward passed into the pleasant
land of Elysium. In the most ancient Greek mythology, however, Hades was a region for all the dead, good and bad, a land
of shadow and dim suggestion.

THE ELYSIAN FIELDS

The Elysian fields appear in some descriptions as a fertile
plain at the utmost ends of the earth, washed by the waters of
Oceanus, and ruled over by the god Rhadamanthus, a fair-haired
deity who exercises a benevolent sway over his perfect kingdom.
The balmy air, mingled with the perfume of sweet-scented
blossoms, is tempered by zephyrs and whispering winds. It is
never too hot nor too cold. Snow and storm have no place in
this delectable country. In Hesiod, in addition to this description, Elysium is said to be ruled over by Cronus, the father
of Rhadamanthus, the latter sharing his sovereignty and
administering judgment. Heroes who never died, but were
transferred from the realms above without pain, were the
principal subjects of Elysium.

A later theory describes Elysium as a part of the Underworld.

THE SLAVONIC PLACE OF THE DEAD

It is testified by Cosmos of Prague and other early writers
that the pagan Slavs believed in the continuance of life after
death, and naturally therefore in an abode of the dead ; but it
is probable that this region was not a place of reward or punishment till the influence of foreign ideas made it so. The abode
of the dead was called by the pre-Christian Slavs *peklo*, *raj*, or
nav, which some authorities have endeavoured to collate with
the Greek *naus*, the Latin *navis*; and colour is lent to this
connexion by the ancient Slav custom of burying their dead in
boats, wherein the soul travelled to its abiding-place. More
probably, however, *nav* is from the root *ny*, which expresses the
idea of death (thus *navi*, the dead, *unaviti*, to kill). The historian Dlugosz identifies a god Nya, ruler of the Underworld
and the souls of the dead, with Pluto ; and another possibility
is that the word *nav* still lingers in the Little Russian *mavka*

INTRODUCTION TO MYTHOLOGY

or *navka*, a species of elf or nymph, believed to be the spirit of an unbaptized child.

It is most likely that the terms *raj* and *peklo* were formerly synonymous with *nav*—that is, designated a Hades where life continued much the same as on the earth; but in later times *raj* came to signify the Elysian fields, *peklo* Tartarus. Both words occur prior to the introduction of Christianity, although Christianity modified their use. The derivation of *raj* cannot be traced with any certainty. It appears elsewhere as *vuirei*, said to be connected with the Elysian *vireta* of Virgil. It is generally pictured as an island far out in the sea, a place of eternal sunshine and happiness, where dwell the souls not only of the dead, but of those who have not yet been born. Here also are the birds that in autumn take flight from the earth-world, and the seeds of the flowers that have perished; types of all things that vanish from the earth in winter are here preserved, to be restored to the waiting world in springtime. The mystic isle of Buyán is one variant of the *raj*. Its name is probably derived from an adjective signifying 'burning,' 'ardent,' or 'fruitful,' and the isle itself is connected with the idea of the sun, of warmth, intense light, and fruitfulness. Buyán is the resting-place of the white stone Alatnir, a potent magical instrument frequently mentioned in spells and charms. Like everything else connected with Buyán, Alatnir is of burning, dazzling brilliance.

Peklo also was associated with the idea of heat, possessing affinities with the verb *pech*, to parch; but whereas *raj* came to signify Paradise, *peklo*, under the influence of Christian ideas, became identified later with the infernal regions, a place of punishment for the wicked dead. In modern folklore we find mention of a subterranean place of the dead called *Ad*, inhabited by demons who torment the souls of evil-doers; the corresponding Heaven (of the "Jack and the Beanstalk" kind) is equally vague and indeterminate; and both have been so evidently influenced by Christian conceptions that they reveal but little of their pagan ancestry.

The *nav* of the ancients was reached by various ways. Sometimes, as has been indicated, the soul had to traverse a wide sea in the boat-shaped coffin provided by relatives left on earth. Sometimes, again, the journey was accomplished on foot, when a pair of boots was provided ; or the soul might have to climb a mountain of iron or glass, and for this the parings of its mortal nails were laid in the coffin. The road leading to the celestial regions was generally the Milky Way, though sometimes the rainbow was trodden by the dead. In either case popular imagination pictured the *nav* a long distance away.

THE CELTIC OTHERWORLD

Besides a belief in a land of the dead, the Celts had an Otherworld to which favoured mortals might penetrate. This region possessed many names—Mag Mor, the Great Plain ; Tir n' Aill, the Otherworld ; Tir-nan-og, the Land of Youth, the Shining Land ; and so forth. It is also called in Celtic myth the Isle of the Men of Falga, Falga being an old name for the Isle of Man, which was connected with the god Manannan, lord of the under-seas.

This Celtic Elysium was sometimes beyond the seas, sometimes under the seas, or it might be situated in the hollow hills ; and sometimes it was the abode of the *Sidhe* or elder gods. It is alluded to in the Voyage of Bran, in the Cuchulainn cycle, and in the tale of Laegaire mac Crimthainn. In Celtic myth it was clearly distinguished from the subterranean place of the dead ; it was a blessed region which only a favoured few might hope to reach during life. The subterranean home of the earth-gods is sometimes a place of the dead, because Celtic myth is predominantly agricultural.

The Otherworld, shrouded by mist, was upon the same plane as the terrestrial, or sometimes co-extensive with it. There dwelt the gods and other supernatural beings. It had some resemblance to the Mohammedan Paradise in its purely material delights, yet was not without its spiritual aspect. It conferred oblivion for a term of years on those who visited it, like that later Land of Faerie where long forgetfulness awaits the wight who wanders in its enchanted glades. The Celtic Elysium is the first step in the evolution of a Heaven.

INTRODUCTION TO MYTHOLOGY

The gods connected with it were Manannan and Lug, the sun-god, probably because it lay in the western sea.

Some think that the Celtic Elysium was coloured by Christian story, but such a very sensuous Paradise possesses little of the character of a Christian Heaven.

THE HEAVEN OF ANCIENT MEXICO

Various destinations awaited the dead in ancient Mexico. Warriors slain in battle repaired to the sun, where they dwelt in bliss with the deity who presided over that luminary; and sacrificed captives also fared thither. These followed the sun in his course, crying aloud and beating upon their shields. "It is also said," writes old Sahagun in his *History of the Affairs of New Spain*,[1] "that in this heaven are trees and forests of diverse sorts. The offerings which the living of this world make to the dead duly arrive at their destination, and are received in this heaven. After four years of sojourn in that place the souls of the dead are changed into diverse species of birds, having rich plumage of the most brilliant colours."[2] These were known as *tzinzonme* ('little bird which flies from flower to flower'), and they flitted from blossom to blossom on earth as well as in Heaven, sucking the rich fragrance from the tropical blooms of the deep valleys of Anahuac.

Tlalocan, an even more material Paradise, was that of the water-god or deity of moisture, Tlaloc. Sahagun calls this a "terrestrial Paradise" "where they feign that there is surfeit of pleasure and refreshment, void for a space of torment." In that delectable region there is plenteousness of green maize, of calabashes, pepper, tomatoes, and haricots, and it is filled with variegated blossoms. There dwell the god Tlaloc and his followers. The persons who gain admittance are those slain by lightning or thunderbolt, the leprous, and the dropsical—those whose deaths have in any way been caused *through the agency of water*—for Tlaloc is god of that element; and existence there is perpetual. The Paradise of Tlaloc was situated in the mountains, in a climate of eternal summer.

[1] Appendix to Book III, chap. iii.
[2] I quote from my own manuscript translation of Sagahun.

PARADISE AND PUNISHMENT

THE AZTEC ABODE OF THE DEAD

The Hades of the Aztec race was Mictlan, presided over by Mictlantecutli (Lord of Mictlan) and his spouse (Mictecaciuatl). The souls of the defunct who fared thither were those who died of disease, chiefs, great personages, or humbler folk. On the day of death the priest harangued the deceased, telling him that he was about to fare to a region "where there is neither light nor window," but all was shadow—a veritable land of chiaroscuro, reached by a route swarming with grisly inimical forms. On arrival at the dreary court of Mictlan the defunct offered gifts to its lord—coloured paper, perfumes, and torches, mantles and other apparel, provided before cremation. It was a four years' journey to the first of the nine Hells of Mictlan, over a deep and wide river, on whose shores dwelt the dogs providently buried with the dead and employed to carry them across the stream.

Above the nine Hells of Mictlan were thirteen Heavens, the first containing planets, the second the Tzitzimime, or demons, the third the Centzon Mimizcoa, or four hundred stars of the Northern Hemisphere. The fourth was inhabited by birds, the fifth by fire-snakes (perhaps comets); the sixth was the home of the winds; the seventh harboured dust; and in the eighth dwelt gods. The remainder were placed at the disposal of the high primal and creative gods, Tonacatecutli and his spouse Tonacaciuatl, whose particular home was in the thirteenth and highest Heaven.

THE RED MAN'S AFTER-LIFE

The red men of North and South America knew no place of future reward or punishment. They regarded the future life merely as a shadowy extension of this—more wonderful, more supernatural, perhaps more desirable because of its material delights, but still of the earth earthy. The land of the sun was for them the land of future bliss.

"Where the sun lives," they informed the earliest foreign visitors, were the villages of the deceased, and the Milky Way which nightly spans the arch of Heaven was, in their opinion,

INTRODUCTION TO MYTHOLOGY

the road thither, and was called the path of souls (*le chemin des âmes*). To *Hueyu ku*, the mansion of the sun, said the Caribs, the soul passes when death overtakes the body. To the warm South-west, whence blows the wind which brings the sunny days and the ripening corn, said the New England natives to Roger Williams, will all souls go.

"Our knowledge is scanty of the doctrines taught by the Incas concerning the soul, but this much we do know, that they looked to the sun, their recognised lord and protector, as he who would care for them at death, and admit them to his palaces. There—not indeed, exquisite joys—but a life ot unruffled placidity, void of labour, vacant of strong emotions, a sort of material Nirvana, awaited them." [1]

From Peru to the coast of Brazil, the savage millions who inhabited that great stretch of watered forest pointed to the west, to the region beyond the mountains or the blessed abode of their ancestors, where in a continual state of intoxication they whiled away the hours of bliss. The people of the Pampas and Patagonia considered the sky to be the home of the dead, where they dwelt as stars. During the night they patrol the sky, but at sunrise flock around the great luminary and are bitten by his beams.

The Hurons, Iroquois, Chippeway, Algonquins, and Dakotas all told of a deep and swift stream that the soul must cross, bridged either by an enormous snake, a slender tree, or by some other precarious means, such as a stone canoe.

In old Peru, Çupay, the shadow, ruled a land of shades in the centre of the earth. To him went all souls not destined to be the companions of the sun. But, like nearly all savage Hells, this was merely a 'place of the dead' and not a place of retribution. Xibalba, the Hades of the Kiches of Guatemala, was a grisly Underworld ruled by a veritable secret society having rules of initiation. The name is derived from a root meaning 'to fear,' from which also comes the Maya term for 'phantom' or 'ghost,' and this derivation shows it to have been a place of the dead. In the *Popol Vuh*, the sacred and traditional book of the Kiches, we find nothing to indicate that

[1] Brinton, *Myths of the New World.*

PARADISE AND PUNISHMENT

Xibalba was a place of punishment. Those who entered it had to undergo tests analogous to those which a Red Indian must endure upon his initiation into any of the numerous esoteric societies still to be found among American barbarians; but torment is otherwise absent. The scenery of Xibalba is varied. It is gloomy, with a river of blood, a stream full of gourds, plantations of calabashes, courts for the ball-game, in which its lords are very expert, and stone buildings. It is ruled by grim lords, One-Death and Seven-Deaths. It is stated in the *Popol Vuh* that these were more 'devils' than gods. " In the old times they did not have much power. They were but avengers and opposers of men, and, in truth, they were not regarded as gods."

THE CHINOOKS

The Chinooks believe that after death the spirit of the deceased drinks at a large hole in the ground, after which it shrinks and passes on to the country of the ghosts, where it is fed with spirit food. After drinking of the water and partaking of the fare of spirit-land, the soul becomes the irrevocable property of the dead, and may not return to earth. But every person is possessed of two spirits, a greater and a lesser, and during sickness it is this lesser soul which is spirited away by the denizens of ghost-land. The Navahos have a similar belief. They assert that in the personal soul there is none of the vital force which animates the body, nor any of the mental power, but a third entity, a sort of spiritual body (like the *ka* of the ancient Egyptians), which may leave its owner and become lost, much to his danger and discomfort. Among the Mexicans a similar spirit-body ('tonal') was recognized, much the same in character, indeed, as the 'astral body' of modern spiritualism. Among them, as with the Maya of Yucatan, it came into existence with the name, and for this reason the personal name was sacred and rarely uttered. It was regarded as part of the individuality, and through it the ego might be injured. This belief is general among the aboriginal peoples of both Americas.

In the country of the ghosts we see a striking analogy to the old classical idea of Hades. It is a place of windless, soundless half-dusk, inhabited by shadows who shrink from tumult of any description, and pass a sort of shadowy extension of earthly life. It is to be sharply distinguished from the country of the 'Supernatural People,' who lead a much more satisfying existence.

There are other and still more mysterious regions in the sky, recorded in the Amerindian myth of Aqas Xenas Xena. It tells how a boy who has slain his mother mounts to the celestial sphere by a chain fastened to the end of an arrow. He first meets the Darkness, and is then accosted by the evening star, who asks if he has seen his game, and explains that he is hunting men. He reaches the house of the evening star, and finds his sons and daughter at home counting over the game-bag of the day—dead folk. The daughter is the moon. The same thing occurs in the house of the morning star, whose daughter is the sun. The sons of the one star are at war with those of the other. He marries the moon, and has children united in the middle. He returns to earth with his wife and progeny, whom Blue Jay separates, and they die, returning to the Sky with their mother and becoming the 'sun-dogs.' In this day and night myth we recognize the widespread belief in celestial regions where man exists not after death, a belief common to nearly all American mythologies.

There is a similar myth relating to the sun, which is kept in the hut of an old woman dwelling in the skies. From her an adventurous hero obtains a blanket to render him immune. The myth was probably invented to explain sunstroke.

In his work on the Lengua Indians of South America Mr W. B. Grubb gives this account of their beliefs:

" The unseen world in its relation to man is naturally much more clearly defined by the Indian. He holds that the *aphangak* or departed souls of men in the shade world (*pischischi*, shadows) merely continue their present life, only of course in a disembodied state. The souls of the departed are supposed, in the ethereal state, to correspond exactly in form and characteristics with the bodies they have left. A tall man and a short man remain tall and short as spirits; a deformed man remains deformed. A kindly-natured man continues so in shade-land. A witch-doctor, or a great chief, feared and respected in the body, is feared and respected in the spirit-world. Those who were related in this world associate with each other in the next. Departed spirits continue the same tribal and clan life as when in the body. The spirit of a child remains a child and does not develop, and for this reason is not feared. Infanticide is not regarded as murder in the same degree as the murder of an adult. No punishment follows the murderer of an infant, nor is its murder attended by the ordinary superstitious fears. A murderer—that is, according to the Indian idea, a man who kills one of his own tribe—is not only executed for the crime, but his body is burnt, and the ashes scattered to the four winds. The Indian believes that after such treatment his spirit cannot take human form, and remains in the after-world shapeless and unrecognizable, and therefore unable to mingle with its kindred spirits, or to enjoy such social intercourse as exists.

"The *aphangak* is supposed to hunt, travel, garden, and carry on more or less his old life, but of course in spirit form, and pursuing only spiritual essences. The spirits of the dead appear to take no interest in the living, nor, beyond causing uncanny feelings when supposed to be hovering about, do they seem in the least to influence those left behind. Their very names are not mentioned, and every effort is made by the living to forget them. . . .

"Speaking generally, three ideas seem to prevail regarding the future abode of the soul. The lower type of Indian holds that the *aphangak* continues to wander disconsolately about the country in company with its kindred spirits, while the more intelligent are of opinion that it moves over to the west, to the cities of the dead, already referred to in dealing with their origin. A few, however, hold a view similar to that prevailing among the Southern tribes—namely, that the dead inhabit a world beneath the earth.

"The lower creation, with the exception of fish and serpents, are supposed to share immortality with men. Birds, cattle, and the carnivora, especially of the leading types, figure largely in their beliefs of the shade-world, as also the dog, jaguar, horse, ostrich, and the thunder-bird."

INTRODUCTION TO MYTHOLOGY

AFRICAN IDEAS OF THE FUTURE LIFE

Among African savages generally the life of the dead is merely an extension of earth-life. In the Kimbunda district of South-west Africa the dead dwell in a region called Kalunga, where they have plenty of provisions and an abundance of female servitors. They engage in the dance and the chase for pastime. In Kalunga the sun shines when it is night in the world of mortals. The Basutos believe in an Otherworld of green valleys, where the dead own herds of hornless and speckled cattle from which they can draw sustenance. Others of the same people believe that the dead wander about in silent reserve, with no feelings of joy or sorrow to agitate them or disturb what seems to be a condition of nescience. There is no moral retribution. The West Africans do not seem to believe in a 'land of heart's desire.' The Dahomans hold that in the Otherworld social status will be unchanged. Thus the king will retain his sovereignty and the slave his serfdom 'for ever.' He also credits the existence of another land beyond the grave, 'Ku-to-men' or Dead Man's Land, a place of ghosts and shadows. Turning southward again, the Zulus think that after death their souls proceed to the land of the Abapansi or underground folk.

BORNEO

In Borneo the Idaan race have a Heaven which is to be seen. Indeed, it is situated on the summit of Mount Kina Balu, on whose peak no native guide would pass the, night. There the adventurous traveller is shown the moss on which the spirits feed, and the hoof-prints of their ghostly herds of buffalo. The Sajera of West Java possess another such Heaven on the summit of Tunung Danka. It took Mr Jonathan Rigg ten years to discover this fact among a population outwardly professing Mohammedanism.[1] The Fijians consider that Bolotu, the island of the gods, lies in the ocean north-west of Tonga. It is extensive and is replete with everything which can make for an existence of physical satisfaction. Like the

[1] *Journal of the Indian Archipelago*, vol. iv, p. 119.

PARADISE AND PUNISHMENT

Norsemen, they believe that the swine slaughtered in their Paradise will reappear when again required for the feast. The Samoan Otherworld is a mere shadowy replica of this.

CONCLUSIONS

From these data several considerations of importance arise. We see that among the classical religions of antiquity—the Egyptian, Babylonian, Hebrew, for example—the idea of judgment, retribution, and reward arose in connexion with their places of bliss and punishment. On the other hand, we find in the myths of the Teutons, Mexicans, and people in the barbaric stages generally that a place of bliss is reserved, in most cases, for the warrior, while those who die a 'straw death' are deemed unfit to enter the Valhalla of the brave. Still further down in the scale of civilization we see that Africans, American Indians, Fijians, and other people in a state of savagery more or less, regard the future dwelling-place of the soul as a pale reflex of the world in which they have been accustomed to dwell—sometimes with mitigating circumstances and improved surroundings. Thus the savage hunts, gorges himself, and wallows in happy intoxication; the more advanced barbarian comports himself as a warrior and feasts homerically; while the civilized man must be judged ere he can betake himself to an immortal destination of bliss or torture. Only in the higher reaches of civilization does any idea of judgment, retribution, or reward, as distinguished from mere sensuous pleasure, enter into the future life.

There is one strange exception to this rule, and that is Greece. This is probably because Greek ethics was nurtured more upon philosophic than religious ideals. We find the exact opposite of the philosophic ethics of Hellas in the drastic religious morality of the Semitic race. The idea of judgment is seen only in early Greek myth.

But the most important question for us, discussing the manufacture and evolution of myth, is: How far have ethical promptings influenced mythic conceptions of a place of future reward or punishment?

They have influenced it very powerfully. Let us regard these beliefs in the line of their evolution. In primitive (*i.e.*, savage) civilization we find a mere home of the dead, like that of the peoples of the north-west coast of America, the Samoans, or the peoples of Western Africa. The dead there may be kings or medicine-men, warriors or slaves, as in the mortal life, but there is no ruler, no Pluto or Satan. Later, in the barbaric stage, we find monarchs or arch-devils, such as Mictlantecutli of Mexico, Çupay of Peru, or Hel of Scandinavia. These, however, are merely there from a supposed necessity for a headship, or because they chance to be corn-spirits like the Greek Persephone ; for agricultural spirits usually reside in the earth. Indeed the myth of Persephone well illustrates the adaptation of a corn-spirit to the lordship (or ladyship) of Hades, and probably represents a fusion of myths in which that of the corn-spirit was grafted on to the already accepted lord of the place of the dead. The daughter of the chief of Xibalba, the Kiche Hell, is also a corn-spirit, as witness her gathering of a basket of maize where no maize had grown before ; and even Osiris, great god of the Egyptian dead, was primarily connected with the 'agricultural interest.'

It is only in the higher stages of religion, when ethical significance has become a *fait accompli*, that we find the god of the Otherworld metamorphosed into a judge who disposes of the souls of men according to their deserts. Thus we find that ethical ideas strongly affect the mythic character of the lords of the Otherworld, and may alter them from mere presiding demons into god-like arbiters of the fate of the soul. Further, the introduction, evolution, or acceptance of ethical ideas may entirely alter the scenery and geography of the Hades myth, and from a nebulous environment of ghostly savagery the place of the dead may on the one hand blossom into a sensuous Paradise or flash into flame as Gehenna.

HEAVEN AND THE SKY

The manner in which Heaven, the place of bliss, came to be associated with the sky and the region of woe with the Underworld is worthy of brief consideration. We have seen that many various peoples—Celts, Indians, Fijians—believed

PARADISE AND PUNISHMENT

their Paradise, their 'land of heart's desire,' to be in the west, where sinks the dying sun. To the mind of primitive man the sun was the source of all good, the nourisher, the giver of light; and no bliss greater than that of accompanying him in his course through the heavens could be imagined. Man beheld him sink and die in the waves of ocean or behind the peaks of the great mountains, and, comparing this with the death of his own kind, concluded that the luminary betook himself to rest in some region beyond the verge of sea or sierra. " If the souls of the dead follow the sun it must be to such a region," he would argue: so would arise the concept of a Tir-nan-og, a sun-Paradise beyond the world's rim.[1]

Not thus did all religious philosophers of old time reason— not thus the mythographers of Babylon, for example, those astrologer-priests who watched from tower and temple the wheelings of the white host of stars which silvered the skies above the city of Bel. These had identified the various gods in their pantheon with the stars and heavenly bodies. Once this had been done it is easy to understand how the gods were conceived as dwelling in the sky. Races who believed in a Paradise beyond the setting sun did not place their great divinities in the sky. The Celtic gods lived in their sunset Elysium; the deities of the Samoan tale dwell in an island Paradise. Roughly, peoples dwelling near the western sea (Celts, West Africans, North-west American Indians, etc.) locate their Paradise beneath the rim of ocean; peoples dwelling at the foot of mountain ranges (Greeks, Javanese, etc). believe the Otherworld to be situated on their summits; while peoples dwelling in plains or deserts (Plains Indians, Babylonians, certain Egyptian castes, etc.) place their Heaven in the sky among the constellations.

HADES AND THE UNDERWORLD

On the other hand, the Otherworld becomes the Under-world, because of the subterranean burial of the dead. Under the earth is the home of the dead, and there rest their shades or spirits. The Greeks believed Hades to be situated only

[1] Compare the recently coined (?) war phrase or idiom ' gone west.'

twelve feet beneath the surface of the soil. Again, the practice of burial in caverns may have assisted this belief. The scenery of the Otherworld, from Homer to Dante, is decidedly cavernous. The lords of Hell are frequently the gods of a conquered or subject race, relegated to the Underworld by the policy or contempt of the conquerors. Thus the Irish Tuatha de Danann, who dwell underground, were once the chief gods of Ireland, and were displaced by an incoming people; and we can trace in the gigantic figure of Osiris the primeval god of an agricultural people placed over the popular world of the Egyptian dead, partly perhaps by the deliberate policy of the priests of Ra, partly by reason of his status as a corn-god, and developing into the great ruler of the realm of the dead.

CHAPTER VIII
FOLKLORE AND MYTH

FOLK-TALE, and indeed folklore of every description, is worthy of study by the student of myth; for not only will he often find that the principles which govern it are identical with those of myth, but he will glean much knowledge of methods from those who work this neighbouring row in the vineyard of tradition.

Some people regard mythology as merely a branch of wider study of folklore, but in the definitions in the first the chapter of this work we called the former "the study of a primitive or early form of religion while it was a living faith," and folklore "the study of primitive religion and customs still practised." Let us now examine the writings of the great authorities on folklore and see what they have to say upon this interesting subject.

Sir George Gomme, in his *Folklore as an Historical Science* (p. 148), says: "The folk-tale is secondary to the myth. It is the primitive myth dislodged from its primitive place. It has become a part of the life of the people independently of its primary form and object and in a different sense. The mythic or historic fact has been obscured, or has been displaced from the life of the people. But the myth lives on through the affections of the people for the traditions of their older life. They love to tell the story which their ancestors revered as myth, even though it has lost its oldest and most impressive significance. The artistic setting of it, born of the years through which it has lived, fashioned by the minds which have handed it down and embellished it through the generations, has helped its life. It has become the fairy tale or the nursery tale. It is told to grown-up people, not as belief, but as what

221

was once believed; it is told to children, not to men; to lovers of romance, not to worshippers of the unknown; it is told by mothers and nurses, not by philosophers or priestesses; in the gathering ground of home life, or in the nursery, not in the hushed sanctity of a great wonder."

Coming down to hard-and-fast definition, Sir George Gomme says: "The myth belongs to the most primitive stages of human thought, and is the recognisable explanation of some natural phenomenon, some forgotten or unknown object of human origin, or some event of lasting influence; the folk-tale is a survival preserved amidst culture-surroundings of a more advanced stage, and deals with events and ideas of primitive times in terms of the experience or of episodes in the lives of unnamed human beings; the legend belongs to an historical personage, locality, or event. These are new definitions, and are suggested in order to give some sort of exactness to the terms in use. All these terms—myth, folk-tale, and legend—are now used indiscriminately with no particular definiteness. The possession of three such distinct terms forms an asset which should be put to its full use, and this cannot be done until we agree upon a definite meaning for each."

Dean Macculloch in his valuable *Childhood of Fiction* (p. 432) says: "The mythological school represented by the writings of De Gubernatis, Cox, Max Müller, and others, have found the origin of folk-tales in the myths of the Aryan race. Folk-tales are the detritus of such Aryan myths, when the meaning of the myths themselves was long forgotten. The whole theory falls to the ground when it is discovered that exactly similar stories are told by non-Aryan races, and that the incidents of such stories are easily explainable by actual customs and ideas of savages and primitive folk everywhere. On the other hand, many folk-tales have originated as myths explanatory of existing customs, or by way of explaining phenomena which seemed to depend on these customs, and when the customs fell into desuetude the myths remained as folk-tales. The incidents of existing folk-tales, again, have frequently been embodied in mythologies—Greek, Celtic,

FOLKLORE AND MYTH

Japanese. Thus there is throughout an intimate connection between mythology and folk-tales, though not of the kind which De Gubernatis and others imagined." Again: "Folk-tales have a vital connection with myth and saga, though the connection is far from that insisted on by Max Müller and the mythological school. Still another link of connection may be perceived in many European *Märchen*, where the gods and mythic figures of an earlier faith have been metamorphosed into ogres, witches, and fairies, and where the dimly-remembered the story of that earlier religion have supplied incidents for ~~a later age."~~

In a note to his *Mythology and Folklore* (p. 7) Sir George Cox furnishes the philological view of the relation of mythology to folklore: "It is, perhaps, open to doubt whether the terms mythology and folklore are likely to retain permanently their present relative meanings. Neither term is altogether satisfactory; but the distinction between tales susceptible of philological analysis and those which are not must nevertheless be carefully maintained, as indispensable to any scientific treatment of the subject. In his introduction to *The Science of Language*, Mr Sayce admits 'that it is often difficult to draw the line between folklore and mythology, to define exactly where the one ends and the other begins, and there are many instances in which the two terms overlap one another.'"

It is demonstrable that the author of the term folklore, the late Mr W. J. Thoms (1803–1885), deputy librarian of the House of Lords and founder and editor of *Notes and Queries*, did not intend it to include mythology. He said that he intended it to designate "that department of the study of antiquities and archæology which embraces everything relating to ancient observances and customs, to the notions, beliefs, traditions, superstitions, and prejudices of the common people." It will be remarked that this definition does not include "the study of a primitive or early religion *while it was a living faith*."

But the study of folklore is, as has been said, greatly capable of assisting the student of myth. A Roman sword or a Saxon cup exhumed after many centuries are no less the blade once wielded by a Roman, or the vessel from which the Saxon imbibed, solely because centuries have elapsed since they were in use by their original owners, nor do they fail to yield us information concerning the lives and habits of those to whom they belonged. In the same manner a story or custom long embedded in the earth of superstition is no less capable of throwing light upon ancient religion and thus upon ancient myth. Many folk-tales are merely ' broken-down ' myths, but by no means *all* folk-tales are so, as numbers were invented for purposes of amusement and partake of the character of fiction.

As an instance of the manner in which ... belief can influence true myth we have only to look at the tales of the Knights of the Round Table. Arthur, Merlin, and many of the lesser figures of the galaxy of Camelot are in reality British Celtic deities metamorphosed into medieval knights. A similar instance, perhaps of added interest because of its novelty, has recently come under the notice of the writer.

THE LEGEND OF ST TRIDUANA

The story of St Triduana and her healing well, situated at Restalrig, near Edinburgh, is a tale of the kind the student of myth delights to encounter; for what may appear to the uninitiated to be an ordinary saintly legend is, he readily sees, a fragment of true myth.

The story of the sainted lady who, in her latter days, dwelt at Restalrig, or Lestalryk, is in the grand style, and combines the poignant pathos of Euripidean tragedy with the fanaticism of mistaken religious zeal. The glorious virgin Triduana of Colosse, we are told, arrived in Scotland from Achaia, in Greece, with the holy St Regulus, or Rule, the traditional founder of St Andrews, at some date between A.D. 237 and the eighth century. This mission was evidently that entrusted to bring the relics of St Andrew to Scotland and charged with the plantation of the Christian faith in that country. The lady found a retreat at Rescobie, in Forfarshire, where she dwelt in great piety; but her Grecian beauty proved a snare for the susceptibilities of the Pictish king Nectanivan or Nechtan, who became hotly enamoured of her. Flying before his zealous wooing, she came to Dunfallandy in Athol, where his emissaries speedily discovered her. Perturbed and seemingly incredulous that a monarch should rate her charms so highly, Triduana asked of the King's messengers what so great a prince desired of her, a poor virgin dedicated to God. The reply was couched in terms which betray the Celt, and we are left with the firm conviction that he who vouchsafed it was none other than the King's *seanachaidh* or bard. " He desireth," said that person, "the most excellent beauty of thine eyes, which if he obtain not he will surely die." Triduana's retort was typical of the Christian martyr, and we are left wondering whether she was possessed with a fanaticism which surpassed her sense of humour, or of a grim penchant for the ridiculous which transcended all fanaticism. "What he seeketh he shall surely have," she exclaimed, and thereupon she plucked out her eyes, skewered them on a thorn, and handed them to the King's messengers with the words : " Take that which your prince desireth." Later she betook herself to Restalrig, where she pursued the life religious until her death.

Throughout the Middle Ages the shrine and well of St Triduana were famous for the cure of blindness, and to it came pilgrims from all parts of Scotland and the north of England. Sir David Lyndsay makes two allusions to it. Devotees thronged to St Tredwell, he says, "to mend their eine," and again he states in his curious inventory of saints in *The Monarchie* :

> Sanct Tredwall, als, thare may be sene
> Quhilk on ane prick hes baith her ene.

At Rescobie, her first place of sojourn in Scotland, each September brought round a St Trodlin's Fair.

Authorities are divided as to the exact site of St Triduana's Well. Indeed, much confusion attaches to the subject. A well dedicated to St Margaret, and roofed by a structure obviously copied from or copied by the chapter-house hard by Restalrig Church, stood for many generations on a site now covered by the locomotive works of the North British Railway Company. (Its groined roof now shelters *another* St Margaret's Well in the

King's Park.) This well I do not believe to have been, as is generally stated, that of St Triduana, afterward known as St Margaret's. I incline to the belief that the building known as the 'chapter-house,' close to Restalrig Church, and almost certainly a chapel of St Triduana, sheltered the original well. This building was erected at the close of the fifteenth century, and was probably the second or third so raised over the miraculous well to which came the stricken from all over broad Scotland. It is a notable fact that since the restoration of this chapter-house modern engineering skill has proved unequal to the task of stemming the flow of water, which constantly remains at the same level here. Was not this, then, the ancient bath-house of the shrine of St Trid, down whose steps groped the sightless in hope of the precious boon of light?

What is the mythical kernel to this saintly tale?

Firstly, be it noted, St Triduana does not figure in the Roman calendar.

Secondly, such wells as hers are by no means uncommon in Britain. Well-worship is still to be traced in the Celtic or semi-Celtic portions of the country—Wales, Lancashire, and Scotland. In Teutonic Southern England, although many wells are still known as 'holy,' no trace of any reason for regarding them as such remains; but a fully developed ritual is still observed in drawing from many wells in Wales. Thus at St Tegla's Well, near Wrexham, coppers are cast into the water, the well is thrice perambulated, and a cock left as an offering by the patient who suffers from epilepsy. Semi-Celtic Shropshire, too, is rich in wells which cure sore eyes, and Miss C. S. Burne of that county, in *Shropshire Folklore*, suggests that the legend in the Scandinavian prose Edda of Odin giving his eye in return for a draught of water from the wisdom-giving well of Mimir might perhaps account for it. I myself had arrived at the same conclusion before perusing Miss Burne's work, and I further think that the theory is strengthened by Odin being a sun-god; the round 'eye' of the sun pierces the depths of the dark water in which it is reflected. Indeed I advanced some such explanation in the article "Mimir" in my *Dictionary of Mythology*, published in 1910.

FOLKLORE AND MYTH

We know that after the introduction of Christianity into ancient Gaul those well-spirits in which Celtic imagination delighted were frequently metamorphosed into saints, and that the teeming Gallic pantheon added many a name to the calendar of Rome. May not the same be true of our Restalrig saint? The name is obviously Latinized. It appears as 'Triduana' in a charter of James IV, but to the people she was St Trid, and we have seen that Rescobie folk called her Trodlin—an affectionate diminutive. We probably have in Trid-well a spot where the mystic rites of some Celtic goddess of the spring were celebrated. Was not the 'Young Tamlane' of Carterhaugh, near Selkirk, such a well-spirit or deity?

> There's nane that goes by Carterhaugh
> But maun leave him a wad

or pledge. Also he was "a wee, wee man." The portion of the ballad that makes him a mortal kidnapped by fairies is only a clumsy late explanation of the older myth of well-sprite or god, obviously lurking beneath. Is Triduana the old British goddess Keridwen who possessed the mystic cauldron Amen, conferring inspiration (or clear sight) on whoever drank of its waters?

Another good example of myth run to seed in folk-tale is the fairly widespread story of the musician who ventures to explore an underground passage, and never returns. The mythological pedigree of this tale is very clear indeed; but it seems better in the interests of the reader (having first reasoned from effect to cause) to reverse the usual method of folklore for once and argue from known cause to effect. Starting, then, with such myths as those of Orpheus, Ishtar, and others, in which the object is to demonstrate how death may be vanquished and the dead restored, we find the plot turned to the uses of folk-lore, the heroes entering upon a quest in the Underworld of Fairyland or the abode of a dishonoured goddess, rather than in the sad shades of Hades. Thus Ogier the Dane essays the Land of Faerie, and Tannhaüser enters the Hill of Venus or Holda—the Hörselberg—as Thomas the Rhymer enters the Hill of Ercildoune. Is there a formula? Can we reduce the general circumstances to a least common denominator something like this?

An adventurous person, usually a musician or maker of poetry, ventures underground (1) in myth to recover a beloved one from the clutches of death, (2) in folklore to gain the love of the Queen of Faerie, or some discredited goddess who takes her place.

But we have not yet plumbed the depths of mythic degeneration. From the allurements of Fairyland we descend still farther to the more dusty shadows of the underground passage. Very numerous are the local tales which tell of these. Thus in Edinburgh a piper accompanied by his dog (for so were the dead ever accompanied in primitive times) dares the dangers of an underground passage from the cliff-perched Castle to Holyrood Palace. The sound of his pipes guides those who follow his progress standing in the streets above, but at a certain point the music ceases and the piper never returns.

A SCOTTISH FAUST

In this volume it has been the policy of the author to give where possible examples which have come within his own personal notice, thus avoiding such as have done service again and again in works on myth and folklore; but to show how a folk-tale of universal fame and interest may become localized we will repeat one of these here. The Faust legend, based upon the pact with Satan, has many variants; but surely it is surprising to a degree to discover it as a local story in a Scottish lowland community.

Persons who sell themselves to the Devil are met with in the popular fiction of all European countries; but the legend of the 'Warlock Laird' of Leith, or its *dénouement* at least, so closely resembles the Faust story that we can hardly help ascribing a common origin to them.

In that part of Leith once known as the Lees quarter resided a person known as the Warlock Laird. His house was dissimilar from those which surrounded it, for although the portion which served as a dwelling was only one story in height, from the back of it rose a tall, circular tower about fifty feet high, enriched with curious little turrets and lit with many strange windows. For what purpose the tower had been erected is not known, and although it had been built for many years when Gordon first took up residence in the cottage attached to it, it was locally understood that he had erected it for the convenience of private consultations with the enemy of mankind. In popular romance a magician usually does business in a tower; *ergo*, a magician must have a tower ; or is it necessary that every tower should have its magician ? However that may be, Gordon, not a native, and well past middle age when he came to reside in Leith, specially selected this house as most suitable to his requirements, whatever those requirements were.

He gave out that he had spent many years at sea. When he first came his resources were slender, and he was glad to accept the situation of a labourer in a cooper's yard for a very small weekly stipend. When he had been for some months in this employment, he requested leave of absence for a week. On his return at the termination of that period it was remarked that he appeared to be better off than before : he looked sleeker, wore good clothes, and had money to spend ; but he continued his work, and matters took their normal course until, a year later, he asked for another holiday. At the expiry of this vacation a still more marked change was visible in his circumstances : he purchased a ruinous old house and gave more for it than was considered fair value. Suspicion began to be aroused among his neighbours. He spent his money freely, and this in itself may have suggested that he must have come by it lightly. It was even whispered that he had been a pirate, and that he was drawing gold from some hidden hoard as necessity arose. Once more he demanded a holiday, and his request was granted as usual, but this time he was not permitted to go away without a watch being set upon his movements. Those who had resolved to observe his actions while on holiday were rather disappointed, as on the first day of his leave he remained at home all the time. But on the following day he took ship for Kirkcaldy, on the sands of which he landed without any suspicions that he was being watched by a person, disguised as an elderly woman, sitting next him in the boat.

When Gordon landed he made straight for an inn, where he ordered a copious supply of liquor. After a brief exit he returned with half a dozen boatmen dressed in their best, and commenced a drinking-bout which lasted until two o'clock next morning. For two successive days after this he loafed about the town and the shore, chatting with the boatmen, much to the annoyance of the person who was engaged to watch his movements. Two days only remained now, and on the morning of the sixth day of his holiday he was seen to embark in a ferryman's boat, in which he proceeded down the Firth alone. His follower found some difficulty in hiring a craft, and by the time he had procured one Gordon's little vessel was concealed behind the huge bulk of Inchkeith. The boatman who hired out the vessel to the spy insisted on accompanying him, and he had perforce to assent to this. After they had passed Inchkeith, Gordon's boat was seen far in advance and close inshore on the Midlothian side of the river. On the right, near North Berwick, Gordon steered his craft inside of the rocky islet known as the Lamb, nearly opposite to where the picturesque village of Dirleton now stands. Here the Leith man shipped his oars, and gazing ahead fancied that he saw two gigantic figures moving to and fro, busily engaged in digging. At this point the boatman refused to approach any farther, rowed his passenger back, and landed him at Prestonpans, whence he made his way home.

Gordon returned as usual, but on the very same day he gave a week's notice of his intention to leave his situation. At the end of that time it was rumoured that he had bought up nearly the entire buildings on one side of the Broad Wynd, and it was this gigantic investment which gave rise to the story that he must have sold himself to the Devil. He was now known and addressed as 'Laird' Gordon, visited his tenants in turn, and when they announced their intention of giving up their houses "because they disliked becoming tenants of the Deil," he passed no comment upon their resolution. But there was not much house-room in Leith in those days, and one by one the objectors returned; but they never succeeded in getting an interview with Gordon, for when they called upon him he was either deeply engaged or had just left the house. As term-time drew nigh frantic endeavours were made to see him, but he could never be found alone: a tall dark man of authoritative mien always accompanied him. This personage was silent unless directly appealed to, but he seemed to control the Warlock Laird's every movement. On one occasion Gordon summoned all the tenants together, and, entering alone the room where they were met, he desired such of them as were in earnest in their applications to stand on their heads and strike their feet against the wall. This they very naturally refused to do, whereupon his sombre-looking companion appeared, and at once every man found himself standing on his head and kicking his heels in the air. Those who wished to retain their houses were allowed to do so, but were subjected to many annoyances by Gordon and his familiar, who paid them visits at all manner of unreasonable hours. On one occasion they were brought together into one house and compelled to dance until they fell down through sheer exhaustion. Those who had occupied new dwellings were so persecuted and tormented that they were glad to return to the Broad Wynd in order to free themselves of annoyance. But one day these cantrips ceased, and for many weeks nothing was seen of the Warlock Laird. When the day came round to call upon him and disburse rents, the tenants went in a body to the Yard-heads. A strange-looking man opened the door of Gordon's house at their summons and they were ushered into an apartment where they did not remain long before they heard piercing shrieks of agony mingled with prayers for mercy proceeding from the room directly overhead. They were about to leave the house, when the door of the room they were in was dashed open and Gordon rushed into their midst, closely pursued by his fiendish companion. He earnestly besought their protection, but they were so paralysed with fear as to be incapable of assisting him in any way. The dark and sinister-looking being who had companioned him so long threw himself on the trembling wretch and dragged him forcibly into the passage outside. A great slamming of doors and clanking of chains followed : then a terrible explosion shook the house from cellar to garret. Terrified beyond expression, Gordon's tenants made what haste they could to escape from so dangerous a locality, and on reaching the doorway they discovered that the tower connected with the house had been hurled to earth and that a strong sulphurous odour hung about its ruins. Some of them even asserted that as they crossed the threshold the ground in front of the house opened and they saw Gordon descending through it, accompanied by his mysterious companion. Nevermore was Anthony Gordon seen in the streets of the port, and his house remained a shunned and dreaded spot until time laid the cottage in ruins beside the prostrate tower.

Some twenty years afterward a beggar unacquainted with the local traditions was taking shelter among the ruins of the Warlock's house when he stumbled upon a small iron-bound chest, in which were the titles of the properties in Broad Wynd. With these he immediately absconded, and returning some six months afterward posed as the Warlock's heir and assumed possession of the property; but a curse seemed to rest upon it. The tale says that the dreadful visions by which he was haunted drove him to seek refuge in intoxication, although the converse is more probably true! He drank heavily, and was found dead one morning with his throat cut. So, in this very commonplace manner, the legend ends. The date of it cannot be ascertained, but it is probable that it may be placed somewhere about the end of the seventeenth or the beginning of the eighteenth century.

The manner in which the legend ends bears a strong resemblance to at least one version of the Faust story—that given by Wierus or Wier, the great demonologist, who in his *De præstigiis dæmonum* (Basel, 1563) tells how Faust was found with his neck wrung after the house had been shaken by a terrific din. Some students who occupied a chamber near by said that between twelve and one o'clock at midnight there blew a mighty storm of wind against the house as though it would have shaken the foundations out of their place. The students, alarmed, leapt from their beds, and then they became aware of a hissing in the hall as of thousands of snakes and adders. With that the hall door flew open and Dr Faustus rushed out, crying, "Murder, murder!" but after a little they heard him no more. Next day they found his mangled remains in the hall where the Devil had destroyed him.

There can be very little doubt that the Leith legend was based, in part at least, upon the German one. The story of Faust was commonly known in Britain by the end of the sixteenth century, and so had plenty of time to take on local colour and evolve under local superstition into the shape in which it is here given.

THE 'COMPLEMENTARY' PROCESS

One process in use among folklorists is of interest to students of myth because of its application to mythic material. This process I will call the 'complementary' process for want of a better name. It consists in building up or restoring a ritual act or tale from a number of fragmentary examples, perhaps scattered all over the world. For example, if we find a certain custom in England and an analogous custom in India plus some ritual circumstance which the English custom does not possess, we are justified in believing that the English custom once included it. Or if we find a certain tale in Africa, we may discover another closely resembling it in Ireland and possessing features which explain some break in the African story. The comparative and complementary methods are necessary to both folklorists and mythologists, because an isolated instance is of little use in the study of either science. These must be restored to association with all the known examples of their kind, and the earliest and most complete form may thus be discovered.

Sir George Gomme in his *Folklore as an Historical Science* (p. 171) says that a "restored and complete example is in a position to be compared either with similar survivals in other countries on the same level of culture, or within the same ethnological or political sphere of influence, or with living customs, rites, or beliefs of peoples of a more backward state of culture or in a savage state of culture. Comparison of this kind is of value. Comparison of a less technical or comprehensive kind may be of value in the hands of a great master ; but it is often not only valueless but mischievous in the hands of less experienced writers, who think that comparison is justified wherever similarity is discovered."

One of the common grounds of folklore and myth is that where religious elements obviously enter into folk-belief and custom. These may furnish us with new knowledge of a god or a cult. For example, many fragments of the old religion of Central America still linger in the folklore of the Indians of Guatemala ; the witch-lore of Italy is full of obscure allusions to the classical deities of Rome ; and the folklore of the Arabs of Egypt here and there touches hands with the ancient religion of that country. In Scotland such examples are frequent. That of the thunder-god Brounger has already been alluded to. It is on record that the fishermen of Newhaven, which Brounger haunted, have an almost equal dislike to hearing the name of a certain Johnny Boag or Boggie, and that they have been known to stay from sea because this name had been mentioned in their hearing while on the way to the boats. The Slavonic word for god is *bôg*—a word which has run through a number of modifications, but has finished with us Britons as 'bogy,' or 'bogle,' and 'bugbear' (compare Welsh *brog*, a goblin). At the fishing on the Cromarty Firth a salmon must never be spoken of. If it were, the whole crew would start, grasp the nearest iron thowel, and fervently exclaim, "Cauld iron, cauld iron!" in order to avert the omen. Thus the name was taboo, and it looks as if it were of the class of 'names of power' which may not be spoken. Certain 'hidden' names of the Egyptian deities also must not be spoken, or dire consequences would ensue. "If one of them is uttered on the bank of the river the torrent is set free." [1] It appears then as if 'Salmon' was the appellation of an ancient fish-totem whose name was taboo. Iron is of course the terror of all 'tricksy sprites,' and the theory has been advanced that the prehistoric bronze-users, in

---

[1] *Magical Papyrus* (Harris) 7, 1 *et seq.*

whom some see the fairies of folklore, detested and feared the metal employed by the conquering iron-users, seeing in their trenchant blades, against which the bronze leaf-shaped falchion would shiver into pieces, the evidence of a magic power. " In the North of Ireland an iron poker laid across the table kept away the fairies till the child was baptized,"[1] and the efficacy of iron in warding off fairy attacks is notorious all over the Highlands.

Another name which is taboo in the Highlands is that of the minister. I am at a loss to assign a reason for this, unless as the 'descendant' of the pagan priest he was regarded as 'magical.' More understandable is the terror when such words as cat, pig, dog, and hare were mentioned ; and of this class the salmon name-taboo may be a member. The first two of the above words should be pronounced ' Theebet ' and ' Sandy.' To allude to any animal at sea is unlucky. From Campbell (*op. cit.*, p. 239) we learn that among the Highlanders when in a boat at sea " it is forbidden to call things by the names by which they were known on land." Thus a boat-hook should not be called *croman* in Gaelic, but *a chliob* ; a knife not *sgian* but *a ghair* (the sharp one); a fox, the 'red dog'; and a seal, the 'bald beast.' Even places seen from the sea undergo a change of appellation when the speaker is afloat. It is evident that these precautions were originally adopted from a desire not to incur the displeasure of powerful supernatural beings. Thus when certain tribes of North American Indians periodically sacrifice an eagle, the totem of their tribe, they strive to avert the vengeance of the bird by saying to each other : " A snow-bird has been slain." The supernatural power must be hoodwinked at all costs. What could be the character of a supernatural power who must be deceived in this way ? Although Christianity had a firm grip enough on land, was it a negligible quantity when afloat? It is from such examples as these that folklore may assist the mythologist who gropes for the principles of ancient mythic ideas. The student of the mythic system of any race should apply himself with the utmost earnestness to the study of the folklore of its modern representatives.

[1] Campbell's *Superstitions of the Scottish Highlands*, p. 152.

INTRODUCTION TO MYTHOLOGY

THE MAGIC OF ITALY

As showing how ancient myth may be embedded in modern folklore, the discoveries of the late Charles Godfrey Leland have an importance it would be difficult to overestimate. In his preface to his *Aradia, the Gospel of the Witches of Italy*, he says:

" There are in Italy great numbers of *strege*, fortune-tellers or witches, who divine by cards, perform strange ceremonies in which spirits are supposed to be invoked, make and sell amulets, and, in fact, comport themselves generally as their reputed kind are wont to do, be they Black Voodoos in America or sorceresses anywhere.

" But the Italian *strega* or sorceress is in certain respects a different character from these. In most cases she comes of a family in which her calling or art has been practised for many generations. I have no doubt that there are instances in which the ancestry remounts to mediæval, Roman, or it may be Etruscan times. The result has naturally been the accumulation in such families of much tradition. But in Northern Italy, as its literature indicates, though there has been some slight gathering of fairy tales and popular superstitions by scholars, there has never existed the least interest as regarded the strange lore of the witches, nor any suspicion that it embraced an incredible quantity of old Roman minor myths and legends, such as Ovid has recorded, but of which much escaped him and all other Latin writers.

" This ignorance was greatly aided by the wizards and witches themselves, in making a profound secret of all their traditions, urged thereto by fear of the priests. In fact, the latter all unconsciously actually contributed immensely to the preservation of such lore, since the charm of the forbidden is very great, and witchcraft, like the truffle, grows best and has its raciest flavour when most deeply hidden. However this may be, both priest and wizard are vanishing now with incredible rapidity.

" However, they die slowly, and even yet there are old people in the Romagna of the North who know the Etruscan

FOLKLORE AND MYTH

names of the Twelve Gods, and invocations to Bacchus, Jupiter, and Venus, Mercury, and the Lares or ancestral spirits, and in the cities are women who prepare strange amulets, over which they mutter spells, all known in the old Roman time, and who can astonish even the learned by their legends of Latin gods, mingled with lore which may be found in Cato or Theocritus. With one of these I became intimately acquainted in 1886, and have ever since employed her specially to collect among her sisters of the hidden spell in many places all the traditions of the olden time known to them. It is true that I have drawn from other sources, but this woman by long practice has perfectly learned what few understand, or just what I want, and how to extract it from those of her kind.

"For brief explanation I may say that witchcraft is known to its votaries as *la vecchia religione*, or the old religion, of which Diana is the Goddess, her daughter *Aradia* (or Herodias) the female Messiah, and that this little work sets forth how the latter was born, came down to earth, established witches and witchcraft, and then returned to Heaven. With it are given the ceremonies and invocations or incantations to be addressed to Diana and Aradia, the exorcism of Cain, and the spells of the holy-stone, rue, and verbena, constituting, as the text declares, the regular church-service, so to speak, which is to be chanted or pronounced at the witch-meetings. There are also included the very curious incantations or benedictions of the honey, meal, and salt, or cakes of the witch-supper, which is curiously classical, and evidently a relic of the Roman Mysteries."

CHAPTER IX

RITUAL AND MYTH

RITUAL is worship organized, the detail and circumstance of adoration. The study of ritual is one of the branches of the science of comparative religion, but much light is often cast upon myth by its consideration, and here we have to discuss it only in its relationship to myth.

This almost resolves itself into an argument upon the vexed question whether myth is a product of ritual or not. As this question has been already fully discussed (pp. 62-64), there is no necessity to renew it here; but it possesses a pendent question. When the original reason for a certain ritual became forgotten and lost, a myth might arise to account for it. Such a myth would, of course, be 'secondary' in its nature, and is, properly speaking, more of the nature of folklore than myth. Ritual thus arises from an original myth and gives birth to secondary myth or folklore.

It is not essential that ritual should originate in a definite original myth—a concrete story having *dramatis personæ*, plot, and counterplot. The savage may conceive a deity without endowing it with any characteristics. " The sun-being lives up there," says the savage, or " I fear the wind. I will placate him." The only myth created is: " The supernatural wind-being lives on the earth." All the same this statement is myth; it is primitive theobiography.

Marett thinks that primitive religion was something "to be danced out." The religious dance of the savage is both myth and ritual; it combines myth, tale, and worship. Many myths were and are acted in dance, especially among the aborigines of Australia and America. The Eleusinian mysteries of Greece were almost certainly relics of mythic dances such as

RITUAL AND MYTH

Red Indians and Black-fellows still participate in. We have then a meeting-place for myth and ritual in the tribal dance, which at the same time as it represents the adventures of the gods chants their praises in psalm and hymn (that is, in ritual) and performs the mystic movements that are the most ancient ritual. Dance itself may be purely ritualistic rather than explanatory. When David "danced before the Lord" he did not 'dance out' a myth. He danced ritualistically, with ritual movements—probably traditional and unchangeable—to suit the cadence of his chant or psalm. It is such ritual movements that mechanics unconsciously employ when at work. The blacksmith when he strikes the anvil with his hammer in the intervals of shaping the shoe he holds between the tongs does not do so because he *requires* to. The blows are needless and he gives them because all other craftsmen give them; but they were not always unmeaning. Once, perchance, they filled in the lapses of a song (like that of Joe Gargery in *Great Expectations*), or perhaps he thought they rounded off the music his hammer made on the hot iron he shaped on his stithy. Now they are merely part of the *ritual* of his craft and he is 'forced' by the immemorial usage of his 'mystery' to employ them, just as we all employ certain stereotyped expressions, for custom's sake.

Lack of originality is the disease of ritual. Dullness, pomposity, or mock piety are the pillars of its falling house. Why does Stiggins state that a certain prayer-meeting will take place "D.V."? Because other Stigginses do so, following a habit started in the dim past by some prudent man. Why do some golfers cut such fantastic capers while 'addressing'? Because other conceited golfers do the same, having originally seen it done with effect. It is part of the ritual of later people to do these things, nor can they tear themselves away from them nor appreciate their absurdity—and man is, above all, an imitative and most unoriginal animal!

Ritual, then, enters as much into life as into religion, and secondary myths may arise concerning craft rituals, just as they do about religious ones.

Traces of early ritual in later folk-belief are by no means

rare. Such traces were to be found in the old Scottish festival of Bealltainn which was held on May Day. Of course the pious medieval folk who secured the continuity of the rite did not know that they were celebrating a pagan festival, for the Church, following its age-long policy of propitiating the heathen, tactfully confounded it with the festival of the Rood, the True Cross discovered by the Empress Helena. At Edinburgh and Peebles Bealltainn was held in medieval times on the 3rd of May, the feast day of the Rood, instead of on the first of the month, as at Perth and elsewhere, and the old custom or ritual would unquestionably be superimposed upon the Christian practice of the day. It is notable that two of the Rood churches in Scotland—Holyrood Abbey and Peebles—were reared where the Celtic rite of Bealltainn had been unusually popular—raised, as it were, to confound and supersede the festival. The rite of Bealltainn survived until a generation or two ago, and circumstantial accounts have been bequeathed to us concerning it. Says the parish minister of Callander, writing upon the festival : " In the Parish of Callander, upon the first day of May, all the boys in the town or hamlet meet on the moors. They cut a table on the green sod, of a round shape, to hold the whole company. They kindle the fire, and dress a repast of eggs and milk in the consistence of a custard. They knead a cake of oatmeal, which is baked at the fire upon a stone. After the custard is eaten up, they divide the cake into as many portions, and as similar as possible, as there are persons in the company. They blacken one of these portions with charcoal until it is perfectly black. They put all the bits of cake into a bonnet. Every one blindfolded draws a portion —he who holds the bonnet is entitled to the last. Who draws the black bit is the devoted person to be sacrificed to Baal, whose favour they mean to implore in rendering the year productive of substance for man and beast. There is little doubt of these human sacrifices being once offered in the country, but the youth who has got the black bit must leap through the flame of the fire three times."

In the preceding generations men, not boys, were the celebrants. Thus ritual droops into the hands of the very young, the despised, or the very old. The strong desert it, but the weak pitifully conserve it. "In the Parish of Logierait," says Napier, "Beltane is celebrated by the shepherds and cowherds in the following manner. They assemble in the fields and dress a dinner of milk and eggs. This dish they eat with a sort of cake baked for the occasion, having small lumps or nipples raised all over its surface. These knobs are not eaten, but broken off, and given as offerings to the different supposed powers or influences that protect or destroy their flocks, to the one as a thank-offering, to the other as a peace-offering."

Pennant, in his *Tour through Scotland*, thus described the Bealltainn observances as they were practised at the end of last century. "The herds of every village hold their Beltane (a rural sacrifice). They cut a square trench in the ground, leaving the turf in the middle. On that they make a fire of wood, on which they dress a large caudle of eggs, oatmeal, butter, and milk, and bring besides these plenty of beer and whiskey. Each of the company must contribute something towards the feast. The rites begin by pouring a little of the caudle upon the ground, by way of a libation. Every one then takes a cake of oatmeal, on which are raised nine square knobs, each dedicated to some particular being who is supposed to preserve their herds, or to some animal the destroyer of them. Each person then turns his face to the fire, breaks off a knob, and, flinging it over his shoulder, says—'This I give to thee,' naming the being whom he thanks, 'preserver of my sheep,' etc.; or to the destroyer, 'This I give to thee (O fox or eagle), spare my lambs,' etc. When this ceremony is over they all dine on the caudle."

We thus see that Bealltainn was the survival of the sacrifice of a human being to certain animistic spirits, the preservers of the flocks and herds of the celebrants. Later, cattle must have taken the place of the human victim. Jamieson remarks, quoting O'Brien: "*Ignis Bei Dei Aseatica ea lineheil*, or May-day, so called from large fires which the Druids were used to light on the summits of the highest hills, into which they drove four-footed beasts, using certain ceremonies to expiate for the sins of the people. The Pagan ceremony of lighting these fires in honour of the Asiatic god Belus gave its name to the entire month of May, which to this day is called *Me-na-bealtine*, in the Irish, *Dor Keating*." He says again, speaking of these fires of Baal, that the cattle were driven through them and not sacrificed, the chief design being to avert contagious disorders from them for the year. And quoting from an ancient glossary, O'Brien says: "The Druids lighted two solemn fires every year, and drove all four-footed beasts through them, in order to preserve them from contagious distempers during the current year."

Bealltainn was perhaps an adaptation of one of the names of Bilé, a Celtic god of death and the Underworld, one of the Danann or gods imported from Gaul. Thus we may find in the festival the celebration of a propitiatory festival to the god of death and all his devastating crew, the tempest, the fox, the eagle—the pantheon of destroyers, whom it was hoped to placate and soften into protective agencies.

The collection of dew is a notable circumstance in the May Day festival. It is alluded to by Ferguson, who sings in the ancient metre which Scotland took from France:

> On May day in a fairy ring
> We've seen them round St Anthon's spring
>   Frae grass the caller dew to wring
>   To wet their een
> And water clear as crystal spring
>   To synd them clean.

First-of-May dew preserved the skin from wrinkles and freckles, and gave a glow of youth. Dew collected on the morning of the first day of May is supposed to confer witchcraft on the gatherer, and protect against an evil eye. To be seen in a field at daybreak that morning rendered the person seen an object of fear—perhaps as a witch or wizard.

THE RITES OF DIONYSUS

The manner in which a complicated secondary myth may result from ritual is well exemplified by that which sprang from the rites of Dionysus celebrated at Thebes. A branch or some other symbol of vegetation was carried through the cultivated fields in the neighbourhood of the city by a man

disguised as a woman. A human image was then attached
to the top of a tree-trunk, which was raised from the ground
by ropes and held upright. The tree-spirit is then supposed to
animate the trunk. Then, as happened in Mexico at the feast
of Uitzilopochtli, the image attached to the tree was stoned
and its fragments were scrambled and fought for. The woman
who secured the head hastened to nail it to the temple or
principal house of the community.

The late explanation of these doings, the origin of which
became entirely lost, was that, as whatever was done must
redound to the honour of Dionysus, the being represented on
the top of the tree-trunk was inimical to him. The women,
perhaps, supposed themselves to be enacting the part of
bacchantes crazed with wine. As Roscher and Jevons have
shown, this late story is the framework of the myth of
Pentheus as given in the *Bacchæ* of Euripides. Pentheus,
a monarch, refuses to permit the introduction of the worship
of Dionysus, who bereaves him of his senses and, having
dressed him in woman's garments, leads him through his
own town as a laughing-stock. The women of Thebes, led
by Agave, the mother of Pentheus, accept Dionysus and
become mænads or bacchantes. To enable Pentheus to see
their worship, Dionysus bends down a pine-tree, places him
on the top and then lets it go. He is then attacked by Agave
and the other bacchantes, who tear him limb from limb and set
his head on the front of his own palace.

Whatever the significance of this rite—and it would seem
to have its origin in priapic and bacchic worship—we cannot
fail to observe how far too explanatory and how little ingenious
the foregoing tale appears when adapted to it. As Falstaff says
of his own excuse: "It will not fadge." It is lame and awk-
ward. Pentheus could have beheld the rites of the bacchantes
without the pine-tree being lowered for his convenience; and
had he been bereft of his senses, he would probably have joined
in the bacchic rout instead of tamely witnessing it. The
circumstances point to the real myth behind the ritual being
connected with the secret priapic and seasonal rites of a
feminine cult—for women have their secret cults as well as

men, as has been proved of late by the wonderful and valuable discoveries of Mrs D. Aumary Talbot among the Congo peoples—discoveries which seem destined to throw much light upon a most interesting department of comparative religion.

The student must then be upon his guard against secondary interpretations of ritual, which in most cases can only have reference to an early type of myth.

CHAPTER X
THE WRITTEN SOURCES OF MYTH

AMONG the most important sources of our knowledge of myth are ancient books, which, purporting only to set down the annals of a people, contain numerous important passages concerning the mythology of the race whose deeds they celebrate, the adventures of divine or semi-divine beings, whose godhead we can discern shining beneath the armour of the mortal hero. Such books are the *Iliad* of Homer, the Japanese *Nihongi*, the *Popol Vuh* of the Kiches of Central America, the *Ramayana* of the Hindus, and the *Wallum-Olum* of the Lenapé Indians. Among the pages of these and of similar works where myth shades into history, we will now search for the pure mythic gold, refining it from the dross which surrounds it, and making an attempt to restore it to its pristine condition. In perusing these ancient writings we shall find that although many of the myths which they conserve have undoubtedly changed their original shape, others have as certainly retained it, as well as their ancient simplicity of matter and spirit.

THE SOURCES OF EGYPTIAN MYTH

The more we learn of Egyptian myth the more we realize how little we knew concerning it until recently, and how very much more remains to be discovered. We now know a good deal about the various Egyptian deities and their attributes, from the careful study of Greek and Latin writers, by induction, and from the Pyramid and other hieroglyphic texts; but it is strange how comparatively few Egyptian myths have come down to us. Of the many papyri taken from temple and sarcophagus only a small proportion deals with what may be led literature, and of this only a small part treats of myth. Perhaps the most outstanding contribution to Egyptian myth is that of Plutarch, who in his *Osiride et Iside* tells us practically all we know of Osiris and Isis. Plutarch's information was second-hand at the best, and his version of the myth contains many grievous errors; but it is our one and only guide for the main body of the story, and we must be thankful for it. One of the great repositories of Egyptian ritual, the *Book of the Dead*,[1] is of great indirect value to mythology. It treats of the manner in which the soul of the deceased Egyptian should comport itself in the Otherworld, and also relates the voyage of Ra-Osiris through the realms of night, mentioning numerous deities and spirits who accompany him in his progress. Of this book there were three recensions or versions, the Heliopolitan, the Theban, and the Saïte. The first-mentioned was edited by the priests of the college of On, or Heliopolis, and was based on manuscripts which were probably ancient even in that far-away time. The pyramids of Unas, Teta, and Pepi contain the original texts of this recension. Chapters were added from time to time between the VIth and XIth Dynasties. The favourite version of the *Book of the Dead* from the XVIIIth to the XXIInd Dynasty was the Theban recension, and the Saïte must be still later, by its arrangement. As has been said, the *Book of the Dead* has greatly assisted students of Egyptian myth. Not only does it describe many of the gods and supernatural beings who inhabit the Underworld, but it paints vivid pictures of the scenery of that gloomy region. It was necessary that the dead Egyptian should know the name of every door, door-keeper, watcher, and questioner in the abode of the dead, and those names greatly assist in discovering the exact character of the multitude of beings who inhabited the regions ruled over by Osiris.

Several papyri provide us with mythological items, notably the Westcar Papyrus, written about 1800 B.C., now in the Berlin Museum. The beginning and the end are wanting, yet sufficient remains to show the trend of the whole. Among the several tales it contains is the " Prophecy of Dedi," which recounts the

[1] The title of which has also been translated *The Book of the Coming Forth in Day*.

birth of the sons of Ra. In the history of Setne and his son Se-Osiris, too, we get several mythological glimpses, especially valuable being the vision of Amenti, the abode of the dead, vouchsafed to the child Se-Osiris. From a secret place in the mountains of Memphis he led his father to seven great halls (filled with people of all conditions), symbolic of Amenti. These various halls or circles remind us of the abode of the damned in Dante's 'Malebolge.' In the sixth hall the gods of Amenti held council, and in the seventh sat the god Osiris, with Thoth and Anubis. A judgment scene is described, corresponding to that in the *Book of the Dead*; and parallels such as these provide that 'test of recurrence' insisted upon by Tylor, and the first tenet in the creed of all good mythologists—not, of course, that this recurrence suitably illustrates Tylor's law—*i.e.*, that if mythological phenomena on which a certain theory is based 'recur' in a far distant place the correctness of that theory is proved. Here similar facts only 'recur' concerning the same subject in the accounts of different contemporary writers; but these accounts are therefore almost certain to mirror the current belief on that subject, unless, of course, internal evidence reveals that one writer has slavishly copied from the other.

THE TWO BROTHERS

The "Story of the Two Brothers" contained in the D'Orbiney Papyrus, bought in Italy and acquired by the British Museum in 1857, provides us with a story of great significance to the students of myth and comparative religion. It will be found in the volume of this series which deals with Egyptian mythology, and it is only necessary to state in this place that there were two brothers, Anapou and Bitou, that Anapou's wife sought Bitou's life, and that Bitou had to flee. After meeting the nine gods and receiving the 'Daughter of the gods' for his wife, it was intimated to him by the Seven Hathors that he should die by the sword. He confided to his wife that he had placed his heart, or life,[1] on the summit of an acacia-tree, and that whoever discovered it there would have to

[1] This movable 'life' or heart is known to students of tradition as the 'life-index.' This is a common incident in medieval romance.

247

meet him in combat. It came to the ears of Pharaoh that Bitou had a beautiful wife, and he sent armed men to kill him, but Bitou slew them all. Pharaoh then enticed the girl away. She told him her husband's secret, and he cut down the acacia-tree, whereupon Bitou expired. His brother, opening the tree, discovered therein a berry, which he placed in cold water, and Bitou was restored to life. He then took the shape of a sacred Apis bull, which was led before Pharaoh. The animal entered the harem and addressed his former wife, telling her who he was. She put pressure upon the King to slaughter it, and when this was done, two big drops of blood fell from the animal's neck and became two great trees, one at either side of Pharaoh's portal. Sacrifices were offered to these, and Pharaoh with his wife, or rather Bitou's wife, was carried in his chair of state to sit under the wonderful trees. But the tree under which Bitou's wife was seated whispered its secret to her, and at her desire the trees were cut down. As this was being done a chip flew into her mouth. In due time she had a son, who was none other than Bitou himself; he succeeded the Pharaoh and put his faithless wife to death.

This tale is a blend of several well-known mythologic and folklore elements, the chief of which it may be observed are the slaughter of the bull and the felling of the trees. These incidents show that part of the story at least was originally made to explain the origin of tree and animal worship. At the time it was reduced to writing this tale was probably about four thousand years old, so that it had had every chance to attract to itself other floating incidents, such as the way in which the wickedness of the faithless wife was brought to naught.

The Gilgamesh Epic

An important place in the mythic lore of the Orient falls to the great Chaldean poem known as the Gilgamesh epic, a copy of which, inscribed on fragmentary clay tablets, is still extant in the British Museum. This copy was made at the instance of Assurbanipal (Sardanapalus), King of Assyria, in the seventh century before our era, and was housed in that monarch's famous library at Nineveh. Ere the century in which they were deposited there closed the tablets were buried beneath the ruins of the city, to be recovered only in modern times through the researches of Sir A. H. Layard and others. The epic, written by the Ninevite scribes on twelve tablets, tells the adventures of a mythical or semi-mythical hero called Gilgamesh, and is of the nature of a solar cycle, comprising a number of more or less distinct and complete myths woven into a connected narrative. Some of its episodes are known to be of high antiquity, dating at the latest from some two thousand years before the time of Assurbanipal.

It is possible that there is an historical basis for the character of Gilgamesh, whose name is thought to be of Elamite or Kassite origin. It happens by no means infrequently that a real national hero becomes the nucleus of various legends of gods and supernatural beings, and it is therefore not improbable that Gilgamesh was at one time that prince of Erech which the epic represents him to be. Mythologically, he is the type of the sun-god (as a brief scrutiny of the poem will show), his adventures typifying the course of the solar luminary through the heavens and into the Underworld. Eabani, the mythical type of primitive man, with whom Gilgamesh is associated as friend and fellow-adventurer, also presents solar characteristics. It is not, however, sun legends alone which have found their way into the epic. The myth of Eabani and Ukhut in the Ist tablet approximates to the story of Adam and Eve; there is mention of the seasonal myth of Tammuz and Ishtar in the VIth tablet; most important of all, in the XIth tablet appears the famous Babylonian story of the deluge, forming in itself a complete and separate narrative, connected with the rest of the epic only by the most mechanical of literary devices.

The opening of the poem is rather obscure. A fragment exists which seems to be its earliest lines, a sort of prologue indicating the benefits accruing to those who read the epic. Another fragment thought to belong to this work is about a grievous siege of the city of Erech; but as no mention of Gilgamesh appears, it is doubtful whether the fragment really forms a part of the poem. When Gilgamesh is first introduced in the mutilated text it is as the semi-divine king of Erech, a tyrannous monarch whose people groan beneath the weight of his oppression. There is nothing to indicate how he reached the throne, whether he was a native prince or a conqueror. Like the sun he typifies, his birth is shrouded in mystery. His mother, Rimat-belit, is a priestess of the cult of Shamash ; it is not from her that he has received his strain of divinity. His father, strangely enough, is not once mentioned, and we are left to conjecture that he was the offspring of a god, probably of the sun-god himself, whose worshipper and *protégé* he is.

The people of Erech at length rebel against his cruel treatment, calling on the gods to create a hero to subdue him. The divine beings hearkened, and the goddess Aruru made Eabani, the wild man, from a piece of clay. Eabani haunts the mountains and desolate places, herding with the gazelles as one of them, and it is in this condition that Tsaidu, the hunter, finds him, whether by accident or design is not clear. Tsaidu, after trying in vain to capture him, returns with news of him to Gilgamesh, who, evidently guessing that the wild man was intended by the gods for his downfall, dispatches Tsaidu once more in search of him. This time the huntsman is accompanied by the temple-woman Ukhut, whose snares Gilgamesh trusts will be more effective than those of Tsaidu. Like Adam in the Garden of Eden, the wild man falls before the wiles of a woman, and is led in triumph to Erech, with whose monarch he establishes a close friendship, thus in a measure thwarting the designs of the gods.

In the IInd tablet we find Eabani somewhat dissatisfied with his position at Erech, and lamenting his lost freedom ; but the god Shamash appears to him in a dream and induces him to remain. The two heroes, Gilgamesh and Eabani, project an expedition against Khumbaba, the monster who guards the forest of cedars, and in the IIIrd tablet they obtain the patronage of Shamash for their undertaking, through the good offices of Rimat-belit.

The fearsome aspect of Khumbaba (identified by some writers with an Elamite dynasty which flourished more than two thousand years before our era) is portrayed in the IVth tablet, while the Vth relates the episode of the heroes' approach to the forest of cedars. The portion of the text dealing with the combat is no longer extant, but we gather that the monster is overcome and slain. The encounter with Khumbaba appears to be symbolical of the conflict between light and darkness.

The VIth tablet embodies a myth of different character, representing, perhaps, the wooing of the sun-god, the god of the spring-time, by Ishtar, the patron deity of fertility and of the renewal of vegetation on the earth. Returning from his expedition to the forest of cedars, Gilgamesh lays aside his armour and stained garments and robes himself with becoming state. The goddess Ishtar, beholding him, loves him, and desires him for her bridegroom. "Come, Gilgamesh," she says, "and be thou my bridegroom! I am thy vine, thou art its bond; be thou my husband, and I will be thy wife," and so on, with many fair promises and inducements. But Gilgamesh will have none of her proffered favours. In a speech replete with mythic allusions he taunts her with her treatment of former lovers—of Tammuz the bridegroom of her youth, of Alala the eagle, of a "lion perfect in might" and a "horse glorious in battle," of the shepherd Tabulu and the gardener Isullanu. To all these has she meted out cruel tortures; "and yet," says Gilgamesh, "thou lovest me that thou mayest make me as they are." Ishtar in mingled rage and shame appeals to her father Anu to send a great bull against the hero, and Anu at length consents to do so. However, Gilgamesh and Eabani succeed in slaying the divine animal, while Eabani still further incenses the goddess by his contemptuous treatment of her. After the overthrow of the celestial bull the heroes return to Erech. Up to this point their victorious career has not received a single check; but just as the sun when he reaches the zenith begins to decline in strength, so the might of the two heroes begins to wane after the middle of the epic.

In the VIIth tablet the death of Eabani is foretold to him in a vision. The temple maiden Ukhut (cursed by him in his first bitterness at the loss of freedom, and now dead) appears to him, and in a passage beginning, "Come, descend with me to the house of darkness, the abode of Irkalla," describes the gloomy and wretched aspect of the Netherworld. Soon afterward Eabani becomes ill, no doubt through the malignance of the goddess Ishtar. This tablet and the following, which recounts the death of Eabani, are in a very mutilated condition.

The IXth tablet opens with the lament of Gilgamesh for his deceased friend. "Must I die like Eabani?" asks the hero, and a great dread comes upon him, so that he resolves to go to the abode of his ancestor, Ut-Napishtim, the Babylonian Noah, who has been admitted into the pantheon, and, he trusts, will unveil for him the secret of immortality. It must be remembered that on this journey thitherward Gilgamesh, in his mythical character of sun-god, is travelling downward from the zenith. In due course he reaches the Mountain of the Sunset, lying on the western horizon, and when he has passed its portals, guarded by scorpion-men, he passes through a region of darkness which takes him twenty-four hours to traverse.

The Xth tablet brings him to the seashore, and here he meets with Sabitu, goddess of the sea, who directs him to Ut-Napishtim's ferryman, Arad-Ea. After some persuasion the ferryman consents to row him across the waters of death to the abode of his ancestor. Arrived at the farther shore, the hero (who has meanwhile contracted a sore disease) remains sitting in the boat till Ut-Napishtim comes down to the strand. The survivor of the flood is greatly surprised to see that a mortal man has crossed the dark sea in safety, and he demands to know his errand. Gilgamesh makes known the object of his quest (to learn the secret of perpetual life), whereupon the listener on the shore looks grave, and points out to him that death is the common lot of all men.

To explain how he himself obtained immortality and deification, Ut-Napishtim relates the Babylonian version of the ubiquitous flood-story, which occupies the first portion of the XIth tablet. The flood was decreed, according to this version, by the gods who dwelt in the ancient city of Shurippak. "Their hearts prompted the great gods to send a deluge," says Ut-Napishtim naïvely, and no other cause is assigned for the disaster. Ut-Napishtim was evidently a favourite with Ea, lord of the deep ; he instructed him in a vision how to build a ship in which he and his household might escape. To allay the suspicions of the populace he had to give as the reason for his preparations that he was hated by Bel and was therefore disposed to quit the realms of that deity and repair to the domains of Ea. The building, launching, and loading of the ship occupied seven days, and at eventide on the seventh Ut-Napishtim with his family and household entered the ship, and the torrential rains then commenced. For a season all was storm and chaos, so that even the gods were afraid. On the seventh day the tempest ceased, and finally the ship came to rest on Mount Nitsir. To discover whether the waters were abating this Babylonian Noah sent out a dove, then a swallow, but both returned to the ship ; after a space he sent out a raven, and the raven drew near, "wading and croaking," but did not come back. Then Ut-Napishtim and all his household came out and offered a libation and burnt incense on the mountain-peak. The gods descended and hovered round him, and the lady of the gods swore by her necklace of lapis lazuli (an amulet) that she would not forget the days of the deluge. Bel, who seems to have been the prime mover in the destruction of mankind, was wroth when he discovered the survivors, but at length, on the intervention of the other gods, he decided to raise Ut-Napishtim and his wife to the status of divinities and admit them to the council of the gods. After this, the pair were taken away and made to dwell at 'the mouth of the rivers.'

His recital ended, Ut-Napishtim undertook to cure Gilgamesh of his disease, and for that purpose directed him to a magic spring of healing virtue. The hero, once more strong and healthy, returned to his ancestor's dwelling and again demanded the secret of life. Ut-Napishtim, though he had previously pointed out the hopelessness of the quest, now told Gilgamesh how he might obtain the plant of life, and with Arad-Ea for his pilot the hero set out. He was successful in finding the magic plant, but ere he could make use of it a

serpent-monster stole it from him, and with his quest still
unfulfilled he was obliged to return to Erech.

The mythological significance of this tablet is, of course,
that the sun-god can never attain immortality, he must 'die'
inevitably at eventide, cross the waters of death, and sojourn
until morning in the Underworld. Just as Gilgamesh is healed
and restored to Erech, so is the sun restored to the world at
dawn, his quest still unsatisfied, for he must 'perish' again
when night comes round.

The XIIth and last tablet concerns the return of Eabani's
ghost (*utukka*) from the Underworld. Gilgamesh still mourns
for his friend, and begs the gods to restore him to life. At
length Ea hearkens and intercedes with Nergal, god of the
Netherworld, who consents to release the spirit for a little while.
The passage containing Gilgamesh's interview with the ghost is
of interest as setting forth the Babylonian doctrine of care for
the dead. Eabani describes the conditions of life in the Underworld, showing that the dead who are properly buried and
receive offerings are comparatively comfortable, while those who
are uncared for dwell in squalor and wretchedness.

We must not overlook the important astrological aspect of
the Gilgamesh epic. It is generally thought that the division
of the epic into twelve tablets implies a connexion with the
zodiac, though it is also suggested that the association is an
artificial one conceived by the Ninevite scribes who copied the
poem. However this may be, it is obvious that the epic
abounds in astrological allusions. Thus the sign Virgo would
be represented by the wooing of Ishtar in the VIth tablet;
Taurus by the combat with the celestial bull; Scorpio by the
meeting with the scorpion-men at the Mountain of the Sunset,
and also by the traversing of the region of darkness, since the
scorpion typified darkness, and the sign Scorpio was frequently
used both as the seventh and eighth signs of the zodiac.
Capricornus, represented as a fish-tailed goat, may be depicted
by the encounter with Sabitu, goddess of the sea. The deluge
story inserted in the XIth tablet comes under the sign of
Aquarius, the water-bearer; while Pisces, the twelfth sign,
typical of the after-life, corresponds with the ghost-scene in the

XIIth tablet. As has been said, Gilgamesh and Eabani were both of them forms of the sun-god; it is therefore not impossible that they were the mythological equivalents of the sign Gemini, the twins, itself connected with two types of the solar deity. The astrological or zodiacal element in the epic grew in importance with the advance of astrology in Babylonia.

HINDU MYTHICAL LITERATURE: THE VEDAS

The generic term *Veda* ('knowledge') is applied to a collection of ancient Hindu writings forming the Brahmanical scriptures. The *Veda* comprised a group of four distinct collections of sacred literature—namely, the *Rig-veda*, or book of hymns, the *Sama-veda*, or book of chants, the *Yajur-veda*, or book of prayers, and the *Atharva-veda*, or book of the Atharvans—each of these composed of a *Samhita* (a collection of sacred sayings forming the veda proper), to which are appended three other classes of writings, somewhat less authoritative and divine—the *Brahmanas* (prose writings), the *Aranyakas*, dealing with the more esoteric rites, and the *Upanishads*, of a rationalistic and speculative nature. The *Rig-veda*, the work of early Aryan settlers in India, is the oldest and most important of the four, and is believed to be of high antiquity. It is written in a dialect older than classical Sanskrit. The *Sama-veda* and *Yajur-veda* are largely composed of borrowings from the *Rig-veda*, resemblances to which are also apparent in the *Atharva-veda*, though the significance of the latter is less religious and more magical.

With the religious and moral teachings of the Vedas we have here no concern; but the lore of the ancient gods which still lingers in them is of great mythological interest, and reveals to some extent the workings of Indian religious thought in the early Aryan period. The foundation of the early Hindu religion as it is set forth in the Vedic literature was, apparently, a simple animistic cult, wherefrom was gradually evolved a pantheon of deities for the most part anthropomorphic. The natural world was divided, conveniently enough, into three spheres, the earth, the air, and the sky, each of which had its presiding deity with his divine court. Thus arose a constantly changing triad of supreme deities—changing, at all events, in name—and in time the partly monotheistic idea of a spiritual essence or universal soul pervading and animating all things, even the gods themselves.

Despite the lofty moral sentiments of the Vedas, and their spiritual character, we may discern in them traces of barbarism. This is less evident in the Vedic hymns, or Samhitas, than in the prose Brahmanas : many of the myths, complete and fragmentary, in which these latter abound, present a distinctly savage element of irrationality and stupidity.

THE "RAMAYANA" AND "MAHABHARATA"

The *Ramayana* treats of the traditions of two great races, the Kosalas and the Videhas, who dwelt in Northern India between the twelfth and tenth centuries B.C. It is not in these families that our interest centres, but in the numerous mythological allusions which enrich the work. It is, of course, chiefly a hero-tale, but, unlike the *Nibelungenlied*, for example, it abounds in direct allusions to the gods and their various attributes ; and this it is that makes it so interesting to the mythologist. Here is a short catalogue of gods from the fifth book of the *Ramayana* to illustrate its usefulness as a mythological guide. The principal attributes of the various deities are described in a phrase :

> *Brahma* and the flaming *Agni*, *Vishnu* lord of heavenly light,
> *Indra* and benign *Vivasvat* ruler of the azure height,
>
> *Soma* and the radiant *Bhaga*, and *Kuvera* lord of gold,
> And *Vidhatri* great Creator worshipped by the saints of old,
>
> *Vayu* breath of living creature, *Yama* monarch of the dead,
> And *Varuna* with his fetters which the trembling sinners dread,
>
> Holy spirit of *Gayatri*, goddess of the morning prayer,
> *Vasus* and the hooded *Nagas*, golden-winged *Garuda* fair,
>
> *Kartikeya* heavenly leader strong to conquer and to bless,
> *Dharma* god of human duty and of human righteousness.

The adventures of the hero Rama in search of his wife Sita and her eventual discovery, form the principal incidents ; and although the work rings with the clash of battle, it yet possesses infinite wisdom, related in the words of holy hermits and sage priests.

The *Mahabharata*, or 'great poem of the Bharatas,' most wonderful of all Eastern epics, tells of a great war fought some thirteen or fourteen centuries before our era; but the main historical theme has been largely obscured by the medley of mythical, legendary, and religious lore which with the passing of centuries has gradually swelled the epic to more than a hundred thousand couplets. Originating, posibly, some centuries before the Christian era, the poem is believed to have been cast in its present form as early as A.D. 200.

Like the *Ramayana*, the *Mahabharata* is rich in mythic matter—in myths, legends, and hero-tales more or less completely fused with the central narrative. Thus it contains one version of the Indian deluge story, and the Greeks are known to have identified certain of its characters with the beings of their own mythology. The chief religious tendency of the poem in its existing shape is toward the cult of Krishna, who plays a leading part in its development. It has been suggested that the Krishna stratum was superimposed on an earlier Buddhist groundwork at a time when the worship of Vishnu (regarded as being incarnate in Krishna) was in ascendancy.

The "Iliad" and "Odyssey"

Much obscurity enfolds the origin of those famous Greek epics, the *Iliad* and *Odyssey*, whereof the authorship is traditionally assigned to Homer. Beyond the fact of their undoubted antiquity nothing is known of their early history save what may be gleaned from internal evidence; it is not even certain that they are both from the same pen. Much of the matter they contain is extremely ancient, and authorities are generally agreed that they must have been cast in epic form at latest before the ninth century B.C. The literary beauty and power of these noble works need not be dwelt upon here, but both the *Iliad* and *Odyssey* are rich in mythological matter, and it is this

257

INTRODUCTION TO MYTHOLOGY

which calls for our attention. Gods and men mingle freely in both narratives.

Thus we learn that in Homeric times the gods were definitely personalized and anthropomorphic ; yet not to such an extent as to lose theriomorphic traits which indicate their origin. They could, for instance, assume animal shape at will, even Athene herself, who has but few savage elements in her nature, becoming a bird on occasion. Apollo, too, and Dionysus, and other deities possess this faculty of metamorphosis as an inheritance from a more barbarous age.

The Homeric myths, in whatever form they reached the Greek poet (or poets) known to us as Homer, are singularly free from the grosser elements which appear in the Hesiodic tales of the gods. Zeus and Hera, Apollo and Artemis, all the gods whose classic lineaments were fixed for all time by the pen of Homer, are portrayed by him in noble and beautiful aspect, with only here and there a reminiscence of some primitive *chronique scandaleuse*, or a trace of that barbaric element of irrationality characteristic of myth in its primitive stages.

Zeus was, of course, the supreme deity of the Homeric pantheon, and is represented as a just and pitiful god, a father to his people and an avenger of the wrongs of the weak. To him is paid genuine religious veneration, and submission to his supreme and righteous will is obviously one of the first duties of man. Round him are grouped the other gods and goddesses, likewise anthropomorphic and rational beings. The divine government consists of a simple monarchic state, probably drawn up on the model of the Greek government of the period. Between gods and mortals a general spirit of friendliness and confidence exists, giving to the religion of the Homeric period a pleasant and spontaneous character not always evident in later times.

It is notable that both the *Iliad* and *Odyssey* were unhesitatingly ascribed to Homer until the eve of the Christian era, when certain Greek writers advanced the thesis that the epics were the work of different authors. Thus was commenced a controversy which has never been entirely settled. It was urged, again, that the *Iliad* was composed of numerous short folk-poems taken from oral tradition and woven by the poet into a connected narrative ; but this theory in turn has been examined and found lacking, for the literary unity and co-herence of the poem, failing only in a few minor instances, stamps it as an original work. This, of course, does not imply that myth has been excluded from the main structure of the poem, for, as has been shown, it has not. It has likewise been brought forward, as proof of the separate authorship of the epics, that various deities appear in a different aspect in the *Odyssey* from that which they wear in the *Iliad*, but this in all probability is due rather to the exigencies of composition than to a different author.

These great epics are of the widest mythological importance, determining, as they do, as much as the Hesiodic poems, the character and status of the Greek divinities. And still more surely than Hesiod does Homer mark the transition from the barbarous or semi-barbarous mythical period to the full splendour of the classic age. For many centuries the works of the ancient poet formed the scriptures of the Greek religion, the very foundation-stone of the mythological "glory that was Greece."

Japanese Mythic Literature

Japan is rich in mythic literature, perhaps the most valuable of its mythic books being the *Kojiki*, or "Record of Ancient Matters." The traditions embraced in it are said to have been recited by a court lady, Hiyeda No Ra Rae, endowed with an extraordinary memory, and commanded by the Emperor Temmu, who flourished at the end of the seventh century A.D., to absorb all the mythical and historical materials she could and then to dictate them to a scribe. But the emperor died before he could give final instructions concerning the scheme, and for twenty-five years Hiyeda carried these mythic annals in her brain, patiently awaiting the day when Temmu's suc-cessor could furnish her with a scribe. At length the Empress Gemmyo took the matter up in A.D. 712, and gave her as helper the scribe Yesumaro. The *Kojiki* is written in archaic

INTRODUCTION TO MYTHOLOGY

Japanese, and describes the divine origin of the Japanese race and the story of creation given elsewhere in this book, before it goes on to treat of the annals of early sovereigns. The *Nihongi*, or "Chronicles of Japan," is written in the classical or Chinese style, and goes over much the same ground as the *Kojiki*, the songs of which it occasionally alters slightly, supplementing here and omitting there, but it is by no means so Japanese in character. It is, however, much more valuable as a repository of myth and history. The mythology of these books is, of course, Shintoism. The principal gods and heroes and their adventures, divine and terrestrial, are described, and one of the chief tales recounts the quarrel of the sun-goddess with her brother Susa-no-o. The sun-goddess, Ama-terasu, is, of course, an important figure in these mythic annals, as from her sprang the line of the mikados. The great cycle of myths collected in these annals is known as the "Period of the Gods," and may be compared with the divine cycles of the Celts, or the *Popol Vuh*.

THE EDDAS

The Teutons of the North do not appear to have possessed any very ancient written records of their mythology. The Prose, or Younger, Edda is a miscellaneous group of writings collected by Snorri Sturlason (1178–1241), who completed the work about 1222. The name 'Edda' does not appear to have been originally bestowed upon it by its author, and Scandinavian scholars find some difficulty in explaining it. It was, it is thought, composed by different hands between the years 1140 and 1160. It is divided into four parts, with a preface, which, after the fashion of that period, purports to furnish the reader with a history of human affairs from the beginning. The second part, "Gylfaginning," or "The Delusion of Gylfi," is a valuable compendium of early Scandinavian myth. It deals, in the first place, with the adventures of the mythical king Gylfi and the giantess Gelfion, the manner of creation of the island of Zealand, and the invasion of Sweden by the Æsir, or divine beings, captained by Odin. The third part, the "Bragaræthur," or "Sayings of Bragi," contains mythical poems attributed to

260

Bragi, the god of poetry. The remainder of the Younger Edda deals with the poetic art, and therefore does not fall to be described here. Sturlason's collection is fortified by another work called the *Ynglinga Saga*, which describes how the hero-gods of the Scandinavian race advanced from the Black Sea northward through Russia and westward through Esthonia, overrunning the south of Scandinavia and founding kingdoms there. Of this work three important manuscripts are still extant, the Wurm Manuscript, the Codex Regius, and, most important of all, the Upsala Codex, probably written about the year 1300.

The Elder Edda, or the Poetic Edda, discovered by Bishop Sveinsson in 1643, was attributed by him to Sæmund Sigfusson, a royal Norwegian who flourished in Iceland from about 1055 to 1132. He was mistaken, for the fragmentary poems it contains are probably rather earlier. They deal with the myths of early Scandinavian civilization, and are composed in a simple and archaic form of Icelandic. Who composed them we do not know, but they were almost certainly collected from oral tradition. The most important and interesting of these ancient poems is the " Völuspá," or prophecy of the Völva, or Sybil, who from her lofty seat addresses Odin, singing of the primeval times before even the gods were created, of the origin of the Jötunn of men and dwarfs, and of the last dreadful doom in the 'twilight of the gods' at Ragnorök. The whole composition is intensely mystical in both atmosphere and wording, shows knowledge of a cosmology different from that of later Scandinavian times, and is on the whole extremely difficult to understand. Next we have " Hávamál " (" Lesson of the High One "), a collection of saws and proverbs, containing a series of stories told by Odin to his own discomfiture. This is true matter of mythology, and is the sort of material which strengthens the theory of Lang and others that myth possesses no religious significance, that it is exoteric to religion, the truth, of course, being that the above is only one type of myth—the secular as opposed to the sacred. The cosmogony and chronology of the Scandinavian religion are set forth in the " Vafprúthnismál," or " Lesson of Vafprúthnir," a giant who is visited by Odin in disguise and catechized by him. Many burlesque stories of the gods are also told in "The Journey of Skirnir," "The Lay of Hoarbeard," and "The Brewing of Ægir." In the "Song of Thrym" we are told how a giant of that name stole the hammer of Thor, refusing to restore it unless the goddess Freya was given him to wife, and how Thor, dressed in female garments, took her place, slew the giant, and recovered his hammer. A myth which recounts how the caste system arose in Scandinavia is met with in "Rígsmál," which tells how the god Hemisdal, taking the human name of Rig, bestowed the power of pro-creation on the two dwarfs Ai and Edda, who became the parents of the race of thralls or bondsmen. A like gift he bestowed on Afi and Ama, who became the parents of the caste of churls. He himself brought up Jarl, the first freeman, instructing him in the arts of war and wisdom. The rest of the Poetic Edda is concerned with pseudo-history, and, among other things, with the long and important series of lays relating to the two heroic families of the Volsungs and the Nibelungs. These, however, are not so much myth as hero-story. The principal manuscript of the Poetic Edda is the Codex Regius in the royal library at Copenhagen, written on forty-five leaves of vellum, probably between 1260 and 1280.

THE "MABINOGION"

The name *Mabinogion* is given to a collection of Welsh tales of much mythological interest.[1] The ancient Britons called a man qualified for bardic honours a *mabinog*, or graduate, and the traditional lore which he had to learn by rote was called *mabinogi* (plural, *mabinogion*). Only a few of these tales are *mabinogion* in the strict sense of the word, and these are the tales of Pwyll, Branwen, Manawyddan, and Math. Certain Arthurian tales are also included in the work, but with these we will not deal here. The veritable *Mabinogion* undoubtedly contain Welsh-Celtic myth. We find in them that process through which

---

[1] These were translated into English by Lady Charlotte Guest, and published in 1849. Eleven of them are taken from the *Red Book of Hergest*, a fourteenth-century manuscript in the library of Jesus College, Oxford. The tale of Taliesin is included with these, but is taken from a much later manuscript.

divine beings degenerate into demigods or hero-gods, thereby bridging the gulf between mythology and romance. The manuscript original dates from the fourteenth century, but the tales are of the period between the eleventh and twelfth centuries. This is not to say, however, that they originated then, as elements in many of them may be traced back to dim primeval days. It is only possible to elucidate these fragments of bardic literature by the help of the Welsh *Triads* and the analogies of early Irish literature. Thus in the Irish Tuatha de Danann we find the counterparts of the Children of Don, also divine. So also with others of the characters in the *Mabinogion*; Manawyddan mab Llyr is a variant of Manannan mac Lir, lord of the Irish Hades, while Govannon may be equated with the Irish smith Goibniu. Several theories have been advanced to account for the resemblance between the Welsh and Irish tales. One asserts that the *mabinogi* tales were learned by the Welsh Celts from the earlier Gaelic population of Wales, while another, equally well supported, suggests that the Irish were the borrowers. This last theory is rendered untenable by the fact that the *Mabinogion* has no affinities with the predominant Ulster cycle of the ninth century (in which the tales are alleged to have been borrowed), but rather with the older cycle of the Tuatha de Danann, regarded even in the tenth century as of old mythological origin. A third and more probable explanation is that both Welsh and Irish tales belong to a period when those branches of the Celtic family were as yet unseparated. Similarities of detail may of course result from later borrowings, but these belong to a different category.

As literature the tales of the *Mabinogion* far surpass any contemporary productions, whether English, French, or German. Their imaginative glamour leaves them without a rival in the literary annals of any period.

SOURCES OF MEXICAN MYTH

The principal sources of Mexican myth are the writings and observations of the Spanish *Conquistadores* in the train of the conquering Cortéz and his immediate successors in the country. The most important document for the study of Mexican mythology is the work of Father Bernardino Sahagun, a monk who flourished in Mexico in the sixteenth century.

His great work, the *History of the Affairs of New Spain* (as Mexico was then called), is the result of years of close study of the people and their folklore. Not content to take at second-hand mythological or other details reported to him, he submitted them to a committee of old and experienced Mexicans, thoroughly acquainted with the antiquities of their country. After this committee had approved of the inclusion of the item in his manuscript, Sahagun consulted still other native authorities, so that his book remains our chief and most reliable source of information upon Mexican myth. Even so, the account he gives us of the various deities, their character- istics and attributes, is very brief and not a little disappointing in its lack of detail, occupying as it does only about forty pages of print. The second book deals with calendars and festivals, and in this he supplements in some degree the information regarding the divine beings treated of in the first book. The third book is the most valuable to us, for it provides us with a number of myths relating to the Mexican gods. It acquaints us with the circumstances of the birth of Uitzilopochtli, of the manner in which Quetzalcoatl, god of the Toltecs, was half lured, half driven from the land by Tezcatlipoca, of how the inhabitants of Tollan, the city of the Toltecs, were decimated by the malign necromancy of the same deity working on behalf of less civilized tribes. The remaining books are occupied with the astrology and customs of the Mexicans.

Torquemada, a later priest, wrote a similar work which, however, was based upon the matter contained in Sahagun's treatise, still in manuscript when the former wrote.

A magnificent example of an aboriginal work teeming with mythical allusions is the *Popol Vuh*, or "Collection of Written Leaves," of the Kiche Indians of Guatemala, already alluded to in the chapter on cosmogony. The history of the discovery of the *Popol Vuh* has already been related, and it only remains to furnish some account of its contents. It embraces the creation story of that people, the tale of the downfall of the earth-giants, the wanderings of the Kiche race, the adventures

WRITTEN SOURCES OF MYTH

of certain hero-gods in the Underworld, and Kiche history up to a fairly late date. It is divided into four books, the first of which is the story of the creation and what occurred shortly after. The universe was dark and in a chaotic condition when the god Hurakan, the 'Heart of Heaven,' passed over the abyss, and called out "Earth!" At the word the solid land appeared. Hurakan then summoned the other gods to consultation regarding their future course of action, among them Gucumatz and the mother- and father-gods, primeval deities who are also called 'the Serpents covered with Green Feathers.' The council of deities agreed that animals should be created, and this was done. They next resolved to make man, and fashioned certain mannikins out of wood; but these failed to pay them reverence, and in great wrath the gods sent a mighty flood accompanied by a resinous rain upon them. The wretched mannikins, taken unawares, were overwhelmed and nearly all destroyed; only a few succeeded in getting away, and their descendants to-day, we are told, are the little monkeys which infest the forests.

After this unlucky experiment the gods turned their attention to another denizen of the earth, called Vukub-Cakix, a name to be translated 'the great Macaw.' He seems to have been a primitive sun- or moon-god, but he offended the pantheon of Heaven by his overweening pride, which at last became so offensive to the gods that they resolved to destroy him. He had indeed a person to be proud of, for his teeth were of emerald and he shone resplendent with gold and silver. He had two sons, Zipacna and Cabrakan, who were earth-giants like the Titans of Greek myth. Like their father, they aroused the enmity of the gods, who dispatched to earth the heavenly brothers Hun-Apu and Xbalanque to bring about the downfall of these blasphemous boasters.

Vukub-Cakix noticed them alight in the tapal-tree, which he regarded as his own especial property. They began to pluck its fruit, and this so irritated him that he was about to attack them when Hun-Apu discharged a dart from a blowpipe at him, striking him in the mouth and causing him to topple to the earth from the tree into which he had climbed. He succeeded, however, in tearing off Hun-Apu's arm, which he hung over his fire at home. This use of 'sympathetic magic,' of course, caused the hero-god great pain, so in order to recover the arm he begged the assistance of two magicians, probably the father- and mother-gods. These disguised themselves as physicians, and pretending that they desired to cure Vukub-Cakix, extracted his teeth. With the teeth his power departed from him and he died. The giant's wife had been basting Hun-Apu's arm at the fire, but seizing it the hero-god gave it to the magicians, who replaced it upon his shoulder. Zipacna and Cabrakan, who personified the earthquake, were next reduced. Four hundred young men (the stars) requested Zipacna to dig the foundations of a new house for them, intending to bury him alive while occupied in the task; but when they had erected their dwelling above him he reared his mighty bulk beneath it and shot them into Heaven, where they have since remained. Zipacna, however, tumbling down a ravine, was killed by Hun-Apu and Xbalanque by having a mountain thrown upon him. Cabrakan was next destroyed, partly by poison and partly by overstraining himself by throwing mountains at the instigation of the heavenly brothers.

The father- and mother-gods had two sons, Hunhun-Apu and Vukub-Hunapu, who were much devoted to the game of ball, the national pastime of the peoples of Mexico and Central America. The noise they made while playing attracted the attention of the lords of the Underworld, who sent them a challenge to a game. The challenge was accepted, and Hunhun-Apu and his brother took their way to the grim territory of Xibalba, where they were received by its rulers Hun-Came and Vukub-Came. It would seem from what follows that the condition of affairs in Xibalba closely resembled those of some of the secret societies still in vogue among the Indians all over North America. The brothers were subjected to numerous tests, at all of which they failed, and they were then sacrificed by having their hearts torn out. Hunhun-Apu's head was placed among the branches of a tree from which calabashes sprouted in such a manner that the gory trophy could not be distinguished from the fruit. Although the inhabitants of Xibalba were forbidden to approach the tree, Xquiq, daughter of one of its high officials, did so. By magical influence Hunhun-Apu became the father of her children, and when her father discovered her disgrace she was given up to the owls, the messengers of Xibalba, to be slain. She bribed them, and succeeded in escaping to the earth, where she sought out the dwelling of Xmucane, mother of Hunhun-Apu, and gave birth to Hun-Apu and Xbalanque, who overthrew Vukub-Cakix. These children were persecuted by two other sons of Hunhun-Apu, also living with their grandmother, but by magic they turned their tormentors into monkeys, and thus rid themselves of them. By the aid of a rat they discovered a set of implements for the ball game which had belonged to their father and uncle, and they engaged in the pastime. The lords of Xibalba, hearing them at play, once more sent a challenge, which was again accepted. But, more astute than their forbears, ere they reached the confines of Xibalba, Hun-Apu created from a hair on his leg a small insect called Xan. This, preceding the brothers, found the lords of Xibalba sitting among a number of wooden figures. It bit them, and when they spoke to one another concerning the insect's onslaught, the brothers discovered their names. When Hun-Apu and Xbalanque arrived they were thus enabled to salute each of the Xibalbans by his name, and they passed all the other tests successfully. They were shut up for the night in the House of Gloom with certain torches which they must keep alight all night, but they affixed red feathers to the torches, and thus cheated the Xibalbans. In the House of Bats, Camazotz, the chief of the bats, cut off the head of Hun-Apu, but a friendly tortoise passing by affixed itself to the body in place of the head. Xbalanque then played ball with the Xibalbans, and hit the ball close to the ring, whereupon a rabbit concealed near it leaped out and ran away. The Xibalbans, taking it for the ball, pursued it, and Xbalanque, observing Hun-Apu's head suspended in the ball court, hung up the tortoise in its place, and affixed Hun-Apu's head to his body and resuscitated him. The hero-gods then sacrificed themselves, but returned after a space of five days. Disguised as magicians, they performed many miracles, resurrecting people, burning houses and restoring them again, and so forth. Hun-Came and Vukub-Came considered the resurrection trick so clever that they desired to have it performed upon themselves. The heroes sacrificed them, but did not revive them. This completed the subjugation of Xibalba, the people being reduced to a subservient condition. The aristocratic privilege of the ball game was withdrawn from them, and they were doomed to keep bees and make pots and perform suchlike ignoble work. *Postmortem* honours were paid to Hunhun-Apu and Vukub-Hunapu, who became the sun and moon respectively, while the four hundred youths slain by Zipacna remained in Heaven as the stars.

The *Popol Vuh* further relates the mythical history of the Kiche tribes. Four men, Balam-quitze, Balam-agab, Mahucutah, and Iqibalam, were created by the gods, and the first three were the ancestors of the three Kiche divisions, Cavek-, Nihaib-, and Ahau-Kiches, the fourth being without descendants. These were not alone in the world, as the Yaqui, or Mexicans, also existed, and other cognate tribes dwelt to the east. The ancestors of the Kiches had been formed too perfectly by the gods, who, alarmed at their omniscience, cast a veil over their intellects. Wives were created for them, but they dwelt in darkness, without sunlight or the comforts of religion. Setting out on a wandering life, they came to Tulan-Zuiva, where each tribe received a special god to itself. The want of fire was felt, and the god Tohil, a thunder-deity, struck his flint-shod feet together and produced it as required. The other tribes requested the Kiches to give them fire, but a bat messenger from Xibalba advised them against acquiescence unless the recipients should consent to be united with their god " beneath their girdles and beneath their armpits." All agreed except the Kakchiquel, whose bat-god purloined the seeds of fire. The riddle-like condition portended that the tribes which consented should give up their hearts for sacrifice. A general migration followed, the Kiches as well as other tribes journeying to Guatemala, where on a mountain-side they sat down to await the dawn. The morning star swam into view, followed by the great luminary of day, and at sight of it the tribal gods were turned into stone. The original Kiche ancestors too withdrew in hermit-like seclusion from mankind, being seen only at intervals in the wild places in converse with the gods. Human sacrifice was instituted, and wars with neighbouring peoples began to be waged. A great attack was made upon the Kiches, who dwelt in a settlement on the mountains surrounded by a stockade, the object evidently being to capture the Kiche gods; but the attack was repulsed with great loss to the invaders. The death day of the first Kiche men was now at hand, and calling the people together they sang the song with which they had first greeted the rising of the new-found sun. They then vanished, leaving behind them a bundle which was afterward known as the 'majesty enveloped,' and was probably of the same type as the medicine bundles of the North American Indians.

From this point the *Popol Vuh* begins to shade into history. The sons of the first men, desirous of wielding the power possessed by their fathers, set out on a pilgrimage to the east, to obtain the insignia of royalty. The Kiches became more civilized, stone-built cities were raised, and a definite political existence arose. A policy of conquest was embarked upon, and many of the neighbouring tribes were conquered and subjected to Kiche rule. What follows probably contains but little of the matter of myth, and we may conclude that for the most part it is traditional history.

As has been said, it would be difficult to over-estimate the importance to mythology in general, and to American myth in particular, of such a document as the *Popol Vuh*. When we can be sure of its aboriginal character, and that is not seldom, American myth has the greatest importance because of its isolated nature. When we first encounter it, it is untouched by European or Asiatic myth, and this makes it of the greatest value for comparison. If we can parallel an old-world myth with a well-authenticated American example, then we have proved the universal nature of the principles of mythic evolution. Everything relating to the *Popol Vuh* proves to the hilt its genuine aboriginal character; and this being so, it is of the greatest assistance to mythologists. Unfortunately, no adequate translation exists. The Kiche language in which it was written is most difficult, and for the present we have to rely on the Spanish version of Ximenez and the French translation of the original by the Abbé Brasseur de Bourbourg. However, more than one translation is either meditated or in course of completion; and there is an abridgement in English by the present writer. An English translation of the whole appeared in an American magazine entitled *The Word* during 1906 and 1907, from the pen of Dr Kenneth Sylvan Guthrie, but whether from the Spanish or original Kiche, I do not know. It is, moreover, couched in Scriptural language, and such a treatment assists the vulgar error that the *Popol Vuh* is merely a native travesty of portions of the Old Testament.

AMERICAN INDIAN MYTHIC WRITINGS

The red man of North America also has his epics. Charles Godfrey Leland, in the introduction to his book *Kuloskap* [or Glooscap] *the Master*, says: "Very few persons are aware that there has perished or is rapidly perishing among the Red Indians of North America far more poetry than was ever written by all the white inhabitants, and that this native verse is often of a very high order, for the Indian sagas, or legends, or traditions, were in fact all songs. . . . After I had published my legends, however, I was made aware by Louis Mitchell, a Passamaquoddy Indian, who had been in the Legislature of Maine, and had collected and written out for me, with strictest literalness, a great number of manuscripts, that there were in existence certain narratives and poems quite different in kind from anything which I possessed. Among the former was a history of the Passamaquoddy tribe, illustrated with numerous designs of the Birch-bark school of art, which I transferred to my friend the late Dr D. G. Brinton as its most appropriate possessor. Three of the poems Mitchell wrote out for me in exact, though often quite ungrammatical language, which was so close to the original that the metres betrayed themselves throughout. I regret that, though I had certainly acquired some knowledge of 'Indian,' it was, as a Passamaquoddy friend one day amiably observed, 'only baby Injun now, grow bigger some day like Mikumwess s'posin' you want to,' in

WRITTEN SOURCES OF MYTH

reference to a small goblin who is believed to have the power of increasing his stature at will. However, I with great care put the Mitchell Anglo-Algonkin into English metre, having been impressed, while at the work, with the exquisitely naïve and fresh character of the original, which, while it often reminded me of Norse poetry, in many passages had strictly a life and beauty of its own." Leland tells how he began to correspond on the subject with Professor J. Dyneley Prince of Columbia University, translator of the celebrated Algonquin *Wampum Record*, recited annually in bygone days at the council of the tribes. He continues : " Few indeed and far between are those who ever suspected till of late years that every hill and dale in New England had its romantic legend, its beautiful poem, or its marvellous myth—the latter equal in conception and form to those of the Edda—or that a vast collection of these traditions still survives in perfect preservation among the few remaining Indians of New England and the North-east Coast, or the *Wabano*. This assertion is, I trust, verified by what is given in the Micmac tales by the late Rev. S. Rand, the collection made by Miss Abbey Alger, of Boston, and my own *Algonquin Legends of New England*, which I, *sit venia*, may mention was the first to appear of the series. And I venture to say from the deepest conviction that it will be no small occasion of astonishment and chagrin, a hundred years hence, when the last Algonkin Indian of the *Wabano* shall have passed away, that so few among our literary or cultured folk cared enough to collect this connected aboriginal literature."

The lore of the New England Indians centres chiefly round the figure of Kuloskap, or Glooscap, as good an example of Matthew Arnold's 'magnified non-natural man,' so beloved of Lang, as can well be imagined. A detailed account of this being and his adventures will be found in the volume of this series which deals with the North American Indians. His brother Malsum the Wolf probably typifies the power of evil. In the myths collected by Messrs Leland and Prince we first read of the birth of Glooscap and the death of Malsum the Wolf, his twin brother. Malsum, having slain his mother, desired also to slay Glooscap, but a supernatural power guarded

271

him, and Malsum's attempts were frustrated. He asked Glooscap several times what would slay him, but Glooscap invariably told him a falsehood, until at length, sitting by a stream, Glooscap muttered that a rush would cause his death. The beaver, hearing this, acquainted Malsum of the fact and asked as a reward to be provided with wings; but the Evil One, amused at his request, insulted him so outrageously that at last he betook himself to Glooscap, who, plucking a fern, sought Malsum, and having found him smote him with it so that he fell dead.

The creation of man and the animals is then sung of. First were born the fairies of the forest, the elves, the little men who dwelt in rocks (the red man's equivalent for elves and gnomes), the small animistic spirits which swarm through nature, lending her life and animation and filling up her crevices. Then Glooscap took his bow and arrows and shot at an ash-tree. From the hole made by the arrow men came forth, the first of the human kind. Then Glooscap created animals. At first he made them of colossal size, but seeing that they were too strong he made them smaller and weaker in order that man might be able to hunt them. In the beginning the beaver was the enemy of Glooscap, having on one occasion disobeyed the Master by drinking from a stream which was taboo. The god tore up a rock and hurled it at him from a distance of many leagues, but the beaver dodged it and ran into a mountain, where he has remained unto this day.

The third part of the epic of Glooscap tells how at one time the rattlesnakes were Indians. When the great flood was coming Glooscap gave them fair warning of it, but they answered that they did not care, and mocked him, shaking their rattles, which were made of turtle-shell containing small pebbles. The rain began to fall, the thunder roared, and the lightning flashed, but still the rattlesnakes jeered. Glooscap had not the heart to drown them, but he changed them all to serpent form. Glooscap then named the animals and found that man was the lord of all. He was extremely kind to the creatures he had made. To begin with all was in darkness, so that men could not even see to slay their enemies. But Glooscap brought light into the world, and taught mankind the arts of life, the noble art of hunting, how to build huts and canoes, how to net the salmon and to make weapons. He showed to men the hidden virtues of plants and roots and blossoms, taught them the names of the stars, and acted throughout as a beneficent father to them.

By and by Glooscap withdrew himself from the haunts of men, yet he did not quit the earth for many years, but dwelt in a remote and almost inaccessible place. And he made it known to men that whoever should find him might have one wish granted, whatever that wish might be. For this reason many Indians sought his abode, though the way was long and arduous, and not all who set out reached their destination. Some of the wishers were wise and some foolish. The foolish wishers, or those who disobeyed the Master, found that the fulfilment of their wishes brought them no good, but the gifts which the wise ones received were generous in the extreme. This befell three Indians who visited the abode of Glooscap. One was a simple, honest Indian, who desired to excel in the chase. Another was a vain youth who wished to win the hearts of many maidens. The third was a buffoon whose only care was to create laughter; he therefore desired the power to utter an unusual cry, known to sorcerers in old time, which gladdened the hearts of all who heard it. The first received a magic pipe which would attract all animals to his nets, and the fulfilment of his wish brought him wealth and content. The second received a bag, tightly tied, which he was warned not to open till he reached home. Curiosity overcame him, however, and on the homeward journey he opened the bag, wherefrom issued a host of witches in the form of beautiful women, who strangled him with their embraces. The third received a magic root, and Glooscap warned him not to eat it till he reached his dwelling. He likewise disobeyed the command, and found himself gifted with the power to utter the magic cry; but, to his discomfiture, he could not always restrain it. The people of the town, at first delighted with the sound, soon tired of it, and avoided him who uttered it. This so preyed upon his mind that he betook himself to the woods and committed suicide.

The fourth portion of the epic contains Glooscap's adventures with the beasts—the loons, beaver, serpent, turtle, frog, and eagle. Very curious are the tales which describe the origin of the turtle, Glooscap's uncle, or relate how that crafty being endeavoured to overthrow the Master and make himself lord over beasts and men; and those that paint in picturesque language the binding of the Great Eagle, the Bird-who-blows-the-winds. Many of these stories are legendary, and purport to explain the existence of certain islands, streams, and other geographical features, as well as the physical structure and peculiarities of various animals. Thus the blowing of a whale is ingeniously explained by the fact that Glooscap at one time gave the animal a pipe and tobacco; it is smoking!

The fifth part of the epic treats mainly of the god's encounter with witches and sorcerers, and of his final departure from the earth. Toward the close of the poem a beautiful nature myth recounts how Glooscap found the Summer. Long years ago the deity travelled northward till he came to the lodge of the giant Winter. He entered and sat down, and his host told him tales of enchantment which cast him into a death-like sleep. Six months elapsed ere he awoke and proceeded homeward. With every step the air grew warmer, the earth greener and more beautiful. At length he came to a shady dell, where fairies were dancing joyfully, and, seizing their queen, whose name was Summer, he hid her in his bosom. Then he retraced his steps northward. The giant Winter still sat in his lodge, and at the coming of Glooscap he determined to throw the deity into a sleep that would last for ever; but this time the hidden presence of Summer spoiled the enchantments; tears of melting ice ran down the cheeks of the giant, and soon both he and his dwelling were changed to water, while signs of returning life and vegetation were everywhere apparent. Once more Glooscap turned his face southward, but the summer-elf he left behind him in the northern country.

Finally Glooscap abandoned the world, because of the evil that was in it. For long years he bore with the sinful ways of man, for whom he had cleared the land of evil demons and monsters, but at length his patience was exhausted. He made a great farewell feast, and afterward sailed away in his great canoe. And now he dwells in a splendid wigwam, continually making arrows. When the lodge is full of them he will make war on all mankind, and the world will pass away.

MYTH IN ENGLISH POETRY

How have the written myths we have just reviewed reflected upon the literature of our own race? Poetry and mythology are connected by an indissoluble bond. By mythology phenomena are endowed by the barbarian mind with all the attributes of life and reason. The process is clearly a poetical one, and by it the savage intelligence is brought very near to nature. Poetry, in some of its earliest and perhaps purest forms, is the direct outcome of a series of natural impressions on the mind; and both poetry and mythology are thus emanations from nature. In a barbarian state of society the one great theme of poetry is the story of the divine beings who sway the destinies of humankind. Thus the odes of Pindar, the epics of the *Iliad* and *Odyssey* of Homer, the sagas of the early Norsemen, the *Nihongi* of Japan, the tribal lays of the American Indians, all celebrate the triumphs, loves, wars, and destinies of the gods of these several peoples.

It has often been thought peculiar that mythology should have continued to be the theme of poetry many centuries after the faiths of Greece and Rome had become extinct. This was because at the period of the Renaissance, or rebirth of learning and art, in the later Middle Ages, it became the fashion for literary men to model their writings upon the classical authors of antiquity. This custom was nowhere more powerful than in France, whence it was borrowed by English authors, who began to make large use of classical and mythological allusions in the wondrous era of letters known as the Elizabethan. Thus we find the works of Marlowe, Fletcher, Shakespeare, Massinger, Ford, full of allusions to the principal figures of Latin and Greek mythology. From that period, indeed, down to our own day the beautiful and heroic myths of Greece have been the subject upon which many English poets have exercised their art; and those of them who have not woven tales around these exquisite fables have made plenteous use of them in the illustration and ornamentation of more homely themes. The works of all our great poets abound in allusions to the central figures of Greek mythology. Spenser, Milton, Dryden, Shelley, Byron, Keats have all embodied in their verse, or frequently allude to, the immortal tales of Hellas; and, advancing more nearly to our own time, Tennyson, Morris, and Swinburne, as well as many minor singers, have written of the deeds and loves and deaths of the mighty heroes around whom the ancient epics ebb and flow.

The following paragraphs describe the manner in which the myths of ancient Greece and Rome have been made use of by English poets, so that the reader may be enabled to regard the myth in the light of poetry and the poem in the light of mythology. Thus a double and mutual light may be cast upon both myth and song. Let us take as an example Shelley's *Prometheus Unbound*. Whoso knows the poem but not the myth from which it took its origin is robbed of much pleasure in reading the sublime verse, the ecstatic measures and magical lyrics with their constant allusions to the greater mythological characters. Who, for example, are Ione and Panthea? What is the nature of Demogorgon? For what crime against Jupiter is Prometheus, the Titan,

> Nailed to this wall of eagle-baffling mountain,
> Black, wintry, dead, unmeasured?

Unless these allusions are understood, much of the beauty of such a work is absolutely lost. Let us see, then, how some of our greatest singers have regarded the denizens of Olympus and the mortals whose destinies they swayed.

Ere yet Jupiter seized on the lordship of Heaven and earth, Opion and Eurynome ruled in Olympus. They were dethroned by Saturn and Rhea, who in turn were hurled from power by Zeus, or Jupiter, and Juno. Keats draws a touching picture of the old, forsaken god Saturn, left to meditations of a lost empire:

> Deep in the shady sadness of a vale
> Far sunken from the healthy breath of morn,
> Far from the fiery noon, and eve's one star,
> Sat grey-haired Saturn, quiet as a stone,

276

Still as the silence round about his lair ;
Forest on forest hung about his head,
Like cloud on cloud.   No stir of air was there,
Not so much life as on a summer's day
Robs not one light seed from the feather'd grass,
But where the dead leaf fell, there did it rest.
A stream went voiceless by, still deaden'd more
By reason of his fallen divinity,
Spreading a shade.

A marvellous picture of shattered power! The grey quiet of
the soundless vale, the unnatural stillness of leaf, and the noise-
less stream, symbolize the inertia of the divinity who was once
creative.

In the catalogue of gods in the first book of *Paradise Lost*,
Milton summarizes the usurpation of the heavenly sceptre first
by Saturn and then by Jupiter in four telling lines :

Titan, Heaven's first born,
With his enormous brood, and birthright seized
By younger Saturn, he from mightier Jove,
His own and Rhea's son like measure found ;
So Jove usurping reigned.

An effective picture of the vanquished and fallen Titans is
also drawn by Keats, who says of them :

Scarce images of life, one here, one there,
Lay vast and edgeways ; like a dismal cirque
Of Druid stones, upon a forlorn moor.

The simile of the giant and fallen forms to the lightning-
shattered monoliths of some deserted Druid circle is magnificent.   Such passages show how great are the themes which
bring forth those stupendous images, the mightiest offspring of
imagination.   A great poet might sing of the things of to-day
throughout a lifetime, and yet never so thrill the imagination
as with the dead things which have the glamour of ages upon
them.

Jupiter, as we know, was in the habit of abducting mortals
from the earth, and transferring those who were very beautiful
to the bright clime of Olympus.   For this reason he seized

INTRODUCTION TO MYTHOLOGY

upon the shepherd lad Ganymede, whom he made cup-bearer to the gods, and Asteria, the mother of Hecate, one of the infernal deities. To effect these captures he usually took the shape of an eagle. Spenser in *The Faerie Queene* says of him :

> Twice was he seen in soaring Eagle's shape,
> And with wide wings to beat the buxom air :
> Once, when he with Asterie did scape ;
> Again, when as the Trojan boy so fair
> He snatched from Ida hill, and with him bare :
> Wondrous delight it was there to behold
> How the rude Shepherds after him did stare,
> Trembling through fear lest down he fallen should,
> And often to him calling to take surer hold.[1]

Spenser has another beautiful passage upon one of the captures made by Jupiter :

> Behold how goodly my fair love does lie,
> In proud humility !
> Like unto Maia, when as Jove her took
> In Tempe, lying on the flowery grass,
> 'Twixt sleep and wake, after she weary was
> With bathing in the Acidalian brook.

In the second book of *Paradise Lost* Milton makes Sin spring from the head of Satan, and it is reasonably conjectured that when he composed it he must have had in mind the myth of the marvellous birth of the goddess of wisdom, Pallas Athene. It is Sin who addresses the fallen archangel :

> All on a sudden miserable pain
> Surprised thee, dim thine eyes and dizzy swum
> In darkness, while thy head flames thick and fast
> Threw forth, till on the left side opening wide,
> Likest to thee in shape and countenance bright,
> Then shining heavenly fair, a goddess armed
> Out of thy head I sprung.

In times of peace Minerva assisted mankind in the manual crafts, and she also presided over the fortunes of war. She possessed a shield called the *ægis*, bearing the severed head of a

---

[1] Book III, canto xi, 34.

278

monster named the Gorgon, which possessed the magical property of changing into stone anyone who beheld it. Milton renders her more spiritually formidable by conceiving that her purity and chastity, not the horrid head of the Gorgon, froze the hearts of evildoers into terror :

> What was that snaky-headed Gorgon shield
> That wise Minerva wore, unconquered virgin,
> Wherewith she freez'd her foes to congeal'd stone,
> But rigid looks of chaste austerity,
> And noble grace that dash'd brute violence
> With sudden adoration and blank awe?[1]

Shelley has a wonderful and not often quoted poem on this Gorgon head, torn from the body of the monster Medusa to front the *ægis* of the goddess of divine wisdom :

> It lieth, gazing on the midnight sky,
> Upon the cloudy mountain peak supine ;
> Below, far lands are seen tremblingly ;
> Its horror and its beauty are divine.
> Upon its lips and eyelids seem to lie
> Loveliness like a shadow, from which shine,
> Fiery and lurid, struggling underneath,
> The agonies of anguish and of death.
>
> Yet it is less the horror than the grace
> Which turns the gazer's spirit into stone,
> Whereon the lineaments of that dead face
> Are graven, till the characters be grown
> Into itself, and thought no more can trace ;
> 'Tis the melodious hues of beauty thrown
> Athwart the darkness and the glare of pain,
> Which humanise and harmonise the strain.

Vulcan, or Hephæstus, was the god of fire, both in its forms of lurid conflagration and the more kindly glow of the domestic hearth, and his story is occasionally sung by our British poets. He was a craftsman of marvellous excellence in all the arts, and made the thunderbolts wielded by Jupiter. He was also the husband of Venus. His mother Juno having quarrelled with

[1] *Comus.*

the King of Heaven, Vulcan took her part and was cast from Olympus by his enraged sire. He took an entire day to fall to earth, and at last alighted in the island of Lemnos:

> From morn
> To noon he fell, from noon to dewy eve,
> A summer's day, and with the setting sun
> Dropped from the zenith like a falling star
> On Lemnos, th' Ægean isle.[1]

In his amusing "Execration upon Vulcan," which was occasioned by the fire which destroyed his library and manuscripts, Ben Jonson alludes to Vulcan as the "lame lord of fire," and continues:

> 'Twas Jupiter that hurled thee headlong down,
> And Mars that gave thee a lanthorn for a crown.
> Was it because thou wert of old denied,
> By Jove, to have Minerva for thy bride;
> That since, thou tak'st all envious care and pain
> To ruin every issue of the brain?

Venus, goddess of love, has ever been a theme of delight to poets. She was the daughter of Jupiter, but is sometimes referred to as springing from the foam of the sea, as, for example, in the enchanting lines of Swinburne's "Hymn to Proserpine":

> White rose of the rose-white water, a silver splendour, a flame.

Lord de Tabley also refers to the foam-birth of Venus in the following stanza:

> Uranian Aphrodite, fair,
> From ripples of the ocean spray;
> Sweet as the sea-blooms in thy hair
> Rosed with the blush of early day,
> O hear us from thy temple steep
> Where Eryx crowns the Dorian deep.

The attributes and symbols of Venus are neatly described

---

[1] Milton, *Paradise Lost*, Book I.

WRITTEN SOURCES OF MYTH

by Ben Jonson in his masque of *Love's Triumph through Callipolis.* Venus is supposed to say :

> Here, here I present am,
> Both in my girdle and my flame ;
> Wherein are woven all the powers
> The Graces gave me, or the Hours,
> My nurses once, with all the arts
> Of gaining and of holding hearts.

CHAPTER XI
THE GREAT MYTHIC SYSTEMS OF THE WORLD

IT is now time to review briefly the great mythic systems of the world and to examine and analyse as far as practicable their nature and outstanding figures. This *résumé* is added here merely for completeness, because exhaustive works dealing with the several mythological systems alluded to in these pages are included in this series, and to these the student can refer.

GRÆCO-ROMAN MYTH

Starting with the mythic system practically common to Greece and Rome as that with which our readers are likely to be most familiar, we find a mythology a good deal more human than divine; although it would be untrue to say that it possessed no divine characteristics. However, we are not in this chapter dealing with the cults or religions underlying the mythologies we treat of, but *with the mythologies themselves*, or, as we have elsewhere named it, the theobiography, the gods, their lives and histories. What status did the gods of Greece occupy in the minds of those who believed in them? This, of course, differed with the centuries, but there is pretty good evidence that as they grew more enlightened the Hellenic people paid less and less reverence to Olympus, until at last it became almost a byword among them.

In Greece more than in any other country religion and mythology were two things separate and distinct. In Homer, the Greek gods, headed by Zeus, dwelt in a condition of society very much akin to that of mortals in the Homeric Age. Their government appears to have been modelled upon the social

282

THE GREAT MYTHIC SYSTEMS

polities of the various Hellenic city-states ; and when republics became the fashion, the gods, partaking of the older order of affairs, fell somewhat into disrepute, just as the elder dynasties of Cronus and Uranus, who represented the tribal system of government, had given place to Zeus when a monarchical system came into vogue.

ZEUS—JUPITER

Zeus, the head of the Greek pantheon, was supposed to dwell on the summit of Mount Olympus, where he disposed of the affairs both of the gods and of men. He was probably originally a sky-god, symbolizing the bright, clear expanse of the heavens, being later, like many other sky-gods, anthropomorphized. The many stories told of his amorous adventures in animal form are obviously totemic and fetishistic legacies which as a great mythical figure he would undoubtedly attract to himself. As a sky-god he wields the thunder and lightning, conquers the Titans, and overcomes Gæa, probably the original Earth-Mother—just as in Babylonian myth Merodach conquered Tiawath. He had several spouses, the chief of whom was Hera. He was by no means a creative deity, but he won a wide popularity, and through this and other causes he came to be head of the pantheon, composed of other gods as well as of his parents, children, brothers, sisters, or wives. Lang points out that he may well have begun as a kindly supreme being, and his mythic character may have been ultimately swamped by the accumulation around his name of myths concerning older deities. The corresponding Roman god is Jupiter.

APOLLO

Apollo in tradition is usually a solar deity, but also a civilizer or culture-hero, and his functions and attributes are manifold. He superintends the measurement of time, protects herds and flocks, and is a patron of music and poetry. He has a very active solar connexion when, for example, he slays with his golden arrows the Python, the serpent of night or winter. His oracle at Delphi was the most famous in Greece, and his priestesses were famed as prophetesses. He was usually portrayed as a young and handsome man crowned with laurel and holding a lyre in his hand. There is little doubt that many different and perhaps contradictory myths went to the making of the personality and character of Apollo, and he has decidedly totemic connexions, as, for example, the dolphin, the wolf, and the mouse; and perhaps with lizards, hawks, swans, ravens, and crows. Like Zeus, he attracted to himself the legends of a great many lesser divinities of the same type.

HERMES—MERCURY

Hermes, called by the Romans Mercury, was the son of Zeus and the messenger of the gods. Quick-witted, ready-tongued, and thievish, he is the traditional patron of light-fingered, sharp people, who can charm the senses of others as well as the money out of their pockets.

HEPHÆSTUS—VULCAN

Hephæstus or Vulcan was the god of fire, and the great artist among the gods. It was he who constructed the shining palaces of Olympus, the marvellous armour of Achilles, and the necklace of Harmonia. He also invented the thunderbolt. As a later type of deity, he is the smith or artificer deified, probably evolved from an older fire-god or thunder-god.

HERA—JUNO

Among the goddesses of the Greek pantheon Hera, the Juno of the Romans, was paramount because of her status as wife and sister of Zeus. She is the divine prototype of the wife and mother and the special patroness of marriage.

ATHENE—MINERVA

Pallas Athene, the Minerva of the Romans, is another composite deity. She seems to have been a queen of the air or a storm-goddess, and probably became a war-goddess through her possession of the lightning-spear. In peace she was looked upon as a patroness of useful crafts and even of abstract wisdom. She is often depicted with the owl and the serpent, both emblems of wisdom. It is unusual to discover a war- or storm-deity posing as the patron of learning, and the exact manner in which Athene attained to the latter position is extremely obscure.

APHRODITE—VENUS

Aphrodite or Venus, the goddess of love and beauty, was probably a deity of Asiatic origin, and her birth from the sea-foam and home in Cyprus, where her cult was very strong, confirm the identification of her myth with that of Ashtaroth or Astarte.

EGYPTIAN MYTH

A good deal has been said in this volume about the mythology of Egypt, and in especial Osiris, Thoth, and Ptah have already been considered, so that we may say more here of some other important gods of the Nile country. The reader is reminded that no definite Egyptian pantheon ever existed, for as dynasties rose and fell, and as the various priestly colleges throughout the land came into favour in turn, the deities whose cults they represented rose and fell in popularity— that is, at no time was there a fixed divine hierarchy like that of Greece.

RA

Ra, the great god of the sun, figured as the head of a hawk, voyaged daily across the heavenly expanse in his bark. For many dynasties he was regarded as the greatest of all the gods of Egypt. He is by no means an intricate mythological figure, and it is plain that he is neither more nor less than a personification of the sun.

ANUBIS

Anubis, the jackal, or dog-headed protector of the dead, pre-sides over the process of embalming. He seems to have evolved from the dog who among many primitive people accompanies the deceased in the journey to the Otherworld.

INTRODUCTION TO MYTHOLOGY

HORUS

Horus, the son of Osiris and Isis, was a sun-god with many shapes, some perhaps local, but most of which typified the various stages of the sun's journey—its rising, its midday strength, its evening decline. He was the eternal enemy of Set, the night-god, a deity of darkness with whom he waged constant combat. From being a god of night and darkness pure and simple, Set came to be regarded as a deity of evil, and was placed in dualistic opposition to Horus, Ra, or Osiris, who thus symbolize moral good, the emblem of which is light.

ISIS

Among the most important Egyptian goddesses is Isis, sister and wife of Osiris, probably, like her husband, connected with the corn-plant, although there are also indications that she is a wind-goddess. She is the great corn-mother of Egypt, perhaps only because of her connexion with Osiris, and she has the wings of a wind deity, restoring Osiris to life by fanning him with them. She is a great traveller, and unceasingly moans and sobs. At times she shrieks so loudly as to frighten children to death. She typifies not only the dreaded blast, but the revivifying power of the spring wind wailing and sobbing over the grave of the sleeping grain.

Nephthys, her sister, is the female counterpart of Set and the personification of darkness. As such she is also a funerary goddess.

BABYLONIAN MYTH

As with Egyptian religion, the faith of the Babylonians and Assyrians varied with dynasties, for it depended upon the rise to power of a certain city or province, whose god then became temporarily supreme. Thus we find Merodach regarded as the chief god in Babylonia, while farther north in Assyria Asshur held sway, and Merodach had a fairly long line of predecessors whose powers and dignities he had taken over. Indeed, we find that he actually appropriated their myths. For example, in the creation myth cited in our chapter on cosmogony, Merodach is

286

the hero-god who succeeded in slaying Tiawath, the monster of the abyss ; but in an older version of the story her slayer is the god En-lil, whose place Merodach usurped later. Round the figure of Merodach, alluded to as the Bel, the Babylonian title for the highest divinity, are grouped the other deities in descending degrees of importance, for, as in the worldly State, the king of the gods was surrounded by officials of diverse rank.

MERODACH

Merodach, chief god of Babylon, possessed a solar significance ; but it may be improper to connect him in any manner with the sun in its seasonal stages. He is, in fact, more the lord of light than of the sun in any special aspect. Although there is evidence that he was regarded as the spring sun, this was probably a secondary or derived conception of him, like that which made him a god of battle.

EA

Ea was the Babylonian Neptune. He was figured as half man, half fish, and was a great culture-hero and the lord of wisdom, probably because of the depths whence he emanated, symbolic of the profundity of knowledge. He came every day to the city of Eridu to instruct its inhabitants in the arts of life, and he was the inventor of writing, geometry, and law.

BEL

Bel, called the 'older Bel' to distinguish him from Bel-Merodach, was also called Mul-lil or En-lil. He was a god of the Underworld and may have been relegated thence, like many other deities, on the coming to power of Merodach.

> Better to reign in Hell than serve in Heaven

seems to have been the thought of other ancient divinities than Milton's Satan.

The Babylonians themselves seemed rather doubtful as to the exact status of this god.

Nirig was a favourite deity in Assyria, and is called in inscriptions 'god of war.'

Anu was the father of the great gods. He may at one time have been the supreme being of the Babylonian religion, and his cult is of extreme antiquity.

Nusku was the messenger of the gods and without him the King of Heaven could not pass judgment upon anything. He seems to have personified flame or light.

Shamash was the sun in a different sense from Merodach, and he seems also to have been looked upon as the great judge of the universe, probably because the sun is able to direct his beams into the darkest places. He it was who gave the famous code of laws into the hands of King Hammurabi—according to the 'sun-god tablet' in the British Museum.

ISHTAR

Ishtar, the Queen of Heaven, was the great mother-goddess and sexual goddess of Babylon, and among the Assyrians appears to have been looked upon as a goddess of battle. She was identified with the planet Venus, and her cult was associated with that of Tammuz. Her descent into the Underworld stamps her as a corn-mother, like the Greek Demeter, the reappearance of whose daughter Persephone clothes the earth with fertility.

Allatu was the goddess of the Babylonian Otherworld. Nergal assisted her, and he was also a god of conflict, disease, and pestilence, symbolizing the misery and destruction which accompanies warfare.

Sin was the moon-god, and, probably from his connexion with the calendar, was called 'lord of wisdom.' His worship was surrounded by much mystery, and a beautiful and touching prayer in the library of Assurbanipal describes him as being "full of love like the far-off heaven and the broad ocean."

ASSHUR

Asshur, the head of the Assyrian pantheon, had attained to the position of chief god in it because his city of Asshur was the capital of Assyria. At the same time his worship was even more strongly national than that of Merodach in Babylonia. He was the sun personalized, and he was probably identical in

288

most respects with Merodach. He was, in fact, the national god
of Assyria grafted on to a Babylonian myth.

HINDU MYTH

According to one of the oldest commentators on the Vedas,
three principal deities were known to the Hindus in Vedic
times—Agni, Vayu or Indra, and Surya. Agni appears to
personify three forms of fire—sun, lightning, and sacrificial fire.
Indra was a god of the sky or firmament, twin brother of Agni
and king of the gods. Surya was the sun himself. These three
formed a triad. In later Vedic times the number of the gods
was increased to thirty-three, but behind all these are two more
ancient gods of the father and mother type—Dyaus (equated
with the Greek Zeus and an abstract deity of the sky), and
Prithivi, the Earth-Mother. Mitra was perhaps identical with
the Persian Mithra and seems to have ruled over day, while
Varuna his companion, also a sky-god, combined the divine
attributes of the other gods. He was the possessor of law and
wisdom and ordered all earthly and heavenly phenomena. Indra
also appears to have been a god of the firmament, but, in another
sense, he was a god of storm and battle ; while Soma has been
well described as " the Indian Bacchus."

The gods of the later ages of Hinduism naturally differ considerably from those of the Vedic period, as might well be
expected, considering the time between the two epochs. It is
true that the *Ramayana* and the *Mahabharata* still keep the
personnel of the old pantheon, but whatever was animistic in the
gods in Vedic times became in the later Puranic period (named
after the written Puranas or traditional myths) wholly anthropomorphic. Moreover, a definite attempt to arrange a pantheon
is discernible. Eight of the principal gods are revealed as
guardians of the universe, each having rule over a definite
domain. Some of them have even changed their character
entirely. For example, we now find Varuna a god of water ;
Indra has all the characteristics of a great earthly chief who
has dealings with terrestrial monarchs and who may be defeated
by them in battle. In Hanuman, the monkey king, we perhaps
find a representative of the aboriginal tribes of Southern India.

INTRODUCTION TO MYTHOLOGY

BRAHMA

More important than all these is Brahma. Only a few hymns of the Vedas appear to deal with him as the one divine, self-existent, and omnipresent being, but in the later Puranic literature we find him described as an abstract supreme spirit. With Brahma Hinduism reached its greatest heights of mystical and metaphysical thought. Such questions are asked in the *Vishnu Purana*, for example, as: How can a creative agency be attributed to Brahma, who, as an abstract spirit, is without qualities, illimitable, and free from imperfection? The answer is that the essential properties of existent things are objects of observation, of which no foreknowledge is attainable, and the innumerable phenomena are manifestations of Brahma, as inseparable parts of his essence as heat from fire. Again, this Purana says: "There are two states of this Brahma—one with, and one without shape; one perishable, one imperishable; which are inherent in all beings. The imperishable is the supreme being; the perishable is all the world. The blaze of fire burning in one spot diffuses light and heat around; so the world is nothing more than the manifested energy of the supreme Brahma; and inasmuch as the light and heat are stronger or feebler as we are near to the fire or far off from it, so the energy of the supreme is more or less intense in the beings that are less or more remote from him. Brahma, Vishnu, and Siva are the most powerful energies of God; next to them are the inferior deities; then the attendant spirits; then men; then animals, birds, insects, vegetables; each becoming more and more feeble as they are farther from their primitive source."

The *Vishnu Purana* gives the following derivation of the word Brahma: It "is derived from the root *vriha* (to increase) because it is infinite (spirit), and because it is the cause by which the Vedas (and all things) are developed." Then follows this hymn to Brahma: "Glory to Brahma, who is addressed by that mystic word (*Om*), associated eternally with the triple universe (earth, sky, and heaven), and who is one with the four Vedas. Glory to Brahma, who alike in the destruction and

290

renovation of the world is called the great and mysterious cause of the intellectual principle ; who is without limit in time or space, and exempt from diminution and decay. . . . He is the invisible, imperishable Brahma ; varying in form, invariable in substance ; the chief principle, self-engendered ; who is said to illuminate the caverns of the heart, who is indivisible, radiant, undecaying, multiform. To that supreme Brahma be for ever adoration."

Brahma had his mythological side as Brahmā, apparently a development specially intended for his employment in myth. There he appears as the Creator of the world, born from a golden egg which floated on the waters at the beginning. He went through many avatars or bodily changes, and is thus the active manifestation of the First Cause, Brahma. He was connected with two other gods, Vishnu and Siva.

Vishnu is the preserver, as Brahmā is the creator, and he is closely associated with Indra, whom he assisted to combat the powers of evil. He it was who rendered the universe habitable for man, "made the atmosphere wide and stretched out the world." He is a sort of demiurge patrolling the earth and may have evolved from the idea that the sun was a great watchful eye ever looking down to inspect what was occurring on the world below, as do several other deities.

Siva, a development of a Vedic storm-god Rudra, was regarded as a destroyer or regenerator. He is a god of reproduction and restoration, but he has a dark side to his character, and has given rise to one of the most revolting cults of any religion. Durga is a goddess of war and destruction and the wife of Siva. She is also known as Kali, and, like her husband, is placated by dreadful rites. Ganesa, the son of Siva, is an elephant-headed god of wisdom and of good luck. He is also a patron of learning and literature. He rather resembles the Egyptian Thoth.

A host of lesser deities follow these, notably the Gandharvas, who in Vedic times constituted the body-guard of Soma, but in Puranic days became heavenly minstrels, plying their art at the Court of Indra. The Apsaras are the houris of Indra's court. Indian epics contain many notices of numerous demi-gods, and the planets are also deified.

It may be said that in later times the fervour of Hindu worship has concentrated itself round the two figures of Vishnu and Siva, who from unimportant Vedic beginnings have evolved into deities of the first importance. There is a certain rivalry between them, but they are also complementary, being the beneficent and evil aspects of the divine spirit. It would seem as if dualism and monotheism had almost met here to form a third condition of godhead.

New gods of inferior kind have arisen in India and a small pantheon has been apportioned to each of them, but they do not require description here.

TEUTONIC MYTH

The mythology of the Teutonic peoples has a strong like-ness to those of the other Aryan races, notably the Greeks, Romans, and Celts. At the head is Odin or Wotan, who in many respects resembles Zeus or Jupiter. He is a divine legislator, cunning in Runic lore, and the creator of mankind. His worshippers pictured him as a one-eyed man of venerable aspect clad in a wide-brimmed hat and voluminous cloak, and travelling through the world to observe the doings of men. With his brothers Vili and Ve he raised the earth out of the waters of chaos. His name of 'All-Father' shows the exact position he held in the minds of Scandinavian and Germanic folk. His wife, Freya, is much akin to Juno or Hera. She was the matron and housewife deified and the patroness of marriage.

LOKI

The malevolent deity was represented by Loki, perhaps originally a fire-god, and ever at the elbow of Odin offering him evil counsel. Loki is one of the most interesting figures in any mythology. He is both friend and foe to the Æsir or divine beings and seems to have reduced to a fine art the policy of running with the hare and hunting with the hounds. We find him assisting at the making of humanity and we also discover him acting as steersman to the ship that brings the forces of evil to combat with the gods on the last great day of reckoning. At times he would employ his natural cunning on behalf of the gods, at other times use it for their ignominious defeat. Protean in character, he could assume any shape he chose at will. He has been alluded to as the great riddle of Teutonic mythology, but it may be that this riddle represents fire in its beneficent and maleficent aspects. Indeed, the name Logi is given elsewhere to a certain fire-demon, and this almost clinches the matter. His many evil deeds were at last punished by his being chained to a rock like Prometheus, while over his head hung a serpent whose venom fell upon his face. The fact that Prometheus, also a fire-god, met the same fate is one of those baffling resemblances which occasionally confront the student of myth, and set him on a lifetime's search for the connexion between the stories. The great danger is that such a seeker may become enamoured of some fantastic solution. Frequently a possible solution leaps into consciousness with all the rapidity of an inspiration; but there are true and false inspirations, and the difficulty is to distinguish between them. They should be ruthlessly subjected to a melting and remelting process in the crucible of comparison until only the pure gold remains. Had this scientific process been rigorously adopted by all mythologists, the scientific value of the study would have been enormously enhanced and it would possess greater uniformity; for although magnificent work has been achieved, far too much loose thinking has been indulged in, and at the present time we are reduced to groping for standards and definitions in a manner quite extraordinary.

THOR

Thor, the god of thunder and lightning, possesses a hammer which symbolizes the thunder, as the spear or arrow of some other gods typifies the lightning. The hammer sometimes symbolizes the world-shaping god, the creative divinity, but perhaps not in regard to Thor. His red beard is probably symptomatic of the lightning, like the red limbs of some American thunder-gods. He is the foe of the Jötunn or giants, and he bulked very largely indeed in the myths of the Norsemen. At the same time, like most thunder-gods who bring in their train the fructifying winds and rains, Thor presided over the crops and was thus the friend of peasants. Indeed his wife, Sif, is usually portrayed as a peasant woman of the Scandinavian type. He is the patron of countrymen, slow of speech and wit, if quick to strike with his hammer Mjolnir.

CELTIC MYTH

The mythology of the Celts shows an early connexion with that of the Teutons on the one hand and the Græco-Roman races on the other. Perhaps originally all possessed a common mythology, which altered upon their geographical separation. The priestly caste placed many of the old myths upon a definite literary footing, but these again were manufactured into pseudo-history by Geoffrey of Monmouth and kindred writers, so that it is often impossible to discover their original significance except by analogy. Animistic myths, however, survived the establishment of anthropomorphic gods among the Celts. Agricultural and seasonal deities were in the ascendant, as became an agricultural people, but not to the exclusion of totemic influences. Later, culture-gods of music, poetry, and the manual arts sprang up or were developed from existing deities. In the Gaulish pantheon, concerning which we have little information, we find Cæsar equating no less than sixteen local gods with the Roman Mercury, many with Apollo (among them Borvo, Belenos, and Grannos), while with Mars other writers equate Camulos, Teutates, Albiorix, and Caturix, probably tribal war-gods. With Minerva was compared the horse-goddess Epona, while Berecyntia, a goddess of Autun, is compared by Gregory of Tours with the Italian Bona Dea. Inscriptions make Aeracura the equivalent of Dispater. Turning to Ireland, we possess later and therefore more satisfactory data, based on mythic tales of a far earlier date. These stories speak of immigrant races named the Tuatha de Danann (children of the goddess Danu), the Fomorians, the Firbolgs, and Milesians, of whom the first two classes are divine. Among these warring elements the Fomorians are a race of Titans. Balor, one of their leaders, is a personification of the evil eye; nothing could live beneath his glance. Bres seems to have been a deity of growth—a vegetation-god. Dea Domnann was a species of Celtic Tiawath (Babylonian goddess of the abyss). Tethra was lord of the Underworld. Nét was a war-god. These were all gods of an early aboriginal race, and in later Irish myth are regarded as uncouth giant monsters.

THE CHILDREN OF DANU

Danu, mother of the race, was considered as a daughter of Dagda. She seems to have been an Earth-Mother.

The Tuatha de Danann, or Tribe of the Goddess Danu, have many congeners in British myth, and their worship appears to have been brought from Gaul or Britain. They were conquered by the Milesians and, retiring to the Underworld, appear to have taken the place of fairies, for they are later called *sidhe* or 'fairy folk.' Dagda (the 'good hand' or 'good god'), father of Danu, played the spring season into being with his harp. He fed the whole earth out of an immense pot or cauldron called Undry, the symbol of plenty. His was the perfection of knowledge and understanding. He is undoubtedly the great Celtic god of growth, and was probably originally a sun-deity, as his harp and his wisdom show. Ængus, his son, who supplanted him, resembled him. Nuada of the Silver Hand is a culture-hero and a cunning craftsman. He has a British equivalent, Llud Llaw Ereint, the 'silver-handed,' and both, like all culture-heroes, were connected with the sun and with growth. Manannan is a sea-god, and the Isle of Man may perhaps have taken its name from him when it was regarded as an Elysium. He is the same as the British Manawyddan. Lug (Welsh *Lleu*) is a craftsman and inventor of many arts, and is frequently alluded to as 'Lug of the Long Arm'; whence some authorities have seen in him a solar god, as the beams or arms of the sun reach from heaven to earth.

Ogma is master of poetry and the supposed inventor of the 'ogham' script, which is said to be called after him. His eloquence excited the gods to valour in battle. Diancecht ('swift in power') was a god of the healing art. Goibniu, a god of smith-craft and magic, manufactured arms for the gods and brewed ale for them. Brigit was a goddess of poetry and wisdom, and, like the Greek Pallas Athene, may have been at one time the goddess of a cult especially female. The Morrigan, Naman, and Macha are war-goddesses of sanguinary character.

British Gods

Among purely British gods, Bran, son of Llyr, the sea-god, presided over minstrelsy, and may have been a god of the fertile Underworld or the realm of the dead, the Celtic Elysium. Gwydion, also a bard, is a diviner as well, and, like the Greek Proteus, is expert at changing his form. Amaethon appears to have been an agricultural deity, and the name seems to be connected with *amaeth*, the Welsh for 'plough-man.' He is credited with bringing certain domestic animals from the Land of the Gods to the World of Men, and this suggests totemism. Arianrhod, wife and sister of Gwydion, is perhaps an earth-goddess, but her significance is obscure. Bilé is probably a sun-god, and is equated with Apollo. Keridwen is a goddess dwelling in an under-water Elysium. She is described as a goddess of inspiration and poetry, and possesses a cauldron which is the source of all inspiration. Her son Avaggdu was cursed with hideousness, so his mother resolved to boil the cauldron of inspiration to compensate him for his ugliness. Gwion Bach, requested to watch it until it boils, steals the gift of inspiration for himself. He flees, and is pursued by Keridwen, but changes into various shapes. She follows his example, and at length in the form of a hen she swallows him as a grain of wheat. She later gives birth to him, throws him into the sea, and he becomes the bard Taliesin, famous for his poetic fire, the gift of the cauldron of inspiration.

Mexican Mythology

The mythologies of America are chiefly of interest because they illustrate and supplement the faiths of the Old World, and this is especially the case with the mythology of Mexico, which represents a phase of religious evolution considerably more advanced than the beliefs of the red man of the North American plains or the barbarians of the South American continent. In ancient Mexico we have one of the only three American mythological systems which attained anything like religious cohesion, or exemplified the higher reaches of ethical religious thought. The religion of ancient Mexico has been classified as a religion of the lower cultus, but the folly of such a classification is extreme, and it has, of course, emanated from persons who have made no especial study of the mythology of Mexico. To range it with such religions as those of the aborigines of Australia or those of some African tribes is incorrect, as a brief account of it will prove to the reader.

When the Spaniards finally conquered Mexico the more intelligent among them, although for the most part military men and priests, began to interest themselves in the antiquities and religion of the people they had conquered. The accounts they have left of the Aztec faith are, of course, unscientific, but we can gather a great deal from them by analogy and comparison with Old World faiths. We find that the Aztec population of Mexico worshipped gods who, if they did not form a pantheon or hierarchy, had each a more or less distinct sphere of his own. One of these, Tezcatlipoca, has been called the Jupiter of the Aztec pantheon, and seems to deserve this name.

Bernal Diaz, one of the Spanish conquerors, describes this god as having the face of a bear, and this error has been handed down from generation to generation of writers on Mexican mythology, is repeated in books of reference, and is generally accepted because of its antiquity. As I have shown elsewhere (*Edinburgh Review* for October 1920), Tezcatlipoca was probably a development of the obsidian stone, which was employed for the purpose of making both sacrificial knives and polished mirrors in which future events were supposed to be viewed. This stone, too, was regarded as capable of raising wind or tempests. Tezcatlipoca was supposed to rush through the highways at night, and in this connexion he probably symbolized the night wind, but from analogy with other North American Indian gods of a like character it is most probable that in later times he came to be thought of as a personification of the breath of life. The wind is usually regarded as the giver of breath and the source of immediate life. One of Tezcatlipoca's names was Yoalli Ehecatl, or Night Wind, and this leads us to suspect that he was the giver of all life. In many mythologies the name of the chief deity is derived from the same root as the word 'wind,' and in others the words 'soul' and 'breath' have a common origin. Thus the Hebrew word *ruah* is equivalent to both wind and spirit, as is the name of the Egyptian god Kneph. Strangely enough, however, Tezcatlipoca was also regarded as a death-dealer, and some of the prayers addressed to him are pitiful in their tone of entreaty that he will refrain from slaying his devotees. The probable reason for this is that his worship, however it became so, was so extremely popular as almost to eclipse most other Mexican deities, and owing to this popularity his idea achieved such an enormous significance in the Aztec mind that he began to be regarded as a god of fate and fortune with power to ban or bless as he saw fit, and therefore to be sedulously placated by prayer and sacrifice.

The Aztec War-God [1]

Next to him in importance, but scarcely less in the popular estimation, was Uitzilopochtli, tutelar deity of the Aztec people and god of war. Legends told how he led the Aztec tribes from their home of origin into the valley of Mexico in the shape of a humming-bird. He was represented as wearing a garment of humming-bird's feathers, and his face and limbs were painted black and yellow. Enormous sacrifices of human beings were made at stated intervals to this god, whose great *teocalli* or pyramid temple in the city of Mexico was literally a human shambles, where prisoners of war were immolated on his altar; but he also appears, like some other war-gods, to have an agricultural significance. His mother was the goddess of flowers, and he himself was associated with the summer and its abundance of crops and fruit. This was because of his possession of the war-spear or dart, which with the Aztecs as with

[1] See p. 32.

many another people symbolized the lightning and therefore the thunder-cloud with its fructifying rain.

But the real rain-god, or rather the god of moisture, of the Aztecs was Tlaloc, upon whose co-operation the success of the crops depended. He dwelt in the mountains which surround the Mexican valley, and he is represented in sculpture in a semi-recumbent position, with the upper part of the body raised upon the elbows and the knees half drawn up, to enable him to hold the vase in which the sacred grain was kept. The *tlaloque* or rain-spirits were regarded as his progeny, and he manifested himself in three ways, by the flash, the thunder, and the thunderbolt. His dwelling, Tlalocan, was a fruitful and abounding Paradise where those who were drowned, struck by lightning, or who had died of dropsy were certain to go. In the native paintings part of his face is of a dark colour, probably to represent the thunder-cloud. Numerous children were sacrificed to him annually, and if they wept it was regarded as a happy omen for a rainy season.

One of the most important and picturesque Aztec deities was Quetzalcoatl, probably a god of the pre-Aztec inhabitants of Mexico, the Toltecs. The name signifies 'feathered serpent,' and the myths tell how he played the part of culture-hero in Mexico, teaching the people the arts and sciences; but by the cunning of Tezcatlipoca he was driven from the land, and, embarked upon a raft of serpents, he floated away to the East, the land of sunrise, where dwelt his father, the sun. A number of authorities have seen in Quetzalcoatl a god of the air, and even a moon-deity. He is obviously the trade wind, which carries the rain, and is driven from the country by Tezcatlipoca, the anti-trade wind.

A regular group of gods presided over the food supply and agriculture of Mexico: Xilonen and Chicomecohuatl were maize-goddesses, and Centeotl, a god, also presided to some extent over the maize. The earth-goddess Toci or Teteoinnan was regarded as the progenitrix or mother of the gods. Sun-worship was extremely popular in Mexico, and the sun was regarded as the god *par excellence*. Moreover, he was the deity of warriors to whom he granted victory in battle that they might supply him with food.

CHINOOK MYTH

The Chinook Indians of the north-west coast of America possess a religious system of great interest to the student of myth, and we must deal with it at some length. The Chinooks were divided into two linguistic groups with numerous dialectic differences—Lower Chinook (comprising Chinook proper and the Clatsop), and Upper Chinook (comprising the rest of the tribe). The Lower Chinook dialects are now practically extinct; of persons of pure Chinook blood only about three hundred now exist. Upper Chinook is still spoken by considerable numbers, but the mixture of blood on the Indian Reservation, where they dwell, has been so great that the majority using the dialect are not really Chinooks.

ZOOTHEISM

The stage of religious evolution to which the beliefs of the Chinooks belong is 'zootheism,' where no line of demarcation exists between man and beast, and all phenomena are explained in the mythic history of zoomorphic personages who can hardly be described as gods. The original totemic nature of these beings it would be difficult to gainsay, but they occupy a position between the totem and the god proper—a rank which has been the lot of many evolving deities.

Allied with these beliefs we find shamanistic medico-religious practices invoking assistance for the sick.

Their mythological figures fall into four classes: (1) supernatural beings of a zoomorphic type, with many of the attributes of deity; (2) guardian spirits; (3) evil spirits; (4) culture-heroes.

The first class includes the Coyote, Blue Jay, Robin, Skunk, and Panther, etc. As has been said, there is little doubt that such beings were originally totems of various Chinookan clans, although these clans are without special tribal names, being simply designated as 'those dwelling at such and such a place.' They may, however, have lost their tribal names—a common

300

occurrence when tribes become sedentary — while retaining their totemistic concepts.

Italapas, the Coyote, is one of the Chinook gods of the first class, and may be regarded as the head of the pantheon. Nearly equal to him in importance is Blue Jay, who figures in nearly every myth of Chinook origin; but whereas Italapas the Coyote assisted Ikanam, the Creator, in the making of men, and taught them various arts, Blue Jay's mission is obviously dissension; and he well typifies the bird from which he takes his name, and probably his totem derivation. He figures as a mischievous tale-bearer, braggart, and cunning schemer, and resembles Loki of Scandinavian mythology.

His origin is touched upon in a myth of the journey of the Thunderer through the country of the Supernatural People, where, with Blue Jay's help, the Thunderer and his son-in-law obtain possession of the bows and targets of the inhabitants. They engage in a shooting-match and win at first by using their own targets, but when the Supernatural People suspect craft, they agree to the substitution of shining Supernatural targets for their own, and lose; and, as they had staked their own persons in the match, they fall into the power of the Supernatural beings, who wreak vengeance upon Blue Jay by metamorphosing him into the bird whose name he bears. "Blue Jay shall be your name and you shall sing 'Watsetsetset-setse,' and it shall be a bad omen."

There is a trilogy of myths concerning Blue Jay and his sister Ioi. Ioi begs him to take a wife to share her labour, and Blue Jay takes the corpse of a chief's daughter from her grave and carries her to the land of the Supernatural People, who restore her to life. The chief, her father, discovers the circumstance, and demands Blue Jay's hair in payment for his daughter, but Blue Jay changes himself into his bird shape and flies away—an incident which suggests his frequent adoption of human as well as bird form. When he flees, his wife expires again. The ghosts then buy Ioi, Blue Jay's sister, for a wife, and Blue Jay goes in search of her. Arriving in the country of the ghosts, he finds his sister surrounded by heaps of bones, to which she alludes as her relations by marriage. The ghosts take human shape occasionally, but upon being spoken to by Blue Jay become mere heaps of bones again. He takes a mischievous delight in reducing them to this condition, and in tormenting them in every possible manner, especially by mixing the various heaps of bones, so that, upon materializing, the ghosts find themselves with the wrong heads, legs, and arms. In fact the whole myth is obviously one which recounts the 'Harrying of Hell,' so common in savage and barbarian myth, and probably invented to reassure the savage as to the terrors of the next world, and to instruct him in the best methods of foiling its evil inhabitants. We find the same atmosphere in the myth of the descent into Xibalba of Hun-Apu and Xbalanque in the *Popol Vuh* of the Kiche of Guatemala, hero-gods who outwit and ridicule the lords of Hell.

Skasa-it (Robin) is Blue Jay's elder brother, and his principal occupation is making sententious comments on the mischievous acts of his relative. The Skunk, Panther, Raven, and Crow are similar figures. That most of these were anthropomorphic in shape—probably having animals' or birds' heads upon men's bodies—is proved not only by the protean facility with which they change their shapes, but by a passage in the myth of Anektcxolemix, mentioning "a person who came to the fire with a very sharp beak, and began to cut meat"; and another 'person' splits logs for firewood with his beak. Such ideas are notoriously incomprehensible to those unfamiliar with the distorted appearance of Nature—due to an intense familiarity with and nearness to her—in the savage mind.

Evil spirits are many and various. The most terrible appears to be the insatiable Glutton, who devours everything in a house, and when the meat supply comes to an end kills and eats the occupants. In the myth of Okulam he pursues five brothers, after eating all their meat, and devours them one by one, except the youngest, who escapes by the good offices of the Thunderer, Ikenuwakcom, a being of the nature of a thunder-god, and marries his daughter.

Besides being reckoned as deities of zoomorphic or sometimes anthropomorphic type, Blue Jay, Italapas, and the others may be regarded as hero-gods or culture-heroes, although not always prompted by the highest motives in their activities. They are markedly egotistical, every action being dictated by a desire to prove superior in force and cunning to the foe. To overcome difficulties by craft is the delight of the savage, and those gods who are most skilled in such methods he honours most. In the myths of Blue Jay and his sister Ioi, Blue Jay repeatedly scores against his adversaries, but in the end he is punished himself, and it is difficult to say whether or not the world was any the wiser or better for his efforts. The idea of good accomplished is a purely relative one in the savage mind, and cannot be appreciated to any extent by uncivilized persons.

The shamans of the Chinooks were a medico-religious fraternity, the members of which worked individually, as a general rule, but sometimes in concert. Their methods were much the same as those of the medicine-men of other Indian tribes in a similar state of belief, but were differentiated from them by various thaumaturgical practices which they made use of in their medical duties. These were usually undertaken by three shamans acting in concert for the purpose of rescuing the 'astral body' of a sick patient from the Land of Spirits. The three shamans who undertook the search for the sick man's spiritual body threw themselves into a state of clairvoyance; their souls, temporarily detached from their bodies, then followed the spiritual track of the sick man's soul. The soul of the shaman with a strong guardian spirit was placed first, the next in degree last, and that of the priest with the weakest guardian spirit in the middle. When the trail of the sick man's soul foreshadowed danger or the proximity of any supernatural evil, the soul of the foremost shaman sang a magical chant to ward it off; and if a danger approached from behind, the shaman in the rear did likewise. The soul was usually thought to be reached about the time of the rising of the morning star. If possible, it was laid hands on and brought back, after a sojourn of one or perhaps two nights in the regions of the supernatural. The shamans next replaced the soul in the body of their patient, who forthwith recovered. Should the soul of a sick person take the trail to the left, the pursuing shamans would say, "He will die"; whereas, if it took a trail toward the right, they would say, "We shall cure him."

When the spirits of the shamans reached the well in the Land of the Ghosts where the shades of the departed drink, their first care was to ascertain if the soul of him they sought had drunk of these waters; had it done so, all hope of cure was past. If they laid hold of a soul that had drunk of the water, it shrank as they neared home, so that it would not fill the sick man's body, and he died. The same superstition applied to the spirit eating ghostly food. Did the sick man's soul eat on the astral plain, then was he doomed indeed. In this belief we have a Greek parallel: Persephone, the daughter of Demeter, the corn-mother, might not return to earth permanently, because Pluto had given her to eat of the seed of a pomegranate. The taboo regarding the eating of the food of the dead is almost universal. We find it in the Finnish *Kalevala*, where Waïnamoïnen, visiting Tuonela, the place of the dead, refuses to drink, and in Japanese and Melanesian myth-cycles. Likewise, if the spirit enters the house of the ghosts, it cannot return to earth. These beliefs apply not only to human beings, but also to animals, and even to inanimate objects. For example, if the astral counterpart of a horse or a canoe be seen in ghost-land, unless they are rescued from thence by the shaman they are doomed.

CHOCTAW MYTH

Another interesting North American mythology is that of the Choctaw Indians, formerly occupying Middle and South Mississippi from Tombigbee River to the borders of Dallas County, Georgia. The Choctaw religion is almost unique among the North American Indian religions, as it is a union of animism and sun-worship, or, more correctly speaking, the two systems may be observed side by side among this and allied peoples of the Muskhogean stock. They have a supreme being whom they designate Yuba Paik, 'Our Father Above'; but whether this conception arose from contact with missionaries or is genuinely aboriginal it is impossible to say. The term may be collective, like the Hebrew *Elohim* or the Latin *Superi*, and may include all the powers of the air. It is perhaps more likely that it evolved from the word for sky, as did Zeus, the Nottoway Qui-oki, the Iroquois Garonhia, and the ancient Powhatan Oki. This supposition is strengthened by the cognate Greek expression, signifying 'He who lives in the sky.' As usual among North American Indian tribes, the Choctaws confound the sun with fire ; at least they refer to fire as Shahli miko, 'the greater chief,' and speak of it as Hashe ittiapa, ' He who accompanies the sun and the sun him.' On going to war they call for assistance from both sun and fire, but, except as fire, they do not address the sun, nor does he stand in any other relation to their religious thought. He is not personified, as, for example, among the Peruvians, or worshipped as the supreme symbol of fire. In American religions, generally speaking, what appears on the surface to be sun-worship pure and simple usually resolves itself, upon closer examination, into the worship of light and fire. Indeed the cognate Natchez word for 'sun' is derived from that for 'fire,' and the sun is referred to as 'the great fire.' The expression 'sun-worship' must, then, be understood to imply an adoration of all fire, symbolized by the sun.

The Muskhogean tribes, according to tradition, were originally banded in one common confederacy, and unanimously located their earliest ancestry near an artificial eminence in the Valley of the Big Black River in the Natchez country, whence they believed they had emerged. Gregg states[1] that they described this to him and another traveller, and calls it "an elevation of earth, about half a mile square, and fifteen or twenty feet high. From its north-east corner a wall of equal height extends for nearly half a mile to the high land."[2] This eminence they designated Nunne Chaha, or Nunne Hamgeh, ' the High Hill,' or ' the Bending Hill,' known to the Muskhogees as Rvne em mekko, or 'King of Mountains.' This looks as if the Choctaws alluded to some of those immense artificial mounds so common in the Mississippi valley. When De Soto passed through the Gulf State country in 1540–41, the tribes

---

[1] *Commerce of the Prairies*, vol. ii, p. 235.
[2] Heart, *Trans. Am. Phil. Soc.*, vol. iii, p. 216.

inhabiting it—Creeks, Choctaws, etc.—were still using, and probably constructing, mounds; and from this it is inferred that they and no others were the famous 'Mound-builders' of American archæology—a theory now adopted by the officials of the U.S. Bureau of Ethnology and the majority of modern Americanists. Wilson, writing in 1875, considerably before the modern theory of the 'Mound-builders' gained general credence, states that "analogies to these structures have been traced in the works of Indian tribes formerly in occupation of Carolina and Georgia. They were accustomed to erect a circular terrace or platform on which their council-house stood. In front of this a quadrangular area was enclosed with earthen embankments, within which public games were played and captives tortured. . . . Upon the circular platform it is also affirmed that the sacred fire was maintained by the Creek Indians as part of their most cherished rites as worshippers of the sun."[1] He adds that, although the evidence does not seem very clear, analogies point "to the possibility of some of the Indian tribes having perpetuated on a greatly inferior scale some maimed rites borrowed from their civilized precursors."

Several proved analogies between the worship of the 'Mound-builders' and the Indians exist: for example, there is unmistakable evidence that one of the sacred altars of 'Mound City' was specially devoted to nicotian rites and offerings. The discarded stones, also, found in the mound country are the same as those used by the Muskhogean people in the name of *chunkey*, which has probably a solar significance.

Like the other Muskhogean tribes, the Choctaws believed that before the Creation a great body of water alone was visible. Two pigeons flew to and fro over its waves, and at last espied a blade of grass rising above the surface. Dry land gradually followed, and the islands and mainland took their present shapes. In the centre of the hill Nunne Chaha, already mentioned, was a cave, the house of the Master of Breath (Esaugetuh Emissee). There he took clay, and fashioned the first men; and, as at that period the waters covered the earth, he raised a great wall

[1] *Prehistoric Man*, vol. i, p. 276 (London, 1876).

to dry them on. When the soft mud had hardened into flesh and bone, he directed the waters to their present places, and gave the dry land to the men he had made. The fact that the Choctaws were divided into eight clans has been cited by Brinton [1] in confirmation of the view that the myth of their origin was akin to those American legends which give to the majority of the Indian tribes a descent from four or eight brothers who emanated from a cave. Such a myth was in vogue among the Tupi-Guarani of Brazil, the Muyscas of Bogota, the Nahua of Mexico, and many other tribes. They possessed an ancient tradition that the present world will be consumed by a general conflagration, after which it will be made a much more pleasant place than it now is, and that then the spirits of the dead will return to the bones in the bone-mound, become covered with flesh, and once more occupy their ancient territory.

The Choctaws believe that after death those "who have behaved well" are taken under the care of Esaugetuh Emissee ('Master of Breath') and well looked after; that those who have behaved ill are left "to shift for themselves"; and that there is no further punishment. They also believe that when they die the spirit flies westward "as the sun goes," and there joins its family and friends "who went before it." They do not believe in a place of punishment, or in any infernal power.

Although the sun appears to have been their chief deity, the Choctaws conceived Esaugetuh Emissee, or the 'Master of Breath,' as the creative agency, at least where man was concerned, so that he may have acted as a demiurge. This deity has many counterparts in American mythologies, and appears to be the personification of the wind, the name being onomatopoetic. The deification of the wind as soul or breath is common to many mythologies.

We see a totemic significance in the fact that the alligator was worshipped, or at least venerated, by the coast and river tribes of the Muskhogeans, and never by any chance destroyed by them. The myth of the horned serpent was also in vogue

[1] *Myths of the New World*, p. 101 (1896).

among them, and was practically identical with that told by the Cherokees to Lieutenant Timberlake ; and the charm which they presented to their young men when they set out on the war-path was composed of the bones of the panther and the horn of the fabulous horned snake.

This snake dwelt in the waters, and the old people went to the shore and sang sacred songs to it. It rose a little out of the water ; the magic chant was repeated, and it then showed its horns. They cut off the horns, and, when occasion necessitated, placed a fragment of them in their 'war-physic,' to ward off the arrows of enemies.

The priests of the Choctaws, as is usual among Indian tribes, were medicine-men and diviners. The office of high priest, or 'Great Beloved Man,' as he was called, was kept in one family, passing from father to eldest son. The junior priests are described as dressed in white robes and carrying on their head or arm a great owl-skin stuffed very ingeniously, as a symbol of wisdom and divination. They were distinguished from the rest of the tribe by their taciturnity, grave and solemn countenance, and dignified carriage, and went about the settlements singing to themselves in a low, almost inaudible voice. They possessed an apparently esoteric language, which examination by competent scholars has proved to be merely a modification of the ordinary speech. It contains some words unknown in the idiom of daily life, but they are archaisms, or borrowed from other peoples, along with the ceremonies or myths to which they refer.

ARAUCANIAN MYTH

One of the best examples of a South American religion is that of the Araucanian Indians of Chile. Early accounts credit them with a fairly exalted theogony, with a supreme being, the author of all things, called Pillan—a name derived from *pulli* or *pilli*, 'the soul,' and signifying Supreme Essence. Pillan is, according to the Austrian missionary Dobrizhoffer,[1] their word for thunder. They also called him Guenu-pillan, 'the Spirit of Heaven,' and Annolu, 'the

[1] *Abipones*, vol. ii, p. 101 (London, 1822).

Infinite,' besides many other lesser names. The native tribal life was but a microcosm of his celestial existence; everything was modelled upon the heavenly polity of Pillan, who was called, in his aspect of Supreme Ruler, Toquichen, or 'the Great Chief' of the invisible world. He had his *apo-ulmenes* and his *ulmenes*, or greater and lesser sub-chiefs, like the chief of any prairie confederacy; and to them he entrusted the administration of his affairs of lesser importance.

In Pillan it is easy to trace a mythological conception widely prevalent among the indigenous American peoples. He is unquestionably a thunder-god, similar to such deities as the Hurakan of the Kiches of Guatemala, the Tlaloc of the Mexicans, and the Con or Cun, the thunder-god of the Collao of Peru. The gathering of clouds round great mountain peaks like those of the Andes, and the resultant phenomena of thunder and lightning, kindle in the savage mind the idea that the summits of these mountains are the dwelling-place of some powerful supernatural being, who manifests his presence by the agencies of fire and terrifying sound. Supernatural beings of this kind are usually described by the Indians as red in colour, having neither arms nor legs, but moving with incredible swiftness, difficult of approach because of their irascibility, but generous to those who succeed in gaining their favour. They are in general placated by libations of native spirit poured into the pools below the snow-line, and in case of drought are roused from inactivity by the sympathetic magic of 'rain-making,' in which the magician or priest sprinkles water from a gourd over the thirsty soil.

The *apo-ulmenes*, or greater deities, subservient to Pillan are several in number. The chief is Epunamun, or god of war, whose name is apparently of Peruvian origin. He may have been a type adopted from the Incan sun-idol Punchau Inca, or the 'Sun-Inca,' depicted as a warrior armed with darts. There can be little doubt that the mythology of the Araucanians, as opposed to their mere demon-worship, was highly coloured by, if not altogether adopted from, that of their Peruvian neighbours, the Aymara. And when we find that this Peruvian sun-idol was originally brought to the Incan court by a chief of the Collao who worshipped Cun (adored by the Araucanians under the name of Pillan), it would seem as though Epunamun, with his Peruvian name and probable likeness to Punchau, was also of northern origin, or had been adopted by the Araucanians from the Aymara. Other inferior deities were Meulen, a benevolent protector of the human race; and the Guecubu, a malignant being, author of all evil, also known as Algue or Aka-Kanet—at least, the similarity between him and the deities or demons bearing these names is strong, although Aka-Kanet, throned in the Pleiades, sends fruits and flowers to the earth, and is called 'Grandfather.' As Müller remarks: "Dualism is not very striking among these tribes"; and again: "The good gods do more evil than good." [1] Molina, who lived among the Araucanians for many years, says, speaking of Guecubu: "From hence it appears that the doctrine of two adverse principles, improperly called Manicheism, is very extensive, or, in other words, is found to be established among almost all the barbarous natives of both continents." [2] He goes on to compare the Guecubu with the Persian Ahriman, and states that, according to the general opinion of the Araucanians, he is the cause of all the misfortunes that occur. If a horse tires, it is because the Guecubu has ridden him. If the earth trembles, it is because the Guecubu has given it a shock; nor does anyone die who is not suffocated by the Guecubu. The name is spelt 'Huecuvu' by Falkner in his *Description of Patagonia*, and is translated as 'the wanderer without,' an evil demon, hostile to humanity, who lurks outside the encampment or on the outskirts of any human habitation for the express purpose of working malignant mischief upon unwary tribesmen—a very familiar figure to the student of anthropology and folklore.

It is not clear to which of their gods the Araucanians gave the credit for the creation of all things, and it is probable that they imagined that one or other of the totemic beings from whom they were supposed to be descended had fashioned the universe. They had, however, a very clear tradition of a deluge, from which they were saved by a great hill called

[1] *Amer. Urreligionen*, pp. 265, 272 (Basel, 1855).
[2] *History of Chile*, vol. ii, p. 85 (1809).

Theg-Theg, 'the Thunderer,' with three peaks, and possessing the property of moving upon the waters. Whenever an earthquake threatens they fly to any hill shaped like the traditional Theg-Theg, believing that it will save them in this cataclysm as it did in the last, and that its only inconvenience is that it approaches too near the sun. To avoid being scorched, says Molina, they always kept ready wooden bowls to act as parasols.

The *ulmenes*, or lesser spirits of the celestial hierarchy of the Araucanians, are the *gen* ('lords'), who have the charge of created things, and who, with the benevolent Meulen, attempt to stem the power of the Guecubu. They are of both sexes, the females being designated *amei-malghen*, or spiritual nymphs, who are pure and lead an existence of chastity, propagation being unknown in the Araucanian spiritual world. These beings, especially the females, perform for men the offices of familiar spirits, and all Araucanians believe that they have one of these minor deities or angels in their service. "*Nien cai gni amehi-malghen*" ("I still keep my guardian spirit") is a common expression when they succeed in any undertaking. These minor deities remind us forcibly of the totemic familiars who are adopted by the members of many North American Indian tribes at puberty, and appear to them in dreams and hypnotic trances to warn them concerning future events; and it is probable that the *gen* and *amei-malghen* are the remnants of a totemic system.

The likeness between things spiritual and things material is carried still further by the Araucanians; for, as their earthly *ulmenes* have no right to impose any contribution or service upon the common people, so they deny to supernatural beings worship or gifts. Thus no outward homage is ordinarily paid to them. There is probably no parallel to this lack of worship in the case of a people possessing clearly defined religious ideas and conceptions of supernatural beings. "They possess neither temples nor idols, nor are they in the habit of offering any sacrifice except in some severe calamity, or on concluding a peace."[1] Upon such occasions the offerings were usually animals

---

[1] Molina, *op. cit.*, vol. ii, p. 87.

and tobacco, the latter being burned as incense and supposed to be peculiarly agreeable to their gods. This custom recalls that of the North American Indian peoples, with whom the Araucanians exhibit some points of resemblance in the ceremonial use of tobacco, such as blowing the smoke to the four cardinal points, as a sacrifice to the god of the elements, probably Pillan. On urgent occasions only were these sacrificial rites employed, when Pillan and Meulen chiefly were adored and implored to assist their people. The absolute indifference of the Araucanians to mere ritual was well exemplified by the manner in which they ignored the elaborate ritualistic practices of the early Roman Catholic missionaries, although they displayed no hostility to the new creed, but tolerated its institution throughout their territories.

Although the Araucanians did not practise any rites, they were not behind other American aboriginal peoples in superstition. They were firm believers in divination, and paid marked attention to favourable or unfavourable omens. Appearances in dreams, the songs and flight of birds, and all the usual machinery of augury were pressed into the service of their priests or diviners ; and the savage who dreaded naught on the field of battle would tremble violently at the mere sight of an owl.

The priests, or rather diviners, were called by the Araucanians *gligua* or *dugol*, and were subdivided into *guenguenu*, *genpugnu*, and *genpiru*, meaning respectively ' masters of the heavens,' ' of epidemics,' and ' of insects or worms.' There was also a sect called *calcu*, or ' sorcerers,' who dwelt in caves and were served by *ivunches*, or ' man-animals,' to whom they taught their terrible arts. The Araucanians believed that these wizards had the power to transform themselves at night into nocturnal birds, to fly through the air, and to shoot invisible arrows at their enemies, besides indulging in the malicious mischief with which folklore credits the wizards of all countries. Their priests proper they believed to possess numerous familiars who were attached to them after death. Thus they resemble the 'magicians' of the Middle Ages. These priests were celibate, and led an existence apart from the tribe, in some communities being garbed as women. The tales told of their magical prowess lead us to believe that they were either natural epileptics or ecstatics, or excited themselves by drugs. The Araucanians also held that the knowledge of their real personal names gave dangerous magic power over them.

They firmly believed in the immortality of the soul. They held that the composition of man was twofold—the *anca*, or corruptible body, and the *am* or *pulli*, the soul, which they believed to be *ancanolu* ('incorporeal'), and *mugcalu* ('eternal' or 'existing for ever'). So thoroughly a matter of everyday allusion had these distinctions become that they frequently made use of the word *anca* in a metaphorical sense, to denote a part, the half, or the subject of anything. They differed about details of life after death. All held that after death they would go west, beyond the sea—a conception of the soul's flight held by many other American tribes. The west, the 'grave' of the sun, was supposed also to be the goal of man in the evening of his days—a place where the tired soul might find rest.

"The old notion among us," said an old chief, "is that, when we die, the spirit goes the way the sun goes, to the west, and there joins its family and friends who went before it."[1] The country to which the Araucanians believed their dead went was called Gulcheman, 'the dwelling of the men beyond the mountains.' The general conception of this Otherworld was that it was divided into two parts, one pleasant, and filled with everything that is delightful, the abode of the good; and the other desolate and in want of everything, the habitation of the wicked. Some of the Araucanians held, however, that all indiscriminately enjoyed eternal pleasures, saying that earthly behaviour had no effect upon the immortal state. The amount of spirituality in their belief is shown by their funerary practices.

The relatives of the deceased person seated themselves round his body and wept for a long time, afterward exposing it for a space upon a raised bier, called *pilluay*, where it remained during the night. During this time they watched over and 'waked' it, eating and drinking with those who came to console

[1] Hawkins, *Sketch of the Creek Country*, p. 80 (Savannah, 1848).

them. This meeting was called *curicahuin*, or the 'black entertainment,' as black was the symbolical colour of mourning with them. About the second or third day the body was laid to rest in the *eltum*, or family burying-ground. The *eltum* was usually situated in a wood or on a hill, and the procession to it was preceded by two young men on horseback, riding full speed. The bier was carried by the nearest relatives of the deceased, and surrounded by women who mourned and wept during the entire ceremony. On arrival at the *eltum* the corpse was laid on the ground and surrounded by arms in the case of a man, or by feminine implements in that of a woman. Provisions, *chica* (native spirit), wine, and sometimes even a dead horse were placed beside the deceased to serve him in the Otherworld. The Pehuenches believed that the Other- world was cold, and so sought to warm the corpse with fire, after which they bound it to a horse, placed the bridle in its hand, killed the steed, and buried both together in the grave. The relatives and friends of the dead man then wished him a prosperous journey, and covered the body with a pyramid or cairn of stones, over which they poured large quantities of *chica*.

After they had departed, an old woman called Tempuleague came to the grave in the shape of a whale, and transported the soul of the deceased to the Otherworld. Probably the Arau- canians of the Chilean coast were acquainted with the sperma- ceti, or southern variety of whale, and regarded it as the only method of locomotion for a spirit across the great waters, or it is probable that they borrowed the conception from the Peruvians of the coast, who regarded the sea as the most powerful among the gods, and called it Mama-cocha or 'Mother Sea.' The whale was a general object of worship all along the Peruvian coast, while each of the Peruvian coastal districts worshipped the particular species of fish that was taken there in the greatest abundance. This fish-worship was not mere superstition, and it was very elaborate, the fish- ancestor of each variety or 'tribe' of fish holding a special place in the heavens in the form of a constellation. The Collao tribes to the south, on the shores of Lake Titicaca, some fifty miles or so from the Chilean frontier, also worshipped a fish-god ; so that in all likelihood the fish-goddess of the Araucanians was originally borrowed from the Collao, who were probably ethnologically akin to the Araucanian tribes. This theory is confirmed by the nature of the fish-deity worshipped by the Collao ; its name was Copacahuana, 'valuable stone to be looked upon,' the idol being carved from a bluish-green stone, with the body of a fish surmounted by a rude human head. This deity, like Tempuleague, was female.

The deceased, however, must pay a toll to another old woman, of malicious character, for permission to pass a narrow strait on the road ; otherwise she would deprive him of an eye.

The life after death was very similar to earthly existence, but without fatigue or satiety. Husbands had the same wives as on earth, but had no children, as the Otherworld was inhabited by the spirits of the dead alone.

Certain vestiges of sun- and moon-worship were known among some tribes, who called the sun Anti, and the moon Kayan ; but recognition of these luminaries as deities was intermittent and probably seasonal.

INDEX

A

INDEX

INDEX

INDEX

INDEX

Ishtar and Tammuz, myth of, 251 ; described, 288

Isis, Egyptian goddess, 129–130, 246, 286

Italapas, coyote-god of the Chinook Indians, 301, 303

Italy, modern magic in, 236–237

Ivy, as sacred plant, 94–95

Izanagi, Japanese creative god, 168

Izanami, Japanese creative goddess, 168

J

JACK-IN-THE-GREEN, 137

Jacy, Tupi Indian moon-god, 184

Japanese, creation myth of, 147, 168, 194 ; culture myth of, 150 ; place of punishment of, 154 ; adventures in Underworld of, 155 ; mythic literature, 259–260

Jevons, Dr F. B., on myths, 86 ; his *Introduction to the History of Religion*, 86

Joskeha (White One), Huron Indian deity, 37, 191

Jötunn, Norse giants alluded to in the " Völuspá," 261, 293

" Journey of Skirnir, The," Norse mythic book, 261

Juno, 80 ; as mother of Vulcan, 279

Jupiter, myth of, as swan, 28 ; equated with Zeus and Tyr, 48 ; as thunder-deity, 124 ; Leland on invocation to, 237 ; in Shelley's *Prometheus Unbound*, 276 ; in Milton's *Paradise Lost*, 277 ; Spenser on, 278

Jurupari, Brazilian Indian deity, 192

K

KALI, Hindu goddess, variant of Durga, 291

Kame, Carib Indian hero-god, 182

Karaya Indians, star myth of, 140 ; their myth about Milky Way, 141; their myth about Orion, 141

Karma, Hindu deity, 159

Kartikeya, Hindu god, 256

Karu, hero-god of the Mundruku Indians, 183

Keri, hero-god of Bakairi (Carib) Indians, 182

Keridwen, British goddess, 227, 296

Khepera, Egyptian creative deity, 163 ; Osiris takes form of, 164

Khnemu, creative acts of, 165

Kiche Indians (Guatemala), creation myth of, 147, 172, 264–265 ; their myth of origin of man, 148 ; their myth of origin of heroes, 149, 265–268 ; Underworld of, 212; mythical history of, 268 *et seq.*

Kinder- und Hausmärchen, Brothers Grimm's, 90

King, as tree-spirit, 76

King of Tars, The, English romance, mythical references in, 43

Kingu, Babylonian monster, 35

Klaatsch, Dr, on Australians, 37

Kneph, Egyptian god, 298

Kodoyanpe, Maidu Indian creation myth of, 180

Kojiki, Japanese mythic book, 259

Krimen, Tupi-Guarani Indian hero, 183

Krishna, Hindu deity, cult of, 257

Kuhn, and meteorological myths, 51

Kuni-toko-tachi, Japanese god, 168

Kuvera, Hindu deity, 256

L

LADAKS of Tibet, place of punishment of, 154

Laestrin, his interpretation of myths from nebular phenomena, 51

Lafitau, his interpretation of Indian totems, 29 ; indicates savage element in myth, 45

Lang, Andrew, on solar myth, 54 ; on Spencer's theories, 60 ; works of, 66 *et seq.*; his position, 66 ; distrust of Müller's conclusions, 66 ; on ' disease of language,' 67 ; on the sacred and frivolous in religion, 67 ; his conception of myth, arguments against, 69 ; his general thesis, 69 ; his theory attached to evolutionary systems, 70 ; his three stages of myth, 70 ; his *Modern Mythology*, 71–72 ; his anti-animistic hypothesis, 72–73 ; his *Making of Religion*, 72–74 ; his ' All-Father ' theory and sky-gods, 74 *n.*; his criticism of Frazer's *Golden Bough*, 75–77

Language and formation of myth, 56

Lares, the, 237

Latin earth-gods, 134

325

INDEX

ment of, 154; star myth of, 156.
See also Aztecs

Mexican myth, flint-gods in, 26 *et seq.*; of Uitzilopochtli, 32; creation myths, 171–172; Heaven, 210–211; Hades, 211; sources of, 263–270; mythology described, 296 *et seq.*

Mexico, Payne on mythology of, 84; Mother-goddess in, 98; blood-sacrifice in, 113

Michabo, Algonquin Indian creative god, 139, 177

Mictecaciuatl, wife of Mictlantecutli, 211

Mictlantecutli, lord of the Mexican Hades, 196, 211, 218

Milky Way, in South American myth, 141; as Slavonic path to Heaven, 209; as American Indian route to Paradise, 211–212

Milton, mythology of, 44

Minerva, 278; Ben Jonson mentions, 280; described, 284

Minos, 206

Mithra, Persian deity, 289

Mitra, Hindu deity, 289

Mixcoatl, Mexican god, 124

Mjolnir, hammer of Thor, 294

Modern Mythology, Lang's, 66, 71

Mohammed confused with gods, 43

Mohammedans, soul myth of, 152

Monan, deity of Tupi-Guarani Indians, attempts destruction of world, 139, 183

Monotheism, causes of, 30

Moon-gods, 126–127; their qualities, 127; connexion with water, 127; goddess, her connexion with fertility, 127; with love, 127; myths classified, 155–156

Morrigan, Irish war-goddess, 296

Mother-goddess in Mexico, 98

Mound-building in America, 305–306

Moxos Indians, star myth of, 140

Müller, K. O., his view of mythic science, 46

Müller, Professor Max, definition of religion, 14; on character of early thought, 21 *et seq.*; his interpretation of myth, 47 *et seq.*; 50–51; applied methods of comparative philology to myth, 48; described myth as 'a disease of language,' 48; his critics, 49–50; opposed by anthropological

school, 52; his theory of effect of gender-terminations upon beliefs regarding natural phenomena, 52; Mannhardt on his theory, 53

Mummification, theory of soul developed from, 79

Mummu, Babylonian monster, 34–35, 166

Mundruku Indians, creation myth of, 183

Murri tribe, fire-stealing myth of, 149

Muskhogean Indians, traditions of, 305

Muyscas Indians, flood myth of, 153; moon myth of, 156

Mysteries, Greek, 19

Myth, definitions of, 11, 12 *et seq.*, 87; regarded by some as religious in character, 13, 20, 63, 88; its inter-relation with comparative religion, 14 *et seq.*; elements of, 15 *n.*; its relations with history, 15 *n.*, 34, 42, 58, 90–91, 92; savage and irrational element in, 15, 16, 18 *et seq.*, 45, 65, 67, 69 90; editing of, 16, 18, 33–35; and early science, 20; invention of, 21; development of, 30–31, 58; and spirit of sanctity, 32–33; fusion in, 33; purgation of, 33; explanation of, lost, 34; antiquity of, 33–34; causes of its change, 33–34; classification of, 35 *et seq.*; distribution of, 35–36; theory of origin of, in one centre, 36; fixity of, 38, 55–56; authenticity of, 39; Christian fathers on, 43; 'psychic' explanation of, 43; scientific treatment of, 46; its comprehension through language, 48, *and see* Müller; as natural phenomena, 43; 'pragmatical' explanation of, 43; Müller's interpretation of, 50; personalism in, 56; among races of low culture, 56; and natural phenomena, 57; names in, 57–58; its regularity of development, 58; regarded by some as non-religious in character, 61, 68, 87, 92; and ritual, 61, 64, 89, 238; as primitive philosophy, 62; interpreted by allegory, renders ancient forms significant, 62; non-ethical nature of, 64; difference between, and religion, 68; early, not essentially absurd or blasphemous, 69; difference be-

327

INDEX

Z

ZEALAND, creation of island of, 260

Zephyrs, as west wind, 133

Zeus, Greek deity, birth of, 18 ; as principle of life, 41 ; equation of, with Jupiter and Tyr, 48 ; philological school and his name, 48, 53, 289 ; as woodpecker, 94 ; oak the dwelling-place of, 94 ; father of Apollo, as the sky, 121, 305 ; father of Hephæstus, 130 ; casts him from Olympus, 131 ; transforms the Pleiades into doves, 142 ; brother of Pluto, 206 ; as portrayed by Homer, 258 ; described, 283

Zipacna, earth-giant in Kiche myth, 265 et seq.

Zootheism, 300,

Zulus, creation myth of, 147 ; myth of origin of man of, 148 ; culture myth of, 150

Zuñi Indians, dismemberment myth of, 146 ; creation myths of, 147, 183 ; myth of origin of man of, 148